The Complete Fish Cookbook

Top 500 Modern Fish Recipes and the Complete Guide to Choosing the Right Fish for you

Mary R. Ross

Table of Content

Introduction

Oh my goodness, Fish! So much flavour happening here, friends! If you love bold flavors and love fish, the recipes are for you. For a true blue foodie, Fresh fish recipes are simple yet so rustic and spicy. Here come fish recipes from my mother's own kitchen, something which has been in my palate right from my childhood. Fish recipes are very common and one of the most favourite dishes to me and my family. The recipes are as simple as it can get, and goes well with any type of fish. You can find many variations of these dishes with different measurements of the spices used, and here is my take.

Despite having lived in coastal cities where seafood was fresh and bountiful, I never really learned how to cook it. General intimidation, a bigger shopping expense for an unpredictable outcome as well as laziness, it just felt easier to enjoy seafood at a restaurant. Leave it to the pros.

It doesn't matter whether you are a cooking amateur, seasoned chef, a home cook or a culinary student, the recipes in this book always have a piece to offer. You can either learn to master a recipe or even go through stories that help strengthen your instincts on choosing the best catch. The choice is all yours to pick your best option. Complete fish recipes offer a whole new level of excitement for many food lovers. If the skill is mastered, you can explore different flavors from the same base ingredients – be it a delicious dish of tuna avocado burgers or salmon onigiri. The availability of this fish cookbook makes the experience better for all of us. There are so many different kinds of seafood around the world, and seemingly endless numbers of ways to enjoy it—basically, there's a lot to learn. Fortunately, that's where this cookbook comes in. The wealth of seafood is worth exploring and we've pulled out the most authentic fish recipes that you can try and enjoy at home. Happy cooking Folks..!

Chapter 1 Complete Guide to Fish-Eating Lifestyle

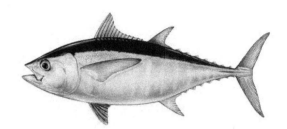

Fish is delicious and is one of the healthiest proteins you can add to your diet. Fish offers a variety of health benefits, including having many essential nutrients and helping with brain function, vision, and sleep.

Benefits of Eating Fish

There are lots of benefits in eating fish.

- The main benefit of eating fish as opposed to meat is that fish is far healthier. It is a complete protein and white fish in particular is very low in fat and calories and therefore useful if you are dieting.

- Not only that, but fish does not contain saturated fats, as all meat products and by-products such as butter, cheese and milk do.

- Although some fish are slightly more calorific and fatty than others, these fats are the healthier polyunsaturated fats, which include omega-3 essential fatty acids that benefit the body and prevent certain diseases rather than cause them.

- Fish oils such as cod or halibut liver oil are often taken in the form of capsules in order to keep joints healthy and supple.

- Fish is very easy to digest and therefore for people with digestive disorders or who are generally felling weak and under the weather, a light fish meal can be of use.

- As well as all of the obvious health benefits of consuming fish, buying fish is also easier on the purse and preparing and cooking it can actually save you time in the kitchen, freeing up your time for other activities.

- There are so many varieties of fish available plus many different ways of preparing and presenting it that you will never have to eat the same fish twice in one week or possibly even month.

- Fish can be boiled, grilled, steamed, baked, fried, deep-fried, smoked, pickled, soused, stewed or poached and can be served in a sandwich, pie, tartlet, salad, croquette, fish cake, whole, in breadcrumbs, battered, in a pastie or on toast. It can even be consumed for breakfast, lunch or dinner!

The Best Fish

There are many fish for you to choose from, and this book will help break down for you the fish we've selected. We based our selection on availability, price point, sustainability, and, of course, health.

1. Accessible to Many

When you think about cooking fish, the first thing that comes to mind is perhaps a beautifully displayed fish counter with heaps of ice and beds of fresh kelp. Or maybe a large assortment of frozen fish.

Whatever you envision, the recipes in this book can bring more variety to your table, regardless of the types of fish that are available to you. We will offer plenty of substitutions so you can adjust recipes based on what is available in your area— fresh, frozen, or canned. Go with what's appropriate and available and you'll never make the wrong choice.

2. Cost Conscious

Buying fresh fish can be expensive, especially when you are looking for wild-caught and sustainable choices. However, frozen and canned fish are widely available and shouldn't be overlooked.

Frozen fish is generally more affordable than fresh fish and can be used in many recipes without compromising flavor and texture. In other recipes, canned fish has the starring role, where fresh or frozen can't compete.

The point is, the cost of fish shouldn't be a deterrent to eating more fish. There is an available fish to fit everyone's budget; and with some creativity and know-how, you can transform the most basic, cheapest piece of fish into a fantastically delicious dish.

3. Good for Your Health

The American Heart Association recommends eating fish at least twice a week—especially fatty fish, such as salmon, mackerel, sardines, trout, and tuna, which are high in omega-3 fatty acids. Eating a diet rich in omega-3s lowers your risk of developing cardiovascular disease. It can also lower your blood pressure and keep harmful plaque from building up in your arteries. What's more, these fatty acids also reduce inflammation in the body, can help curb depression and anxiety, and are great for your skin. Fish is also a great source of protein without any saturated fats.

4. Eco-Friendly

Even though consumers are encouraged to eat more fish and seafood for health reasons, social awareness over some fishing industry methods that compromise and threaten ocean ecosystems has made it challenging. As consumers, we have a responsibility to be mindful when we make our choices. In the last 20 years, our efforts have paid off, but we can't stop there. We have to keep sustainable seafood a priority.

Sustainable seafood is seafood that is managed and fished using practices that will ensure there will be more to catch in the future. It's making sure seafood farming yields the highest nutritional value as though it were caught in the wild, while at the same time not harming the environment.

Aquaculture, as it is now called, is still working on ways to increase sustainable practices, but now more than ever, consumers have options to make the right choices. Here is the list of fish and seafood we are covering in this book, as well as a brief description of the best choices, alternatives, and what to avoid, with thanks to Seafood Watch.

It's easier now to make good choices when shopping for seafood. The food labeling law passed by Congress in 2004 requires grocery stores to label their seafood for sale under a "country of origin labeling" (or COOL). For seafood products to be labeled with "United States" as the country of origin, they must be derived exclusively from fish or shellfish hatched, raised, and processed in the United States.

Tuna: Tuna is a large category to navigate, as it is found all over the world. Tuna that has been caught using handline, hand-operated pole and line, or trolling are all good choices. Types of tuna that are particularly good include albacore (from the Atlantic or Pacific Oceans), skipjack, and yellowfin.

Sardines: Fresh sardines are high in omega-3s, and because they are so small and grow so quickly, they have very low mercury levels. They are considered to be plentiful at the moment and are also very inexpensive. Canned sardines are also a good choice to consider because many recipes call for them.

Mackerel: If you haven't tried mackerel before, now is your chance. It happens to be one of the most sustainably caught fish on the market. It's rich flavor and high omega-3s are unmatched even by its more popular cousin, salmon.

Tilapia: Tilapia is one of the freshwater fish we are covering in this book. Nearly all tilapia is farmed in indoor recirculating tanks. It's always best to choose tilapia from Peru or Ecuador and avoid fish from China.

Catfish: Catfish is as versatile as chicken, due to its mild flavor. A sustainability success story, nearly all farm-raised catfish come from recirculated fresh indoor pools or ponds in the United States and around the world. Avoid farm-raised catfish from China.

Salmon: Salmon is a popular food. Classified as an oily fish, salmon is considered to be healthy due to the fish's high protein, high omega-3 fatty acids, and high vitamin D content. Salmon is also a source of cholesterol, with a range of 23–214 mg/100 g depending on the species.

Cod: Cod is popular as a food with a mild flavor and a dense, flaky white flesh. Cod livers are processed to make cod liver oil, an important source of vitamin A, vitamin D, vitamin E and omega-3 fatty acids (EPA and DHA).

Swordfish: Swordfish can weigh hundreds of pounds and grow to reach several feet in length. These naturally oily fish are common as grilled steaks with marinades or herbs, and have a dense, sweet flavor that's pleasantly hearty. Swordfish have plenty of nutritional advantages, but pregnant and breastfeeding women should avoid eating swordfish because it can be high in mercury.

Halibut: Raw Pacific or Atlantic halibut meat is 80% water and 19% protein, with negligible fat and no carbohydrates. In a 100-gram (3+1/2-ounce) reference amount, raw halibut contains rich content (20% of more of the Daily Value, DV) of protein, selenium (65% DV), phosphorus (34% DV), vitamin D (32% DV), and several B vitamins: niacin, vitamin B6, and vitamin B12 (42-46% DV). Cooked halibut meat – presumably through the resulting dehydration – has relatively increased protein content and reduced B vitamin content (per 100 grams), while magnesium, phosphorus, and selenium are rich in content.

Snapper: Red snapper is a low-calorie, high-protein fish that contains all nine essential amino acids. It's also packed with Vitamins D and E, the minerals magnesium and selenium, and is a good source of omega-3 fatty acids. It does have moderately high levels of mercury, however, which can pose a health risk.

Trout: Trout farming is the oldest domestic aquaculture industry in North America, beginning in the 1880s in Idaho. Technically, rainbow trout are freshwater cousins of salmon. While rainbow trout are freshwater, steelhead trout are saltwater fish.

Arctic Char: Commercial Arctic char typically weigh between 1 to 2.5 kg (2.2 to 5.5 lb).The flesh is fine-flaked and medium firm. The colour is between light pink and deep red, and the taste is like something between trout and salmon.

Flounder: Flounder is a common, inexpensive, and easy-to-cook whitefish that's tasty as a fillet or can be creatively stuffed. It's particularly low in fat.

Sole: Sole fish are a good source of selenium, vitamin B12 and phosphorus, as well as several other vitamins and minerals. In terms of mercury content, sole fish can be a better alternative to certain types of fish rich in mercury, such as shark, swordfish and king mackerel.

Herring: Herring has been a staple food source since at least 3000 BC. The fish is served numerous ways, and many regional recipes are used: eaten raw, fermented, pickled, or cured by other techniques, such as being smoked as kippers. Herring are very high in the long-chain omega-3 fatty acids EPA and DHA.They are a source of vitamin D.

Sea Bass: Sea Bass provides 6 to 11 percent of your daily value for magnesium and potassium. They're both good sources of selenium which your body depends on to produce antioxidants and to synthesize thyroid hormones.

Haddock: Haddock is rich in minerals that help to build bone strength and regulate your heart rate, and this includes everything from selenium (which has been reported to help prevent cancer, heart disease, diabetes and a weak immune system), to the likes of magnesium, potassium, zinc and iron, all of which strengthen and improve the health of your body.

Branzino: A one-pound branzino has just under 300 calories, making it a healthy choice. This fish is high in omega-3 fatty acids and fish oil. Branzino is also packed with protein and rich in the antioxidant selenium.

Mahi-Mahi: An excellent source of healthy, lean protein, mahi mahi is also rich in Niacin, Vitamin B12, Phosphorus, and Selenium.

Rockfish: The health benefits of rockfish are massively undervalued. Pacific rockfish, also known as rock cod or Pacific snapper, is a lean mild-flavored fish high in protein, vitamin D, and selenium. Everyone has been beaten over the head with health benefits of protein by now.

The Educated Fish Shopper

No matter what cooking technique you're using, there are some universal considerations when purchasing fish, whether you're getting it from your small local fishmonger or a big chain grocery store (make sure the store, no matter the size, has high turnover). Here are our tips for buying quality fish so your meals are tasteful and fresh.

Buying Fillets and Steaks

Fish fillets and steaks should be sold on (but not buried in) ice. Whenever possible, we portion individual fillets from larger center-cut fillets (ones measuring the total poundage called for in the recipe). Larger fillets keep longer and allow for more consistent sizing. Not only do pre-cut portions often have different thicknesses, their proportions could be different, making for a less attractive presentation. Do not be afraid to be picky at the counter; a ragged piece of hake or a tail end of sea bass will be difficult to cook properly. It's important to keep your fish cold, so if you have a long ride, ask your fish-monger for a bag of ice. The fish should smell sweet like the sea (not "fishy" or sour)-though your chances of being able to pre-sniff your fish are slim. The surface should be shiny and bright and uniform in color. The flesh should be firm and elastic; when you press into it, the indentation shouldn't remain.

Buying Whole Fish

Unlike fillets and steaks, whole fish should be buried in ice at the seafood counter. The skin should be bright and reflective, without damage. The smell again should be faintly sweet. You are likely buying a whole fish from a person, not an unattended case so instruct the fishmonger to do what you'd like: gut, scale, and snip off the fins (if these tasks are not already taken care of).

Buying Frozen Fish

Around 85 percent of the seafood consumed in the United States is imported. Seafood's high perishability means that a lot of the seafood you eat - yes, even the "fresh" fish you buy or the seafood counter - has been frozen. Does that make a difference? Modern flash - freezing methods cause less damage to tissue, leading to less moisture loss when thawed and better texture. Most fish is also frozen at the peak of freshness, so some argue that frozen fish is even "fresher" than fresh-caught fish that's been sitting on ice for more than a day. However this doesn't always mean that you'll be happy with the frozen fish you buy. Here are our recommendations for frozen fish.

- **Assess the quality of frozen fish**

Inspect the fillets for signs of poor handling: tears or punctures in packaging that could let in air, ice crystals on the fish ("freezer burn") or in the pack-aging, liquid inside the packaging discolored or soft (partially defrosted) flesh.

- **Ask for frozen fillets**

Instead of buying thawed previously frozen fish at the seafood counter, ask if you can get a frozen piece so you have control over how it is thawed. Store it in the coldest part of your freezer, and use it within four months.

- **Thin fish may freeze betterl**

Of the fish we tested (cod, halibut, tilapia, Atlantic salmon, and wild salmon) tilapia fared the best, with tasters unable to discern which fillets were fresh and which were frozen. Thin fish may freeze more rapidly, leading to less damage to tissues.

- **Don refreeze previously frozen fish**

Previously frozen fish may not always be labeled as such at the grocery store but we don't recommend refreezing previously frozen fish, as its quality will suffer more.

- **Defrost fish properly.**

To defrost fish in the refrigerator overnight, remove the fish from its packaging, place it in a single layer on a rimmed plate, and cover it with plastic wrap. You can also do a "quick thaw" by leaving the vacuum-sealed bags under cool running tap water for 30 minutes. Do not use o microwave to defrost fish; it will alter the texture of the fish or, worse, partially cook it. Dry the fish thoroughly with paper towels.

- **Freeze fresh fish yourself.**

If you have the option to purchase fresh fish from a reputable source (or if you've caught it yourself), vacuum seal it or wrap it in a double layer of plastic wrap, removing any air pockets, and then in aluminum foil.

Buying in Season

Fish like most living things, have seasons when they're available to be caught. It varies by region; what's in season in the Northeast might not be in season at the same time in the Mid Atlantic. A good fishmonger can source from nearly anywhere, and a supermarket gets its fish from everywhere, often previously frozen, so it's not too much of concern. However, if fish such as bluefish, certain kinds of wild salmon, and black sea bass are hard to find, it's probably not their season.

Must-Have Equipment

The idea here isn't to buy specialized tools for fish butchery, but rather to make sure you have the necessary tools and cookware to cook and eat fish. I've put together a short list of must-haves, items that I believe must be in your kitchen for successful home cooking.

Cutting Boards: Your boards should be plastic, wood, bamboo, or composite material and large enough to give you ample space on which to prep your fish and vegetables.

Chef's Knife: The best chef's knife is one that feels the most comfortable in your hand. A sharp knife is a safe knife, so make sure to get your knives sharpened regularly.

Serrated Knife: The sharp serrated teeth of this knife make your work easier when it comes to slicing baguettes, tomatoes, or flaky pastry crust.

Serrated Vegetable Peeler: The micro-teeth on the peeler's blades cut through vegetable skin much easier and stay sharper longer than the straight-edged variety.

Tongs: One of the few times you'll hear me advise that cheaper is better. Kitchen tongs should be lightweight, about 12 inches in length.

Wooden Spoons: A couple of wooden spoons are useful for stirring sauces, stirring batters, and testing fry oil temperatures. Wood doesn't transfer heat as quickly as metal, so it's easier to handle.

Fish-Turning Spatula: The spatula's blade is thin and flexible and its sharp edge slides underneath crispy panfried fish easily. You'll find its edge is slightly angled so you can move it around in tight spaces.

Slotted Spoon: A metal slotted spoon can help scoop dumplings out of frying oil or lift steamed mussels from their cooking liquid.

Fish Tweezers: Perfect for removing the pin bones, the small bones at the ends of nerve endings that radiate out from the spines of fish. They are embedded in the flesh and hard to remove without mangling the fish.

Cast Iron Skillet: This versatile pan is great for heartier fish and fish that you want to develop a crunchy crust. It has a great ability to retain heat and can go from stovetop to oven.

Seafood Cracker And Crab Picks: Seafood tool sets that include seafood crackers and picks make it easier to open the shells and extract the delicate meat inside crab legs and claws.

Ingredients That Build Flavor

Building flavor is a crucial part of any cooking process. With fish, it's even more important, because the protein tends to have a delicate flavor. Fats and oils, citrus and acids, and herbs and spices are perfect cooking companions for any fish or shellfish. With the right combination and use of these aromatics, you can show off your cooking skills like a pro.

Fats and Oils

Oils can be used for cooking, marinating, and finishing fish and seafood. Fats add a lot of flavor, not to mention delivering heat to the fish. **Some of the best medium-to high-temperature oils and fats include:**

- Butter
- Canola oil
- Corn oil
- Grapeseed oil
- Peanut oil
- Pure olive oil (more refined and can be cooked at higher temperatures)
- Rendered bacon fat
- Safflower oil
- Vegetable oil

Citrus and Acid

Another element that can enhance the flavor of fish is citrus, or more broadly, acid. Citrus and fish are a match made in heaven. The juice can neutralize and stop the chemical compounds in fish that give off that fishy smell and taste. **Acidic ingredients that pair nicely with fish include:**

- Capers and olives: Try adding these to mackerel, salmon, and tuna.
- Lemon juice
- Lime juice
- Mustard: Catfish, tilapia, and mussels go especially well with a small amount of mustard.
- Pomegranate juice
- Vinegar: My favorites are red wine, champagne, sherry, and white balsamic.

Herbs and Spices

The last piece of the aromatic picture is herbs and spices. They are a fantastic way to introduce flavor without adding extra fat or calories. If you taste your dish and feel like it needs something, before reaching for more salt or butter, add some herbs or spices. **Try some of these classic combinations:**

- **Chile powder, cumin, and cilantro:** Smoky, spicy, and bright, these spices bring the Southwest to salmon, mackerel, tuna, tilapia, catfish, or shrimp.
- **Fennel seeds and tarragon:** Give salmon and tuna a hint of the south of France using these two with a splash of white wine or lemon juice.
- **Lemon and dill:** This classic pairing is as traditional as it gets and for good reason. They complement each other perfectly.
- **Lemongrass and ginger:** Pair with some lime juice for a Thai-inspired dish on tilapia, catfish, salmon, shrimp, and mussels.
- **Parsley and smoked paprika:** Try using this combination with shrimp, mussels, salmon, and mackerel.
- **Thyme and mustard:** Create a distinctly French flavor for fish like salmon and tuna. You can add a splash of white wine or dry vermouth to make it extra special.

Chapter 2 Tuna

Buttery Tuna with Sweet Potato

Prep time: 10 minutes | Cook time: 15 minutes | Serves 2

2 pounds (907 g) sweet potatoes (cubes)
2 garlic cloves
Salt, to taste
1 tablespoon tuna fish
1 tablespoon sage
1 tablespoon rosemary
2 tablespoons teaspoon butter
2 cups grated cheese

1. Add garlic cloves into the frying pan and cook tuna for 5 minutes.
2. Mix sage, butter and rosemary.
3. Add sweet potatoes with salt.
4. Cook for 10 minutes.
5. When ready, enjoy the tasty meal!

Tasty Tuna and White Beans

Prep time: 10 minutes | Cook time: 20 minutes | Serves 4

2 tablespoons olive oil
2 onion (diced)
3 garlic cloves (minced)
1 tablespoon chili powder
1 tablespoon chipotle powder
1 tablespoon cumin
powder
Salt, to taste
1 small can white beans
2 tomatoes (diced)
1 pound (454 g) tuna fish
2 tablespoons lime juice

Toppings:
Cream
Cheese
Avocado
Cilantro

1. Add oil into the frying pan.
2. Mix onion, garlic cloves, lime juice and tuna.
3. Let it cook for 10 minutes.
4. Now add chili powder, cumin powder, chipotle powder, salt and white beans. Mix well.
5. Add sweet potatoes and let it cook for 10 more minutes.
6. Make sure that the ingredients are mixed well.
7. When done, serve and enjoy!

Avocado Tuna

Prep time: 5 minutes | Cook time: 12 minutes | Serves 2

2 cups salsa
2 tablespoons oil
1 pound (454 g) tuna
fish
2 avocados (diced)
Cheese, to garnish

1. Add oil into the frying pan. Let it heat for 2 minutes.
2. Mix salsa and avocados with tuna.
3. Cook for another 10 minutes.
4. Make sure that the ingredients are mixed well.
5. When done, garnish with shredded cheese and enjoy!

Easy Tuna Salad Sandwiches

Prep time: 10 minutes | Cook time: 0 minutes | Serves 4

3 tablespoons freshly squeezed lemon juice
2 tablespoons extra-virgin olive oil
1 garlic clove, minced
½ teaspoon freshly ground black pepper
2 (5-ounce / 142-g) cans tuna, drained
1 (2.25-ounce / 64-g) can sliced olives, any green or black variety
½ cup chopped fresh fennel, including fronds
8 slices whole-grain crusty bread

1. In a medium bowl, whisk together the lemon juice, oil, garlic, and pepper. Add the tuna, olives and fennel to the bowl. Using a fork, separate the tuna into chunks and stir to incorporate all the ingredients.
2. Divide the tuna salad equally among 4 slices of bread. Top each with the remaining bread slices.
3. Let the sandwiches sit for at least 5 minutes so the zesty filling can soak into the bread before serving.

Fried Tuna with Cauliflower

Prep time: 10 minutes | Cook time: 10 minutes | Serves 3

1 cauliflower (cut)	1 pound (454 g) tuna fish
3 potatoes (peeled and chunks)	2 tomatoes (diced)
1 tablespoon Oil	Salt, to taste
1 tablespoon Cumin seeds	1 teaspoon Curry powder

1. Add oil into the frying pan.
2. Mix curry powder, tuna, tomatoes and cumin seeds.
3. Add cauliflower and potatoes with salt.
4. Cook for 10 minutes.
5. When ready, serve and enjoy!

Easy Tuna Mix

Prep time: 10 minutes | Cook time: 15 minutes | Serves 3

1 pound (454 g) sea-shells	(minced)
1 pack spinach (chopped)	1 pound (454 g) tuna fish
2 tablespoons Oil	1 teaspoon red pepper flakes
2 cups peas (boiled)	Salt, to taste
7 garlic cloves	

1. Add oil into the frying pan.
2. Mix tuna fish, garlic, red pepper flakes, spinach and seashells with salt.
3. Cook for 15 minutes.
4. Add peas.
5. When the pot beeps, serve and enjoy!

Delicious Tuna with Fried Kale

Prep time: 5 minutes | Cook time: 10 minutes | Serves 3

12 cups kale (chopped)	1 tablespoon garlic (minced)
2 tablespoons lemon juice	1 teaspoon soy sauce
1 tablespoon oil	Salt and pepper, to taste
1 can tuna fish	

1. Add oil into the frying pan.
2. Mix tuna fish, garlic, soy sauce, lemon juice, kale and salt and pepper.
3. Cook for 10 minutes.
4. When ready, enjoy!

Corn Tuna Dish

Prep time: 10 minutes | Cook time: 10 minutes | Serves 3

1 tablespoon butter	1 pound (454 g) tuna fish
2 tablespoons corn-starch	1 onion (chopped)
2 tablespoons red pepper flakes	2 potatoes (cubes)
	1 cup corn

1. Add butter into the frying pan.
2. Mix tuna fish, cornstarch, red pepper flakes, onion, potatoes, corn.
3. Cook for 10 minutes.
4. Make sure that the ingredients are mixed well.
5. When ready, serve and enjoy!

Savory Kale and Tuna Chickpeas

Prep time: 15 minutes | Cook time: 10 minutes | Serves 3

2 tablespoons olive oil	(boiled)
2 tomatoes (chopped)	2 cups kale (chopped)
2 potatoes (chopped)	1 pound (454 g) tuna fish
Salt and pepper	
2 cups chickpeas	

1. Add oil into the frying pan.
2. Mix tuna, potatoes, tomatoes, salt and pepper with kale.
3. Cook for 10 minutes.
4. Mix chickpeas.
5. When done, serve and enjoy!

Spicy Tuna Meal

Prep time: 10 minutes | Cook time: 15 minutes | Serves 3

1 tablespoon olive oil	Salt, to taste
1 onion (diced)	3 cups Black beans
1 sweet potato	1 pound (454 g) tuna fish
1 tablespoon chili powder	1 tablespoon lime juice
1 tablespoon cumin powder	2 tomatoes (diced)

1. Add oil into the frying pan.
2. Mix tomatoes, lime juice, black beans, salt, cumin powder, chili powder, sweet potatoes, tuna fish and onion.
3. Cook for 15 minutes.
4. When ready, serve and enjoy!

Zucchini Tuna Patties

Prep time: 10 minutes | Cook time: 12 minutes | Serves 4

3 slices whole-wheat sandwich bread, toasted
2 (5-ounce / 142-g) cans tuna in olive oil, drained
1 cup shredded zucchini
1 large egg, lightly beaten
¼ cup diced red bell pepper
1 tablespoon dried oregano
1 teaspoon lemon zest
¼ teaspoon freshly ground black pepper
¼ teaspoon kosher or sea salt
1 tablespoon extra-virgin olive oil
Salad greens or 4 whole-wheat rolls, for serving (optional)

1. Crumble the toast into bread crumbs with your fingers (or use a knife to cut into ¼-inch cubes) until you have 1 cup of loosely packed crumbs.
2. Pour the crumbs into a large bowl. Add the tuna, zucchini, beaten egg, bell pepper, oregano, lemon zest, black pepper, and salt. Mix well with a fork. With your hands, form the mixture into four (½-cup-size) patties. Place them on a plate, and press each patty flat to about ¾-inch thick.
3. In a large skillet over medium-high heat, heat the oil until it's very hot, about 2 minutes.
4. Add the patties to the hot oil, then reduce the heat down to medium. Cook the patties for 5 minutes, flip with a spatula, and cook for an additional 5 minutes.
5. Serve the patties on salad greens or whole-wheat rolls, if desired.

Tuna Fried with Several Veggies

Prep time: 15 minutes | Cook time: 17 minutes | Serves 3

1 onion (chopped)
2 cloves garlic (chopped)
1 carrot (chopped)
2 stalks celery (sliced)
1 tablespoon ginger root (minced)
½ teaspoon paprika
½ teaspoon cumin powder
½ teaspoon oregano
2 tomatoes (crushed)
1 pound (454 g) tuna fish
1 tablespoon lemon juice
Salt, to taste

1. Add lemon juice into the frying pan.
2. Add onion, garlic, celery, ginger root, oregano, cumin powder, paprika and carrots.
3. Mix tuna and cook for 2 minutes.
4. Add tomatoes along with salt.
5. Cook for 15 minutes.
6. When ready, serve and enjoy!

Tuna Fish Fried with Zucchini

Prep time: 10 minutes | Cook time: 15 minutes | Serves 3

2 tablespoons oil
1 onion (chopped)
2 cups black beans
2 tablespoons chili powder
1 can tuna fish
1 tablespoon cumin powder
2 tablespoons salsa
1 tablespoon lime juice
1 zucchini (sliced)
½ cup chives
Chopped cilantro for dressing

1. Add oil to the frying pan.
2. Mix onion, chives, zucchini, lime juice, salsa, cumin powder, chili powder, tuna and black beans.
3. Cook for 15 minutes.
4. When done, serve with cilantro dressing!

Tuna and Squash Dish

Prep time: 5 minutes | Cook time: 12 minutes | Serves 2

1 pound (454 g) tuna fish
2 cups squash (chopped)
Salt, to taste
2 tablespoons tomato sauce
2 cups beans
1 tablespoon cumin powder

1. Add tuna fish into the frying pan and cook for 2 minutes.
2. Mix squash, tomato sauce, beans and cumin powder.
3. Add salt, and make sure that the ingredients are mixed well.
4. Cook for 10 minutes.
5. When ready, serve and enjoy!

Tuna Fish and Spinach Fried

Prep time: 10 minutes | Cook time: 10 minutes | Serves 2

2 tablespoons butter
1 onion (chopped)
2 garlic cloves
1 tablespoon cumin powder
1 tablespoon paprika
1 can tuna fish

2 tomatoes (chopped)
2 cups vegetable broth
1 small bunch spinach, chopped
Cilantro, for garnishing

1. Add butter into the frying pan.
2. Mix tuna fish, onion, garlic, and cumin powder, paprika and vegetable broth.
3. Add tomatoes and spinach.
4. Make sure that the ingredients are mixed well.
5. Cook for 10 minutes.
6. When ready, enjoy!

Spicy Tuna Fried with Peas

Prep time: 10 minutes | Cook time: 10 minutes | Serves 2

4 cups peas (boiled)
3 onions (chopped)
2 tablespoons olive oil
Salt, to taste
1 pound (454 g) tuna fish

1 tablespoon oregano
1 tablespoon chili powder
½ cup green chilies
Cilantro leaves, to garnish

1. Add oil into the frying pan.
2. Mix onions, tuna fish, salt, oregano, green chilies, and chili powder with peas.
3. Cook for 10 minutes.
4. Make sure that the ingredients are mixed well.
5. When done, serve and enjoy the meal.

Qucik Tuna Veggie Broth

Prep time: 10 minutes | Cook time: 14 minutes | Serves 2

2 tablespoons olive oil
1 onion (chopped)
2 cups vegetable broth
1 pound (454 g) tuna fish

3 potatoes (diced)
1 tablespoon thyme
2 tablespoons apple cider vinegar
2 carrots (sliced)
Parsley, to garnish

1. Add oil into the frying pan.
2. Mix vegetable broth, thyme, apple cider vinegar, tuna, carrots, potatoes and onion.
3. Cook for 14 minutes.
4. Make sure that the ingredients are mixed well.
5. When done, garnish with chopped parsley and serve.

Fried Tuna with Mushrooms

Prep time: 10 minutes | Cook time: 10 minutes | Serves 3

2 tablespoons butter
1 onion (chopped)
Salt, to taste
1 pound (454 g) tuna fish
3 cups mushrooms (chopped)

2 garlic cloves
2 cups thyme (chopped)
2 tablespoons flour
2 cups Parmesan Cheese (shredded)

1. Add butter and onion into the frying pan.
2. Mix mushrooms, tuna fish, garlic cloves, thyme, chicken stock and flour.
3. Add salt.
4. Cook for 10 minutes.
5. Make sure that the ingredients are mixed well.
6. When ready, sprinkle shredded cheese on it and enjoy!

Tuna Mixed with Greenish Veggies

Prep time: 10 minutes | Cook time: 15 minutes | Serves 2

1 pound (454 g) tuna fish
3 stalks celery (chopped)
2 garlic cloves

2 onions (chopped)
Salt and pepper, to taste
2 cups green onion (chopped)

1. Add tuna into the frying pan.
2. Mix celery, garlic, salt and pepper, onion and green onion.
3. Cook for 15 minutes.
4. Make sure that the ingredients are mixed well.
5. When ready, serve and enjoy!

Tuna Mushroom and Bell Pepper Mix

Prep time: 15 minutes | Cook time: 19 minutes | Serves 2

¼ cup oil	2 tomatoes (diced)
¼ cup flour (all-purpose)	3 garlic cloves
1 bell pepper	1 teaspoon soy sauce
1 onion (chopped)	1 teaspoon sugar (white)
1 pound (454 g) tuna fish	Salt and pepper, to taste
4½ ounces (128 g) mushrooms	3 drops hot sauce

1. Add oil into the frying pan.
2. Mix tuna and cook for 4 minutes.
3. Make sure that the ingredients are mixed well.
4. Mix bell pepper, chicken, mushrooms, tomatoes, onion, soy sauce, garlic, sugar and hot sauce.
5. Add salt and pepper with flour.
6. Cook for 15 minutes.
7. When done, serve and enjoy!

Delicious Tuna Avocado Burgers

Prep time: 15 minutes | Cook time: 20 minutes | Serves 4

2 (5-ounce / 142-g) cans water-packed albacore tuna, drained	¼ teaspoon chili powder
1 medium avocado, chopped, plus additional reserved for serving	⅛ teaspoon salt
	⅛ teaspoon freshly ground black pepper
	4 whole-wheat buns, for serving
1 large egg	Romaine lettuce, for serving
1 tablespoon Dijon mustard	Tomato slices, for serving
¼ teaspoon ground cayenne pepper	Onion slices, for serving

1. Preheat the oven to 375°F (190ºC). Line a sheet pan with parchment paper.
2. In a large bowl, flake the tuna. Mix in the avocado, egg, Dijon, cayenne, chili powder, salt, and pepper until well combined. To avoid green burgers, gently mix in avocado. Some chunks should remain.
3. Using a ½ cup measuring cup, scoop the burger mixture to form into a patty. Carefully flatten and place on the prepared sheet pan. Repeat with remaining mixture to form 4 patties.
4. Bake for 10 minutes. Remove the patties from the oven and carefully flip. Return them to the oven to cook for another 10 minutes, until a golden crust forms.
5. Serve on a whole-wheat bun with lettuce, tomato, onion, and more avocado or atop a large salad! Enjoy!

Tuna Fish Fried with Kidney Beans

Prep time: 10 minutes | Cook time: 15 minutes | Serves 3

2 cups kidney beans	sugar
2 cans tuna fish	1 tablespoon fish sauce
2 tablespoons oil	
2 tablespoons curry paste	1 tablespoon coriander powder
1 teaspoon brown	Rice, to serve (boiled)

1. Add oil into the frying pan.
2. Add curry paste, brown sugar, tuna fish, kidney beans, coriander powder and fish sauce.
3. Let it cook for 15 minutes.
4. Make sure that the ingredients are mixed well.
5. When done, serve with rice!

Quick Tuna Dish with Spice

Prep time: 5 minutes | Cook time: 10 minutes | Serves 2

½ large onion (diced)	½ tablespoon chili powder
1 tablespoon olive oil	
1 can tuna fish	Salt and pepper, to taste
2 tomatoes (diced)	

1. Add onion and olive oil into the frying pan.
2. Add tomatoes, tuna fish, chili powder with salt and pepper. Mix well.
3. Let it cook for 10 minutes.
4. Make sure that the ingredients are mixed well.
5. When ready, serve with a bread or any of your favorite side dish!

Tuna Fried with Baby Spinach

Prep time: 10 minutes | Cook time: 15 minutes | Serves 3

2 tablespoons ginger (minced)
4 garlic cloves(minced)
1 tablespoon mustard seeds
1 tablespoon vegetable oil
2 cups vegetable broth
½ tablespoon fenugreek
1 pound (454 g) tuna fish
1 tablespoon coriander powder
1 tablespoon cumin powder
4 cups baby spinach

1. Add oil into the frying pan.
2. Mix tuna fish, mustard seeds, garlic, fenugreek, cumin powder, coriander powder and vegetable broth.
3. Add chopped spinach.
4. Cook for 15 minutes.
5. When ready, serve.

Tuna with Peanut Butter

Prep time: 10 minutes | Cook time: 14 minutes | Serves 3

1 tablespoon canola oil
1 tablespoon peanut butter
2 tablespoons soy sauce
½ cup cilantro (chopped)
1 tablespoon lime
juice
1 pound (454 g) tuna fish
1 tablespoon red pepper flakes
2 tablespoons cornstarch
Green onions, for garnishing

1. Add canola oil in the frying pan.
2. Add tuna fish and cook for 10 minutes.
3. Meanwhile, add peanut butter, cilantro, lime juice, soy sauce, red pepper flakes and cornstarch into a bowl. Stir well.
4. Add to the frying pan and cook for another 4 minutes.
5. When done, serve and enjoy with adding the garnishing of green onion!

Black Beans Tuna Dish

Prep time: 15 minutes | Cook time: 15 minutes | Serves 2

1 tablespoon olive oil
1 onion (chopped)
2 garlic cloves (minced)
½ teaspoon brown sugar
Salt and pepper, to taste
3 cups black beans
1 tablespoon lime
juice
2 cups green onion (chopped)
2 cups corn (boiled)
1 pound (454 g) tuna fish
1 tablespoon oregano powder
1 green bell pepper (chopped)

1. Add olive to the frying pan.
2. Mix onion, corn, green onion and garlic.
3. Add black beans, salt and pepper, brown sugar, lime juice, bell pepper, tuna and oregano powder.
4. Cook for 15 minutes.
5. Make sure that the ingredients are mixed well.
6. When ready, serve!

Vibtant Tomato Paste Tuna Dish

Prep time: 10 minutes | Cook time: 15 minutes | Serves 3

2 onions (chopped)
2 tablespoons oil
2 carrots (sliced)
1 tablespoon cumin powder
1 tablespoon coriander powder
1 tablespoon cayenne powder
½ tablespoon cinnamon powder
1 pound (454 g) tuna fish
2 tablespoons tomato paste
1 tablespoon lemon juice
Cilantro, to garnish

1. Add oil into the frying pan.
2. Mix onions, carrots, coriander powder, cumin powder, cinnamon powder, and tomato paste with lemon juice.
3. Add tuna.
4. Cook for 15 minutes.
5. Make sure that the ingredients are mixed well.
6. When ready, serve and enjoy.

Tuna with Green Beans

Prep time: 10 minutes | Cook time: 15 minutes | Serves 3

3 cups green beans
2 cups corn kernels
Pepper and salt, to taste
1 tablespoon cumin powder

2 tablespoons oil
3 cups spinach (chopped)
1 pound (454 g) tuna fish
Cheese, to garnish

1. Add oil into the frying pan.
2. Mix cumin powder, salt and pepper, corn kernels, green beans and spinach with tuna.
3. Cook for 15 minutes.
4. Make sure that the ingredients are mixed well.
5. When ready, garnish cheese and enjoy!

Easy Nut-Free Tuna Waldorf Salad

Prep time: 10 minutes | Cook time: 0 minutes | Serves 4

1 (5-ounce / 142-g) can water-packed tuna, drained
¼ cup chopped red grapes
¼ cup roasted sunflower seeds
2 tablespoons mayonnaise

1 tablespoon chopped fresh dill
1 tablespoon Dijon mustard
⅛ teaspoon freshly ground black pepper
1 English cucumber, sliced

1. In medium bowl, flake the tuna with a fork. Break up any large pieces.
2. Mix in the grapes, sunflower seeds, mayonnaise, dill, Dijon, and pepper until well combined.
3. Arrange the cucumber slices on a large platter or plate. Place 2 teaspoons of tuna salad on top of each cucumber slice.

Colorful Tuna Salad with Lime Vinaigrette

Prep time: 15 minutes | Cook time: 15 minutes | Serves 4

For the Lime Vinaigrette:

¼ cup finely chopped fresh cilantro
¼ cup freshly squeezed lime juice
3 tablespoons extra-

virgin olive oil
2 tablespoons honey
¼ teaspoon salt
⅛ teaspoon freshly ground black pepper

For the Confetti Farro:

½ cup pearled farro
¼ teaspoon salt
4 cups shredded red cabbage
1 cup shredded carrots
½ cup chopped scallions, both white and green parts
1 red bell pepper,

julienned
1 cup fresh corn kernels
2 (5-ounce / 142-g) cans oil-packed white albacore tuna, drained
¼ teaspoon freshly ground black pepper

To Make the Lime Vinaigrette

1. In a container or jar with a lid, muddle the cilantro leaves with the lime juice and olive oil. Mix in the honey. Season with the salt and pepper. Cover and shake to combine. Set aside.

To Make the Confetti Farro

1. In a medium saucepan, combine 1 cup of water, farro, and salt. Bring to a boil, then reduce heat to low to simmer. Cover and cook for about 15 minutes, until all water is absorbed. Turn off the heat and let it sit covered for another 10 minutes.
2. While the farro cooks, in a large mixing bowl, combine the cabbage, carrots, scallions, bell pepper, and corn. Set aside.
3. When the farro is done cooking, let cool completely. Once cooled, add to the bowl with vegetables. Flake in the tuna and toss together with dressing. Season with pepper.

Chapter 3 Sardines

Sardines Toast

Prep time: 10 minutes | Cook time: 6 minutes | Serves 4

4 rustic sourdough bread slices
1 (4½-ounce / 128-g) can oil-packed sardines, oil drained and reserved
1 garlic clove, peeled
1 (2-ounce / 57-g) jar diced pimentos,
drained
Kosher salt
Freshly ground black pepper
Juice of ½ lemon
1 tablespoon minced fresh flat-leaf parsley, for garnish

1. Brush both sides of the bread with the reserved sardine oil. In a small skillet over medium heat, toast the bread, flipping once, until the bread is golden brown, about 3 minutes per side. It should be crispy but still chewy in the center. Rub the tops of the toast gently with the garlic. Mince the remainder of the garlic and set aside.
2. In the same skillet, heat 1 teaspoon of the reserved sardine oil over medium heat. Add the sardines, pimento, and minced garlic. Season with salt and pepper, and sauté, stirring, until the sardines are just warmed through.
3. Drizzle the lemon juice over the sardines and arrange on the toasts. Garnish with the parsley and serve warm.

Nutritious Sardine Breakfast

Prep time: 10 minutes | Cook time: 23 minutes | Serves 4

2 (4½-ounce / 128-g) cans oil-packed sardines, oil drained and reserved
2 Roma tomatoes, cut into ¼-inch dice
1 small red onion, cut into ¼-inch dice
1 small pasilla pepper, cut into ¼-inch dice
3 garlic cloves, minced
1 tablespoon capers, rinsed and chopped
Kosher salt
Freshly ground black pepper
2 large eggs
1 tablespoon chopped fresh dill, for garnish

1. Preheat the oven to 400°F (205ºC). Place a 10-inch cast iron skillet in the oven.
2. In a mixing bowl, break the sardines into chunks. Mix in the tomatoes, onion, pasilla pepper, garlic, and capers, until thoroughly combined. Season with salt and pepper and add 2 tablespoons of reserved sardine oil.
3. Transfer the mixture to the skillet and bake for 15 minutes.
4. Remove the pan from the oven. Using the back of a large kitchen spoon, make two shallow depressions in the mixture. Crack an egg into each depression and season with salt and pepper. Continue to bake for another 8 minutes, or until the eggs have just set.
5. Remove the pan from the oven and tent with aluminum foil, resting for 2 to 3 minutes. Garnish with the chopped dill and serve immediately.

Sardine Rice Bowl

Prep time: 5 minutes | Cook time: 45 minutes | Serves 4 to 6

4 cups water
2 cups brown rice, rinsed well
½ teaspoon salt
3 (4-ounce / 113-g) cans sardines packed
in water, drained
3 scallions, sliced thin
1-inch piece fresh ginger, grated
4 tablespoons sesame oil

1. Place the water, brown rice, and salt to a large saucepan and stir to combine. Allow the mixture to boil over high heat.
2. Once boiling, reduce the heat to low, and cook covered for 45 to 50 minutes, or until the rice is tender.
3. Meanwhile, roughly mash the sardines with a fork in a medium bowl.
4. When the rice is done, stir in the mashed sardines, scallions, and ginger.
5. Divide the mixture into four bowls. Top each bowl with a drizzle of sesame oil. Serve warm.

Delicious Sardines and Plum Tomato Curry

Prep time: 10 minutes | Cook time: 8¹/₃₀ hours | Serves 4

1 tablespoon olive oil
1 pound (454 g) fresh sardines, cubed
2 plum tomatoes, chopped finely
½ large onion, sliced
1 garlic clove, minced
½ cup tomato purée
Salt and ground black pepper, to taste

1. Select the Sauté function on your Instant pot then add the oil and sardines to it.
2. Let it sauté for 2 minutes then add all the remaining ingredients.
3. Cover the lid and select Slow Cook function for 8 hours.
4. Remove the lid and stir the cooked curry.
5. Serve warm.

Sardines Danish Sandwich

Prep time: 10 minutes | Cook time: 3 minutes | Serves 2

1 shallot, cut crosswise into thin rings
¼ cup red wine vinegar
2 tablespoons Dijon mustard
1 teaspoon prepared horseradish
4 seeded rye bread
slices, toasted
1 large handful baby spinach leaves
2 (4½-ounce / 128-g) cans oil-packed sardines, oil drained and reserved
Kosher salt
Freshly ground black pepper

1. In a small bowl, soak the shallot in the vinegar.
2. In a small bowl, mix together the mustard and horseradish. On each slice of toast, spread the mustard and horseradish evenly and top each with spinach. Set aside on plates.
3. In a small nonstick skillet over medium heat, add 2 teaspoons of the reserved sardine oil and swirl to coat the pan. When shimmery wavy lines run through the oil, add the sardines and fry for 3 minutes on each side, flipping once, until crispy.
4. Divide the sardines between the pieces of toast and top with the pickled shallot rings. Season with salt and pepper and serve.

Sardines Spaghetti Mix

Prep time: 10 minutes | Cook time: 13 minutes | Serves 4

12 ounces (340 g) spaghetti
3 tablespoons extra-virgin olive oil
4 to 6 fresh sardines, butterflied and boned
Kosher salt
Freshly ground black pepper
1 large red bell pepper, cut into thin strips
1 large shallot, coarsely chopped
¼ cup pine nuts
3 garlic cloves, minced
2 tablespoons unsalted butter
Juice of ½ lemon
2 tablespoons coarsely chopped fresh flat-leaf parsley

1. Bring a large pot of water to a boil over medium-high heat. Add the spaghetti and cook according to package instructions until tender, about 10 minutes. Reserve 1 cup of spaghetti water, then drain and set aside.
2. Meanwhile, in a wok or deep sauté pan, heat the olive oil over medium heat. When shimmery wavy lines run through the oil, add the sardines and sear for 6 minutes, flipping them over halfway through. Season with salt and pepper.
3. Using a slotted spoon, transfer the sardines to a plate. Return the pan to medium heat.
4. Add the red bell pepper and shallot and sauté until soft, about 7 minutes. Add the pine nuts, garlic, and butter and sauté until the butter melts and browns slightly.
5. Return the sardines to the pan and fold in gently, breaking them up into smaller chunks and flakes.
6. Transfer the spaghetti back to the stockpot. Toss in the sardine mixture and drizzle in some of the spaghetti water to loosen the sauce, if needed.
7. Add the lemon juice and parsley, tossing to coat, and serve.

Seared Sardines with Fennel and Olives

Prep time: 10 minutes | Cook time: 6 minutes | Serves 4

4 fresh sardines, butterflied and boned
Kosher salt
Freshly ground black pepper
¼ cup extra-virgin olive oil, divided
1 tablespoon freshly squeezed lemon juice
1 fennel bulb, trimmed and thinly sliced, fronds reserved for garnish
½ cup halved pitted green olives
Zest and juice of 1 navel orange
2 tablespoons coarsely chopped fresh flat-leaf parsley

1. Place the sardines on a plate and season both sides with salt and pepper. Drizzle with 2 tablespoons of olive oil.
2. Heat a cast iron skillet or griddle over medium-high heat until it begins to smoke. Place the sardines in the pan and sear for 6 minutes, flipping them halfway through. Drizzle the lemon juice over the sardines, transfer to a platter, and tent with aluminum foil to keep warm.
3. In a mixing bowl, toss the fennel, olives, orange zest, and parsley. Season with salt and pepper. Add 1 tablespoon of orange juice and the remaining 2 tablespoons of olive oil and toss to coat.
4. Transfer the salad to a serving platter and place the sardines on top. Garnish with fennel fronds and serve immediately.

Easy Sardine Ceviche

Prep time: 10 minutes | Cook time: 0 minutes | Serves 4

2 to 4 fresh sardine fillets, filleted and boned, then thinly sliced across the grain
1 large red grapefruit, peel and pith removed and segmented
1 lemon, peel and pith removed and segmented
¼ cup extra-virgin olive oil
2 tablespoons finely chopped red onion
Juice of 2 limes
Pinch red pepper flakes
½ teaspoon kosher salt
2 tablespoons chopped fresh cilantro, for garnish
Tortilla chips or endive spears, for serving

1. In a small bowl, fold together the sardines, grapefruit, lemon, olive oil, onion, lime juice, red pepper flakes, and salt.
2. Cover and refrigerate for 1 hour, or until you are ready to serve.
3. Fold in the cilantro just before serving. Serve with tortilla chips or endive spears.

Baked Sardines with Sambal Oelek

Prep time: 10 minutes | Cook time: 12 minutes | Serves 4

4 cups quartered baby bok choy
2 red bell peppers, seeded and diced
3 celery stalks, thinly sliced on the bias
2 tablespoons olive oil
Sea salt, for seasoning
Freshly ground black pepper, for seasoning
2 (4-ounce / 113-g) cans water-packed sardines, drained
2 teaspoons sambal oelek

1. Preheat the oven to 400°F (205°C). Line a baking sheet with parchment paper and set aside.
2. Toss the bok choy, bell peppers, and celery with the olive oil until evenly coated.
3. Season the vegetables with salt and pepper and spread them out on the prepared baking sheet.
4. Bake until the vegetables are tender, 6 to 7 minutes.
5. Pat the sardines dry with a paper towel and top each piece with sambal oelek, using the back of a spoon to coat the tops evenly.
6. Place the fish on the vegetables and bake for an additional 6 to 7 minutes.

Oil-Packed Sardines and Potato Mix

Prep time: 10 minutes | Cook time: 15 minutes | Serves 6

1 pound (454 g) baby Yukon gold potatoes
¼ cup kosher salt, divided
1 (4½-ounce / 128-g) can oil-packed sardines, oil drained and reserved
2 tablespoons extra-virgin olive oil
2 teaspoons freshly squeezed lemon juice
1 teaspoon whole-grain mustard
2 celery stalks, cut into ¼-inch-thick slices on the bias
1 scallion, thinly sliced (white and green parts)
¼ cup chopped fresh flat-leaf parsley
Freshly ground black pepper

1. In a large saucepan, cover the potatoes by about 1 inch of water and add 3½ tablespoons of salt. Bring the water to a boil over high heat, then lower the heat and simmer for about 15 minutes, until tender. Drain and set aside.
2. Meanwhile, use a fork to gently break up the sardines into chunks and set aside.
3. In a wide shallow bowl, whisk together the olive oil, lemon juice, and mustard, then add the celery, sardines, scallion, and parsley. Add the remaining ½ tablespoon of salt and season with pepper.
4. When the potatoes are cool enough to handle, place them on a cutting board. Use a small plate or saucer to gently flatten them, repeating the process until all the potatoes have been flattened.
5. Gently fold the potatoes into the sardine mixture. It's okay if the potatoes break up slightly or if the fish flakes even more. Drizzle with about 2 teaspoons of the reserved sardine oil and serve warm or at room temperature.

Spicy Sardine with White Beans

Prep time: 10 minutes | Cook time: 6 minutes | Serves 4

3 tablespoons extra-virgin olive oil, or oil drained from the sardine can, divided
1 large red bell pepper, cut into ¼-inch-thick strips
Kosher salt
Freshly ground black pepper
3 garlic cloves, minced
1 (15-ounce / 425-g) can cannellini beans, drained and rinsed
2 teaspoons smoked paprika
1 (4½-ounce / 128-g) can oil-packed sardines, oil drained and reserved
1 tablespoon sherry vinegar or red wine vinegar
2 large handfuls baby kale or wild arugula

1. Heat a nonstick skillet over medium heat. Add 2 tablespoons of olive oil and swirl to coat the pan. When shimmery wavy lines run through the oil, add the peppers and sauté for 4 minutes, or until they begin to soften. Season with salt and pepper.
2. Add the garlic and sauté for a few seconds more. Add the beans and paprika and sauté for 2 minutes, or until the beans start to brown slightly.
3. Add the sardines and toss gently to combine, breaking up the sardines into smaller chunks. Keep folding gently until the sardines are warmed through.
4. Remove the pan from the heat and allow it to cool slightly. Add the vinegar and kale, seasoning with a pinch more salt and pepper. The heat from the beans and vegetables should wilt the kale slightly. Drizzle the remaining 1 tablespoon of oil over the salad and serve warm.

Butterflied Sardines with Lemony Tomato Sauce

Prep time: 10 minutes | Cook time: 40 minutes | Serves 4

2 tablespoons olive oil, divided
4 Roma tomatoes, peeled and chopped, reserve the juice
1 small onion, sliced thinly
Zest of 1 orange
Sea salt and freshly ground pepper, to taste
1 pound (454 g) fresh sardines, rinsed, spine removed, butterflied
½ cup white wine
2 tablespoons whole-wheat breadcrumbs

1. Preheat the oven to 425ºF (220ºC). Grease a baking dish with 1 tablespoon of olive oil.
2. Heat the remaining olive oil in a nonstick skillet over medium-low heat until shimmering.
3. Add the tomatoes with juice, onion, orange zest, salt, and ground pepper to the skillet and simmer for 20 minutes or until it thickens.
4. Pour half of the mixture on the bottom of the baking dish, then top with the butterflied sardines. Pour the remaining mixture and white wine over the sardines.
5. Spread the breadcrumbs on top, then place the baking dish in the preheated oven. Bake for 20 minutes or until the fish is opaque.
6. Remove the baking sheet from the oven and serve the sardines warm.

Sardine Fettuccine with Asparagus

Prep time: 10 minutes | Cook time: 10 minutes | Serves 4

8-ounces (227-g) dry whole-wheat fettuccini
2 tablespoons olive oil
½ sweet onion, finely chopped
1 tablespoon minced garlic
1 bunch asparagus, trimmed and cut into 3-inch pieces
1 (4½-ounce / 128-g) can sardines packed in oil, drained
1 tablespoon capers
Pinch red pepper flakes
Sea salt, for seasoning
Freshly ground black pepper, for seasoning

1. Prepare the pasta according to package instructions.
2. While the pasta is cooking, heat the olive oil in a large skillet over medium-high heat.
3. Sauté the onion and garlic until softened, about 3 minutes.
4. Add the asparagus and sauté until the asparagus is tender-crisp, about 4 minutes.
5. Stir in the sardines, capers, and red pepper flakes and sauté until the sardines are heated through, about 3 minutes.
6. Season with salt and pepper.
7. Stir in the fettuccini, toss to combine, and serve.

Chapter 4 Mackerel

Steamed Whole Mackerel

Prep time: 10 minutes | Cook time: 15⅙ minutes | Serves 4

For the Fish:
1 (2-pound / 907-g) whole mackerel, head on
½ cup kosher salt, for cleaning
Freshly ground white pepper
3 to 4 scallions, cut into 3-inch pieces (white and green parts)
½ bunch cilantro
Kosher salt
1 (4-inch) piece fresh ginger, peeled and thinly sliced
2 tablespoons Shaoxing rice wine or dry sherry

For the Sauce:
2 tablespoons light soy sauce
1 tablespoon sesame oil
2 teaspoons sugar

For the Sizzling Ginger Oil:
3 tablespoons vegetable oil
2 tablespoons julienned peeled fresh ginger, divided
2 scallions, thinly sliced on the bias, divided (white and green parts)

1. To make the fish, clean it by rubbing it inside and out with the kosher salt. Rinse the fish and pat dry with paper towels. Season the fish inside and out with salt and pepper.
2. In a steamer basket or on a plate, make a bed using half of each the scallions, cilantro, and ginger. Place the fish on top and stuff the remaining half of each inside the fish. Pour the wine over the fish.
3. Pour 2 inches of water into a wide skillet and bring to a boil over medium heat. Place the steamer basket or plate in the pan and cover. Steam the fish for 15 minutes (adding 2 minutes for every ½ pound beyond 2 pounds), or until a fork inserted near the head flakes the flesh. If the flesh still sticks together, steam for 2 more minutes.
4. To make the sauce, while the fish is steaming, warm the soy sauce, sesame oil, and sugar in a small pan over low heat. Set aside.
5. Once the fish is cooked, transfer to a clean platter. Discard the cooking liquid and aromatics from the steaming plate. Pour the warm sauce over the fish. Tent with aluminum foil to keep it warm.
6. To make the sizzling ginger oil, in small saucepan, heat the vegetable oil over medium heat. Just before it starts to smoke, add half the ginger and half the scallions and fry for 10 seconds. Pour the sizzling oil over the fish.
7. Garnish with the remaining half of scallions and ginger and serve immediately.

Indonesian Fried Rice with Mackerel Fillets

Prep time: 15 minutes | Cook time: 45 minutes | Serves 4

1 tablespoon olive oil
2 eggs, lightly beaten
1 tablespoon red curry paste
pinch caster sugar
800g cooked basmati rice
small bunch spring onions, sliced
140g frozen peas
2 tablespoons soy sauce , plus extra to serve
4 smoked mackerel fillets, flaked
½ cucumber, cut into half moons

1. Heat the oil in a large frying pan or wok. Tip in the eggs and swirl to coat the base of the pan. Cook for 1 minute, then flip and cook the other side until set. Remove and roughly chop into ribbons.
2. Add the curry paste and sugar and fry for 1 minute. Tip in the rice and stir to coat in the paste, then add the spring onions and peas.
3. Stir-fry for 2 to 3 minutes until everything is really hot. Add the soy sauce, then gently toss through the omelette ribbons and mackerel.
4. Divide between 4 bowls and garnish with the cucumber. Serve with extra soy sauce, if you like.

Roasted Mackerel Fillets with Bread Crumbs

Prep time: 10 minutes | Cook time: 8 minutes | Serves 4

¼ cup plus 1 teaspoon extra-virgin olive oil, divided
4 mackerel fillets (1½ pounds / 680 g), skin on
Kosher salt
Freshly ground black pepper
Zest and juice of 1 lemon, divided
1 cup panko bread crumbs
2 tablespoons coarsely chopped fresh flat-leaf parsley
3 small garlic cloves, minced
1 teaspoon smoked paprika

1. Preheat the oven to 400°F (205ºC). Rub 1 teaspoon of olive oil over the inside of a 9-inch by 13-inch baking dish.
2. Place the mackerel fillets, skin-side down, in a single layer in the prepared baking dish. Drizzle with 2 tablespoons of olive oil and season with salt and pepper. Drizzle 2 teaspoons of lemon juice over the fish and reserve the rest. Roast for 8 minutes.
3. While the fish is roasting, in a nonstick skillet over medium heat, combine the remaining 2 tablespoons of olive oil, the lemon zest, bread crumbs, parsley, garlic, and paprika and cook, stirring occasionally, until the garlic is fragrant and the bread crumbs are golden and toasty. Season with salt and pepper.
4. Remove the fish from the oven and top with the bread crumb mixture. Drizzle the remaining lemon juice over the fish and serve immediately.

Mason Jar Mackerel Sushi Salad

Prep time: 15 minutes | Cook time: 45 minutes | Serves 4

For the Ginger Dressing:
½ cup finely chopped yellow onion
¼ cup shredded carrots
¼ cup rice vinegar
2½ tablespoons finely minced peeled ginger
1½ tablespoons honey
1 tablespoon low-sodium soy sauce
1 teaspoon hot chili sauce
½ teaspoon minced garlic

For the Sushi Salad:
1 cup short-grain brown rice
1 cup shelled edamame, fresh or frozen and thawed
1 cup julienned cucumber
1 cup shredded carrots
6 ounces (170 g) mackerel
2 seaweed sheets, crumbled or cut into thin strips

To Make the Ginger Dressing
1. In a high-powered blender or food processor, combine the onion, carrots, rice vinegar, ginger, honey, soy sauce, chili sauce, garlic, and 2 tablespoons of water. Blend until mostly smooth.

To Make the Sushi Salad
1. In a medium saucepan, combine 2 cups of water and the rice.
2. Bring to a boil, then reduce the heat to low, cover, and simmer for 45 minutes. Allow rice to cool slightly before assembling jars.
3. Divide the dressing among four mason jars. Layer in the rice, edamame, cucumber, carrots, and mackerel. Garnish with shredded seaweed. Shake jars before eating.

Crispy Mackerel Patties

Prep time: 10 minutes | Cook time: 6 minutes | Serves 2

15 ounces (425 g) canned mackerel in brine
2 eggs
¼ cup of grated Parmesan Cheese
½ cup of breadcrumbs
2 tablespoons of mayonnaise
2 tablespoons of mustard
2 tablespoons of chopped chives or scallion vegetable oil for frying

1. Drain mackerel, debone and transfer to a mixing bowl. Flake meat with fork. Flaking mackerel meat with fork.
2. Add the rest of the ingredients, excluding vegetable oil, and mix well. Preparing mixture for mackerel patties.
3. Using ¼ cup as a measure, shape into patties.
4. Fry in small amount of vegetable oil, on medium heat until golden brown (about 3 minutes per side).
5. Serve.

Mackerel Fillets with Escalivada and Toasts

Prep time: 15 minutes | Cook time: 29 minutes | Serves 4

For the Escalivada:

3 very large or 4 medium peppers, a mix of colours
1 red onion, halved and thinly sliced
3 tablespoons extra virgin olive oil
2 medium aubergines
Zest 1 lemon, juice of ½

1 rosemary sprig, finely chopped
2 tablespoons small capers, drained
Small pack flat-leaf parsley, roughly chopped

For the Fish and Toasts:

2 rosemary sprigs, finely chopped
3 garlic cloves, crushed
3 tablespoon extra virgin olive oil, plus extra to serve (optional)

1 large olive ciabatta , cut into 8 slices
¼ teaspoon chilli flakes or hot paprika
4 mackerel fillets, pin-boned and cut in half if large

1. Heat the grill as hot as it will go. Line the grill pan or a large baking tray with foil. Using a potato peeler, remove most of the skin from the peppers, then remove the seeds and slice into 1 cm strips.
2. Toss with the onion and 1 tablespoon oil, then grill for 15 minutes, stirring halfway, until soft and charring here and there.
3. Cut the aubergines into 1cm half moons and brush sparingly with 2 tablespoons oil. Lay the slices over the peppers, season well, then grill for 5 minutes until golden. Turn the aubergines over, scatter with the lemon zest and rosemary, then grill for 5 minutes more until golden and soft in places.
4. Stir the capers and the lemon juice into the vegetables. Season and set aside. Make and chill up to 3 days ahead; the flavours will intensify as it matures. Make sure you serve it just warm, with the parsley folded through it.
5. For the toasts and fish, mix the rosemary, crushed garlic, oil and some seasoning. Brush half of this over one side of the ciabatta slices. Mix the chilli into the remainder, then brush over the fish and let it marinate for anything from 5 minutes to 1 hour in the fridge.
6. Grill the fish, skin-side up (or barbecue skin-side down), for 4 to 5 minutes, depending on the thickness of flesh, until just cooked through and the skin is crisp. Grill the bread until sizzling and golden.
7. Top the toasts with the escalivada, followed by the fish, and serve with another drizzle oil, if you like.

Mackerel Fillet Meunière

Prep time: 10 minutes | Cook time: 9 minutes | Serves 4

4 mackerel fillets (1½ pounds / 680 g), skin and pin bones removed
Kosher salt
Freshly ground black pepper
⅔ cup all-purpose flour
2 tablespoons vegetable oil or

canola oil
8 tablespoons (1 stick) unsalted butter, cut into ½-inch cubes, divided
Juice of ½ lemon
2 tablespoons coarsely chopped fresh flat-leaf parsley
Lemon wedges, for garnish

1. Arrange the mackerel on a plate and season generously on both sides with salt and pepper. Pour the flour into a wide shallow dish and dredge the fish generously on both sides.
2. In a large nonstick skillet, heat the oil over medium-high heat. When shimmery wavy lines run through the oil, add 3 tablespoons of butter and quickly swirl to combine it with the oil. Add the fish and cook for 6 minutes, flipping over halfway through, until both sides are golden brown.
3. Transfer the fish to plates and tent with aluminum foil.
4. To prepare the sauce, pour off the oil from cooking the fish and wipe the pan clean. Return the pan to medium-high heat and add the remaining 5 tablespoons of butter and cook until the milk solids begin to brown, 3 to 4 minutes. Remove from the heat and gently stir in the lemon juice and parsley. Season with salt and pepper and spoon the sauce over the fish.
5. Garnish with lemon wedges and serve.

Miso-Lacquered Meunière Dish

Prep time: 10 minutes | Cook time: 30 minutes | Serves 4

For the Rice Cakes:

1 cup short-grain sushi rice	1 teaspoon kosher salt
1 tablespoon seasoned rice vinegar	2 tablespoons vegetable oil

For the Mackerel:

3 tablespoons vegetable oil, divided	pound / 454 g), skin on and pin bones removed
2 tablespoons soy sauce	4 lemon wedges or slices, for garnish
2 tablespoons yellow miso	2 scallions, thinly sliced on the bias, for garnish (white and green parts)
1 tablespoon toasted sesame oil	
1 tablespoon honey	
4 mackerel fillets (1	

1. Preheat the oven to 400°F (205°C). Line a baking sheet with aluminum foil.
2. To make the rice cakes, cook the rice according to the package instructions, about 20 minutes. While the rice is cooking, stir together the vinegar and salt. Set aside.
3. When the rice is done, transfer it to a mixing bowl and gently fluff with a kitchen spoon, letting it cool. Add the vinegar mixture and stir once more. Divide the rice into four equal balls.
4. With wet hands, shape the balls into tightly compacted 1-inch-thick patties and wrap each patty tightly with plastic wrap.
5. In a nonstick skillet, heat the vegetable oil over medium heat. When shimmery wavy lines run through the oil, unwrap the patties and carefully place them in the skillet.
6. Fry until the undersides are golden brown and crispy, about 5 minutes. Flip the rice cakes over and fry on the other side until golden and crispy, about 4 minutes. Transfer the rice cakes to plates and keep warm.
7. To make the mackerel, in a small bowl, whisk 2 tablespoons of the vegetable oil, soy sauce, miso, sesame oil, and honey together until it forms a thick paste.
8. Spread the remaining 1 tablespoon of oil over the prepared baking sheet. Place the fish on the baking sheet and brush the marinade over the tops of the fish. Roast for 8 minutes. Remove from the oven and brush again with more marinade.
9. Adjust the oven to broil on high and broil for 1 to 2 minutes, or until the tops of the fillets become slightly caramelized. Remove from the broiler and transfer to the plates with the rice cakes.
10. Garnish with the lemon and scallions and serve immediately.

Mackerel with Lemon Beurre Blanc Sauce

Prep time: 10 minutes | Cook time: 13 minutes | Serves 4

2 (6- to 8-ounce / 170- to 277-g) mackerel fillets	chopped
1 tablespoon extra-virgin olive oil	Zest and juice of 1 lemon
Kosher salt	6 tablespoons (¾ stick) unsalted butter, cold and cubed
Freshly ground black pepper	½ cup sliced toasted almonds, for garnish
1 cup dry white wine (such as Sauvignon blanc)	3 tablespoons chopped fresh mint leaves, for garnish
1 shallot, finely	

1. Preheat the oven to 425°F (220°C) or turn on the broiler.
2. Line a baking sheet with aluminum foil and place the mackerel fillets side by side on it. Drizzle with the olive oil and season with salt and pepper.
3. Roast or broil for 8 minutes, until the fish feels firm and has a slightly opaque look. Transfer to a warm platter and tent with foil.
4. In a nonstick skillet over medium-high heat, sauté the wine, shallot, lemon zest, and lemon juice until it reduces and is almost dry, 5 to 7 minutes.
5. Begin to add the cubes of butter, a few at a time, while whisking constantly. Be sure that the butter has completely melted before adding more. This ensures that the sauce is velvety and slightly foamy. Lightly season with salt and pepper.
6. Pour the beurre blanc over the mackerel and garnish with the almonds and mint. Serve hot.

Herb-Stuffed Meunière with Roasted Veggies

Prep time: 10 minutes | Cook time: 0 minutes | Serves 4

2 (2-pound / 907-g) whole mackerel, skin and pin bones removed and butterflied
6 tablespoons extra-virgin olive oil, divided
Kosher salt
Freshly ground black pepper
2 lemons, thinly sliced, divided
½ bunch dill
½ bunch flat-leaf parsley leaves
½ bunch oregano
½ head cauliflower, cut into bite-size florets
3 cups grape tomatoes
½ medium red onion, unpeeled and cut into ½-inch slices
3 tablespoons vegetable oil
2 large handfuls baby arugula, spinach, or kale

1. Preheat the oven to 425°F (220°C). Place a 12-inch cast iron skillet in the oven to preheat for at least 15 minutes.
2. Open a mackerel like a book and place it flat, skin-side down. Drizzle with 2 tablespoons of olive oil and season with salt and pepper.
3. Add 3 lemon slices and half the dill, parsley, and oregano and fold the mackerel over to close. Set aside and repeat the process with the remaining mackerel.
4. Using a sharp knife, score three to four diagonal cuts across the top of each fish, cutting about ¼-inch deep. Halve four lemon slices to create half-moons and stuff them into the scores.
5. Rub 2 tablespoons of olive oil over both sides of the fish and season with salt and pepper.
6. In a medium bowl, toss the cauliflower, tomatoes, and red onion together with the remaining 2 tablespoons of olive oil and season with salt and pepper.
7. Remove the pan from the oven and place on a heat-proof surface. Add the vegetable oil and swirl to coat the pan. When shimmery wavy lines run through the oil, place the mackerel side by side in the pan and toss the vegetables around it, being careful as the hot pan may start sizzling right away.
8. Return the pan to the oven and roast for 20 minutes, or until the vegetables have roasted and caramelized slightly.
9. Create a bed of the arugula on a platter and place the fish on top. Arrange the roasted vegetables around the fish and serve hot.

Meunière Fillet Piperade

Prep time: 10 minutes | Cook time: 23 minutes | Serves 4

4 mackerel fillets (1½ pounds / 680 g), skin and pin bones removed
Kosher salt
Freshly ground black pepper
6 tablespoons extra-virgin olive oil, divided, plus more for garnish
1 medium white onion, cut into ½-inch strips
1 red bell pepper, cut into ½-inch strips
1 green bell pepper, cut into ½-inch strips
2 garlic cloves, minced
1 tablespoon smoked paprika
Pinch cayenne pepper
1 (14-ounce / 397-g) can fire-roasted diced tomatoes, with their juices
1 cup halved pitted green olives
2 tablespoons coarsely chopped fresh flat-leaf parsley, for garnish

1. Season the mackerel fillets with salt and pepper and drizzle 2 tablespoons of olive oil over the fish. Set aside on a plate.
2. In a large wide sauté pan or skillet, heat the remaining 4 tablespoons olive oil over medium-high heat. Add the onion and red and green bell peppers and cook until tender, about 7 minutes. Season with salt and pepper.
3. Add the garlic, paprika, and cayenne and sauté for 1 minute, until the garlic is fragrant.
4. Add the tomatoes and their juices and stir gently to combine. Season with salt and pepper and add the olives. Lower the heat to medium and simmer for 5 minutes.
5. Place the mackerel in the sauce and simmer, covered, for 10 minutes.
6. Serve hot, garnished with the parsley and a drizzle of olive oil.

Delicious Smoked Mackerel Kedgeree

Prep time: 15 minutes | Cook time: 45 minutes | Serves 4

4 whole smoked mackerel fillets, skin on
½ tablespoon olive oil
1 teaspoon coriander seeds
6 to 8 curry leaves
1 teaspoon mustard seeds
1 onion, finely chopped
1 carrot, finely chopped
1 leek, sliced
½ small pack coriander, stalks chopped, leaves picked to garnish

1 bay leaf
2 garlic cloves , crushed
½ cup basmati rice , rinsed
1 teaspoon turmeric
1 teaspoon medium curry powder
1 teaspoon white pepper
hot red chilli powder
½ cup cooked frozen peas
knob of butter
6 eggs, boiled for 7 minutes
1 lime, ½ juiced, ½ cut into wedges

1. Pour 2 cups of boiling water over the fish fillets and set aside. Heat the oil in a large, heavy-bottomed frying pan over a medium-high heat.
2. Add the coriander seeds, curry leaves and mustard seeds, and cook until the seeds start to crackle, about 1 min or so.
3. Add the onion, carrot, leek, coriander stalks, bay leaf and a pinch of salt, turn down the heat and cook for 8 to 10 minutes.
4. Add the garlic and cook for 2 minutes more.
5. Add the rice and stir-fry for a few minutes, making sure that it doesn't stick. Drain the mackerel water into the pan, then stir in the spices and increase the heat. Bring to the boil, then turn the heat down low, cover and cook for 15 to 20 minutes.
6. Remove from the heat and leave the rice to steam- cook with the lid on for 15 minutes. (If the rice is still not cooked through, add some water and return to the heat for a few minutes.)
7. Peel and discard the mackerel skin. Flake up the flesh and stir it into the rice along with the cooked peas and butter, the mackerel should be warmed through by the residual heat, but if not, return to the heat for a couple of minutes, stirring so it doesn't stick. Mix in the lime juice, then chop up two of the eggs and stir through.

8. Serve topped with the remaining eggs cut into quarters, the coriander leaves and some pepper.

Peppered Smoked Mackerel and Onion Salad

Prep time: 15 minutes | Cook time: 45 minutes | Serves 6

240g pack peppered smoked mackerel, torn into pieces
100g bag watercress
For the Dressing:
1 small red onion, very thinly sliced
3 tablespoons sherry

250g pack ready-cooked beetroot
100g bag honey-roasted mixed nuts

vinegar pinch of sugar
4 tablespoons extra virgin olive oil

1. Mix together the onion, vinegar, sugar and a pinch of salt. Leave to pickle while you dice the beetroot and roughly chop the nuts.
2. Divide the watercress and smoked mackerel between six plates. Scatter over the beetroot and nuts, then top with a cluster of the pickled onions.
3. Whisk the oil into the pickling vinegar, then drizzle the dressing around the outside of each plate.

Hoisin Mackerel Fillets Pancakes

Prep time: 15 minutes | Cook time: 45 minutes | Serves 4

3 mackerel fillets, all bones removed, cut into finger-length strips
2 tablespoon hoisin sauce , plus extra for dipping

4 spring onions
½ cucumber
2 Little Gem lettuces
1 teaspoon vegetable oil
10 Chinese pancakes

1. Marinate the mackerel in the hoisin sauce while you prepare the veg.
2. Cut the spring onions and cucumber into thin matchsticks, and separate the lettuce leaves.
3. Heat the oil in a large frying pan over a medium heat.
4. Add the mackerel and fry for 3 to 4 minutes until sticky and caramelised. Heat the pancakes following pack instructions.
5. Serve everything in the middle of the table and let everyone help themselves.

Savory Somked Meunière Pintxos

Prep time: 10 minutes | Cook time: 22 minutes | Serves 4 to 6

1 medium potato, peeled and cut into 1-inch chunks
¼ cup kosher salt, divided
1 baguette, cut into 12 (¼-inch-thick) slices on the bias
¼ cup extra-virgin olive oil, divided
Freshly ground black pepper
4 ounces Spanish chorizo, casing removed and finely chopped

1 small shallot, finely chopped
2 tablespoons unsalted butter
2 smoked mackerel fillets (1 pound / 454 g), broken up into chunks
2 tablespoons coarsely chopped fresh flat-leaf parsley, divided
1 (4-ounce / 113-g) jar pimento strips, drained

1. Preheat the oven to 400°F (205ºC).
2. In a small saucepan, cover the potatoes with water and add 3 tablespoons of kosher salt. Bring to a boil over medium-high heat, then lower the heat to medium-low and simmer for 8 to 10 minutes, until tender. Drain and set aside in a mixing bowl.
3. On a baking sheet, arrange the baguette slices in a single layer and brush the tops lightly with 2 tablespoons of olive oil. Season with ½ tablespoon of salt and pepper and toast for 10 minutes. Remove from the oven and set aside to cool.
4. In a nonstick skillet, heat the remaining 2 tablespoons of olive oil over medium heat. When shimmery wavy lines run through the oil add the chorizo and shallot and sauté until the shallot is soft and translucent, about 4 minutes. Season with the remaining ½ tablespoon of salt and pepper. Add the chorizo mixture to the potato.
5. Return the skillet to medium heat and melt the butter. Add the smoked mackerel, breaking up the fish into smaller flakes and swirling the butter to coat it. Remove from the heat and add to the potato.
6. With a potato masher, mash the potato mixture together until combined and smooth. Fold in 1 tablespoon of parsley and season with salt and pepper.
7. To serve, divide and spread the potato mixture evenly among the toasted baguette and top with a few pimento strips. Sprinkle the remaining 1 tablespoon of parsley over the pintxos and transfer to a platter.
8. Serve warm or at room temperature.

Mackerel Fillets and Green Bean Salad

Prep time: 10 minutes | Cook time: 11 minutes | Serves 2

2 cups green beans
1 tablespoon avocado oil
2 mackerel fillets
4 cups mixed salad greens
2 hard-boiled eggs, sliced

1 avocado, sliced
2 tablespoons lemon juice
2 tablespoons olive oil
1 teaspoon Dijon mustard
Salt and black pepper, to taste

1. Cook the green beans in a medium saucepan of boiling water for about 3 minutes until crisp-tender. Drain and set aside.
2. Melt the avocado oil in a pan over medium heat. Add the mackerel fillets and cook each side for 4 minutes.
3. Divide the greens between two salad bowls. Top with the mackerel, sliced egg, and avocado slices.
4. In another bowl, whisk together the lemon juice, olive oil, mustard, salt, and pepper, and drizzle over the salad. Add the cooked green beans and toss to combine, then serve.

Chapter 5 Tilapia

Tilapia Fillets Tacos with Cabbage Slaw

Prep time: 15 minutes | Cook time: 24 minutes | Serves 4

For the Cabbage Slaw:

½ head green cabbage, finely shredded
½ small red onion, cut into ¼-inch dice
¼ cup loosely packed fresh cilantro leaves
1 small jalapeño, seeded and minced

Kosher salt
Freshly ground black pepper
2 tablespoons sour cream or Mexican crema
1 tablespoon freshly squeezed lime juice

For the Tacos:

2 tilapia fillets (1½ pounds / 680 g), each cut into 4 equal pieces
1 teaspoon ground cumin
½ teaspoon chile powder
Kosher salt

Freshly ground black pepper
3 tablespoons vegetable oil
16 (6-inch) corn tortillas
2 limes, quartered, for garnish

1. To make the cabbage slaw, in a small bowl, toss together the cabbage, onion, cilantro, and jalapeño. Season with salt and pepper. Toss with the sour cream and lime juice and keep covered in the refrigerator.
2. To make the tacos, heat a cast iron skillet over medium-high heat. While the pan is heating, season both sides of the fish with the cumin, chile powder, salt, and pepper.
3. Add the oil to the pan. When the oil reaches its smoke point, add the fish and sear on each side for 4 minutes, flipping once. Transfer the fillets to a clean plate and tent with aluminum foil.
4. Wipe out the pan with dry paper towels and return it to medium-high heat. Toast the tortillas, two at a time, for 1 minute each, flipping halfway through.
5. To assemble, break the fillets into small chunks and arrange on top of eight double stacks of tortillas. Lightly season each taco with salt and pepper and a squeeze of juice from the limes. Top with the cabbage slaw. Serve immediately.

Roasted Tilapia Fillets with Orzo Mixture

Prep time: 10 minutes | Cook time: 24 minutes | Serves 4

1 lemon, zested and cut into ¼-inch slices
4 tilapia fillets (1½ pounds / 680 g)
¼ cup extra-virgin olive oil, divided
Kosher salt
Freshly ground black pepper
2 tablespoons coarsely chopped fresh oregano leaves,

divided
1 shallot, coarsely chopped
2 cups halved grape tomatoes
2 cups cooked orzo
1 tablespoon coarsely chopped fresh flat-leaf parsley
2 tablespoons crumbled feta cheese, for garnish (optional)

1. Preheat the oven to 400°F (205°C). Line a baking sheet with aluminum foil or parchment paper.
2. Arrange the lemon slices in a single layer on the prepared baking sheet and place the tilapia across the lemon slices.
3. Drizzle with 2 tablespoons of olive oil and season with salt and pepper.
4. Rub the oil and seasonings all over both sides of the fish and sprinkle 1 tablespoon of oregano over the fish. Roast for 10 to 15 minutes, or until the fish flakes with a fork.
5. While the fish is roasting, in a sauté pan or skillet, heat the remaining 2 tablespoons of olive oil over medium-high heat.
6. When shimmery wavy lines run through the oil, add the shallot and sauté until soft and translucent, about 4 minutes, then add the tomatoes. Cook for 5 minutes, or until the tomatoes begin to soften and break down.
7. Remove the pan from the heat and stir in the cooked orzo, lemon zest, parsley, and the remaining 1 tablespoon of oregano. Lightly season with salt and pepper and transfer to a serving platter.
8. Carefully transfer each fillet to the a bed of the orzo mixture. Garnish with the feta cheese (if using) and serve hot.

Tilapia Fillets in Mustard Sauce

Prep time: 10 minutes | Cook time: 12 minutes | Serves 4

4 (6-ounce / 170-g) tilapia fillets
Kosher salt
Freshly ground black pepper
2 tablespoons extra-virgin olive oil
1 cup sour cream

2 tablespoons Dijon mustard
2 teaspoons whole-grain mustard
1 small shallot, minced
1 teaspoon coarsely chopped capers

1. Preheat the oven to 400°F (205°C). Line a baking sheet with parchment paper or aluminum foil.
2. Arrange the fish on the prepared baking sheet and season on both sides with salt and pepper. Rub the olive oil all over the fish. Set aside.
3. In a small bowl, stir together the sour cream, Dijon mustard, and whole-grain mustard. Add the shallot and capers, season with salt and pepper, and mix well. Spread the sauce over the fish, completely covering each fillet.
4. Roast for 12 minutes. Remove from the oven and transfer to plates. Serve immediately.

Steamed Tilapia Fillets with Chutney

Prep time: 15 minutes | Cook time: 13 minutes | Serves 2

100g basmati rice
2 large tilapia fillets
2 teaspoon butter
150g pot fat-free

yogurt, to serve
2 small naan bread, to serve

For the Chutney:

handful coriander, roughly chopped
½ green chilli, deseeded
25g desiccated coconut

1 lemon ½ juiced, ½ cut into wedges
1 teaspoon chopped ginger
½ teaspoon ground cumin

1. To make the chutney, put the coriander, chilli, coconut, lemon juice, ginger and cumin in a food processor. Add good pinches of salt and sugar, then pulse until it has a rough salsa-like consistency.

2. Rinse the rice and place in a deep frying pan with 1 cup of water. Bring to the boil, then turn down low, it will take about 8 minutes to cook.
3. After about 3 minutes, place the fish fillets on top of the rice, then dot a teaspoon of butter on each and spread the fresh chutney over in a thick layer. Cover with a lid and cook over a low heat for about 5 minutes until the fish and rice are cooked through.
4. Serve the fish and rice with the yogurt, warmed naan breads and the lemon wedges.

Cajun Tilapia Fillets Po' Boys

Prep time: 15 minutes | Cook time: 5 minutes | Serves 4

1 teaspoon garlic powder
½ teaspoon chili powder
½ teaspoon dried thyme
½ teaspoon paprika
½ teaspoon onion powder
½ teaspoons kosher salt
¼ teaspoon cayenne pepper

3 tablespoons mayonnaise, divided
2 tilapia fillets (1½ pounds / 680 g)
2 French sandwich rolls, split
2 ripe Roma tomatoes, cut into ¼-inch slices
2 to 3 green leaf lettuce leaves, washed and spun dry

1. Preheat the broiler. Line a baking sheet with aluminum foil and set aside.
2. In a small bowl, mix together the garlic powder, chili powder, thyme, paprika, onion powder, salt, and cayenne pepper. Add 1½ tablespoons of mayonnaise and stir to combine.
3. Spread the spiced mayonnaise over both sides of the fish and place the fish on the prepared baking sheet. Broil the fish for 5 minutes on each side (it's OK if the fish blackens a bit), flipping once. Remove from the broiler and tent with foil.
4. Spread out the rolls under the broiler and toast for a few seconds. Transfer the rolls to plates and spread the remaining 1½ tablespoons of mayonnaise on one side of each roll. Transfer a fillet to each roll and top with the tomatoes and lettuce. Serve hot.

Tilapia Fillets in Thai Sauce

Prep time: 10 minutes | Cook time: 2 minutes | Serves 2

4 tilapia fillets
2 tablespoons cornflour
2 tablespoons sunflower oil
4 spring onions, sliced
2 garlic cloves, crushed small piece fresh ginger, finely chopped
2 tablespoon soy sauce
1 tablespoon brown Sugar juice of 1 lime, plus 1 lime chopped into wedges, to serve
1 red chilli, deseeded and sliced
Handful of Thai basil leaves or coriander leaves

1. Coat the fish fillets in the cornflour, then set aside.
2. Heat the oil in a large non-stick frying pan, sizzle the fillets for 2 to 3 minutes on each side until crisp, then remove and keep warm.
3. In the same pan, briefly fry the spring onion, garlic and ginger, then add the soy sauce, brown sugar and lime juice and simmer until slightly syrupy.
4. Spoon the sauce over the fish, scatter with chilli, Thai basil or coriander, then serve with the lime wedges.

Savory Tilapia Piccata

Prep time: 10 minutes | Cook time: 5 minutes | Serves 4

3 tablespoons unsalted butter, divided
2 tablespoons extra-virgin olive oil
4 tilapia fillets (1½ pounds / 680 g), blotted dry
Kosher salt
Freshly ground black pepper
¾ cup all-purpose flour
½ cup dry white wine (such as Sauvignon blanc)
Juice of ½ lemon
2 teaspoons coarsely chopped rinsed capers
2 tablespoons coarsely chopped fresh flat-leaf parsley, for garnish

1. Heat a large nonstick skillet over medium-high heat and melt 2 tablespoons of butter and the oil together.
2. Season both sides of the fish with salt and pepper. Lightly dredge the fillets in the flour and shake off the excess.
3. When the butter has melted, swirl it to combine with the oil. Place the fillets in the pan and sear for 3 to 4 minutes on each side, or until golden brown and crispy. Transfer the fillets to plates and tent with aluminum foil.
4. Lower the heat to medium and add the wine. Using a wooden spoon, scrape up the bits of browned butter and flour. Stir in the lemon juice and capers, and salt and pepper. Simmer for 2 minutes to reduce the sauce.
5. Remove from the heat and add the remaining 1 tablespoon of butter, swirling until it is melted. Divide the sauce among the plates and garnish each with the parsley. Serve immediately.

Savory Baked Piri-PIri Tilapia

Prep time: 10 minutes | Cook time: 35 minutes | Serves 4

600 g small new potatoes
2 red peppers, cut into chunky pieces
1 tablespoon red wine
vinegar drizzle of extra virgin olive oil
4 large pieces tilapia, to serve

For the Piri-Piri Sauce:
6 hot pickled peppers
1 teaspoon chilli flakes
2 garlic cloves
Juice and zest of 1 lemon
1 tablespoon red wine vinegar
2 tablespoons extra virgin olive oil
1 tablespoon smoked paprika

1. Heat oven to 220ºF (104ºC).
2. Boil the potatoes until knife-tender, then drain. Spread out on a large baking tray and gently crush with the back of a spatula. Add the peppers, drizzle with the vinegar and oil, season well and roast for 25 minutes.
3. Put the piri-piri ingredients in a food processor with some salt. Purée until fine, then pour into a bowl. Put the fish on a baking tray and spoon over some of the piri-piri sauce. Season and bake for the final 10 minutes of the potatoes' cooking time.
4. Serve everything with the extra sauce and a green salad on the side.

Steamed Tilapia Fillets with Teriyaki Sauce

Prep time: 10 minutes | Cook time: 15 minutes | Serves 4

3 tablespoons soy sauce
2½ ounces mirin
2 tablespoon sugar
1 lemon, juice ½, ½ sliced
250 g basmati rice, rinsed in cold water

5 ounces (142 g) pieces of tilapia fillets
1¼-inch piece ginger, shredded
1 red chilli, sliced, deseeded if you like
Small bunch spring onions , sliced

1. Pour the soy, mirin and sugar in a small saucepan with the lemon juice. Bring to the boil and simmer for 5 minutes until slightly syrupy. Remove and set aside.
2. Put the rice in a large saucepan and cover with water, about 2 cups. Bring to the boil, then turn down to a simmer. Cook for about 5 minutes, the rice should have absorbed about ¾ of the water. Place the fish fillets on top.
3. Sprinkle each with ginger, chilli and a slice of lemon. Season, cover and cook for about 5 minutes, until the fish and rice are cooked through.
4. Serve with a drizzle of the sauce and sprinkled with the spring onions.

Tangy Tilapia Fillets with Ginger

Prep time: 10 minutes | Cook time: 8 minutes | Serves 4

2 tablespoons olive oil
2 tablespoons fresh lime or lemon juice
1 teaspoon minced fresh ginger
1 clove garlic, minced
1 teaspoon ground turmeric
½ teaspoon kosher

salt
¼ to ½ teaspoon cayenne pepper
1 pound (454 g) tilapia fillets
Olive oil spray
Lime or lemon wedges (optional)

1. In a large bowl, combine the oil, lime juice, ginger, garlic, turmeric, salt, and cayenne. Stir until well combined; set aside.
2. Cut each tilapia fillet into three or four equal-size pieces. Add the fish to the bowl and gently mix until all of the fish is coated in the marinade. Marinate for 10 to 15 minutes at room temperature.
3. Spray the air fryer basket with olive oil spray. Place the fish in the basket and spray the fish.
4. Set the air fryer to 325ºF (163ºC) for 3 minutes to partially cook the fish.
5. Set the air fryer to 400ºF (204ºC) for 5 minutes to finish cooking and crisp up the fish.
6. Carefully remove the fish from the basket. Serve hot, with lemon wedges if desired.

Crispy Tilapia Fillets with Mango Salsa

Prep time: 15 minutes | Cook time: 6 minutes | Serves 2

Salsa:
1 cup chopped mango
2 tablespoons chopped fresh cilantro
2 tablespoons chopped red onion
Tilapia:
1 tablespoon paprika
1 teaspoon onion powder
½ teaspoon dried thyme
½ teaspoon freshly ground black pepper
¼ teaspoon cayenne pepper

2 tablespoons freshly squeezed lime juice
½ jalapeño pepper, seeded and minced
Pinch salt

½ teaspoon garlic powder
¼ teaspoon salt
½ pound (227 g) boneless tilapia fillets
2 teaspoons extra-virgin olive oil
1 lime, cut into wedges, for serving

1. Make the salsa: Place the mango, cilantro, onion, lime juice, jalapeño, and salt in a medium bowl and toss to combine. Set aside.
2. Make the tilapia: Stir together the paprika, onion powder, thyme, black pepper, cayenne pepper, garlic powder, and salt in a small bowl until well mixed. Rub both sides of fillets generously with the mixture.
3. Heat the olive oil in a large skillet over medium heat.
4. Add the fish fillets and cook each side for 3 to 5 minutes until golden brown and cooked through.
5. Divide the fillets among two plates and spoon half of the prepared salsa onto each fillet. Serve the fish alongside the lime wedges.

Thai-Spiced Tilapia Fillets

Prep time: 15 minutes | Cook time: 36 minutes | Serves 4

2 tablespoons coconut oil
1 large shallot, finely chopped
2½ tablespoons Thai green curry paste
1 (15-ounce / 425-g) can coconut milk
¼ cup low-sodium vegetable stock
2 teaspoons fish sauce
Kosher salt
Freshly ground black pepper
4 tilapia fillets (1½ pounds / 680 g)
2 scallions, thinly sliced, for garnish (white and green parts)
2 tablespoons shredded Thai basil, for garnish (about 8 leaves)
1 lime, cut into wedges, for garnish
Cooked rice, for serving

1. Preheat the oven to 350ºF (180ºC).
2. Heat a large oven-safe skillet over medium-high heat. Add the coconut oil and swirl to coat the pan. When the oil has melted, add the shallot and sauté for about 4 minutes, until it is soft and translucent.
3. Add the green curry paste and stir to combine. Lower the heat to medium-low and add the coconut milk. Simmer for 5 minutes, stirring occasionally.
4. Stir in the vegetable stock and fish sauce and lightly season with salt and pepper. Continue to simmer for 2 minutes.
5. Season both sides of the tilapia with salt and pepper and place in the curry sauce. Transfer the pan to the oven. Bake, uncovered, for 25 minutes, or until the tilapia feels firm and flakes slightly when pushed with a fork.
6. Garnish with the scallions, basil, and lime. Serve immediately with cooked rice.

Coconut-Poached Tilapia Fillets

Prep time: 10 minutes | Cook time: 22 minutes | Serves 4

3 tablespoons coconut oil, divided
2 cups thinly sliced and stemmed shiitake mushrooms
2 Fresno peppers, seeded, deveined, and finely chopped
2 (15-ounce / 425-g) cans coconut milk
Zest and juice of 1 lime
Kosher salt
Freshly ground black pepper
4 tilapia fillets (1½ pounds / 680 g)
4 baby bok choy bulbs, leaves and stems coarsely chopped

1. Heat a deep skillet over medium-high heat. Add 2 tablespoons of coconut oil and swirl to coat the pan. When the oil has melted, add the mushrooms and sauté for 5 to 7 minutes, until they are golden brown. Transfer to a plate.
2. Add the remaining 1 tablespoon of coconut oil and the peppers and sauté until they are soft and tender, about 4 minutes. Transfer to the plate with the mushrooms.
3. Lower the heat to medium and add the coconut milk, lime zest, and lime juice. Stir to combine and lightly season with salt and pepper. Bring the mixture to a simmer.
4. While simmering, season the tilapia on both sides with salt and pepper. Lower the heat to medium-low and gently slip the fillets into the coconut milk. The fillets should be partially submerged, if not completely covered, in the milk. Let the heat from the milk gently poach the fish for about 8 minutes. Do not let the coconut milk boil.
5. Carefully lift the tilapia from the coconut milk and place in shallow bowls. Cover with aluminum foil.
6. Add the bok choy to the skillet and cook in the coconut milk until tender, about 5 minutes. Add the mushrooms and peppers and stir together until just warmed through.
7. Spoon the sauce over the fish and divide the vegetables evenly among the bowls. Serve hot.

Classic Tilapia Fillets and Chips

Prep time: 15 minutes | Cook time: 12 minutes | Serves 4

3 large russet potatoes, peeled and cut into 1-by-1½-inch strips
6 cups vegetable oil, for frying
¾ cup all-purpose flour, divided
¼ cup rice flour
¼ cup cornstarch
1 teaspoon baking powder
½ teaspoon cayenne pepper
Kosher salt
Freshly ground black pepper
⅓ cup beer (such as Newcastle Brown Ale, but any beer will do)
⅓ cup sparkling water
4 (4- to 5-ounce / 113- to 142-g) tilapia fillets, each cut into 3 pieces and blotted dry
Malt vinegar, for serving
Lemon wedges, for serving

1. To prepare the chips, in a bowl of cold water, soak the potatoes for up to 30 minutes. Drain and blot dry.
2. In a 3-quart Dutch oven or wide saucepan, heat the oil over medium-high heat to 350°F (180°C). Test the oil by dropping a spoonful of batter into it. If the batter begins to fry immediately and float, the oil is ready for frying.
3. While the oil is heating, in a bowl, whisk together ¼ cup of flour, the rice flour, cornstarch, baking powder, and cayenne. Season with a pinch of salt and pepper. Whisk in the beer and sparkling water until a light, foamy batter develops and the mixture is smooth.
4. Preheat the oven to 300°F (150°C).
5. When the oil is ready, using a wire skimmer, gently lower the chips, working in batches, into the pot. Fry for 7 to 8 minutes, until golden and cooked through. Remove the chips from the oil and transfer to a wire rack set over a baking sheet to drain.
6. Turn off the stove and place the chips in the oven to keep them warm.
7. Season both sides of the fish with salt and pepper. On a wide plate, add the remaining ½ cup of flour and dredge a piece of fish in the flour to evenly coat. Shake off the excess and dip the fish into the batter, making sure the batter completely coats the fish. Repeat the process with the remaining fillets.
8. Turn the heat back on and bring the oil temperature to 375°F (190°C). Using a pair of tongs, lift the fish from the batter and gently lower it into the oil. Cook in batches, up to four pieces of fish at time. Fry for 5 to 6 minutes, or until golden brown and crispy. Using a wire skimmer or slotted spoon, lift the fish out of the oil and place on a plate lined with paper towels. Keep warm in the oven.
9. To serve, arrange the fish and chips on a platter. Drizzle malt vinegar over the fish and garnish with lemon wedges. Serve hot.

Italian Tilapia Fillets with Lemon Pepper

Prep time: 5 minutes | Cook time: 10 minutes | Serves 3

2 teaspoons Italian seasoning
2 teaspoons lemon pepper
⅓ cup whole wheat bread crumbs
⅓ cup egg whites
⅓ cup almond flour
3 tilapia fillets
Olive oil

1. Place the bread crumbs, egg whites, and flour into separate bowls.
2. Mix lemon pepper and Italian seasoning in with bread crumbs.
3. Pat tilapia fillets dry. Dredge in flour, then egg, then bread crumb mixture. Add to air fryer basket and spray lightly with olive oil.
4. Cook 10-11 minutes at 400°F (204°C), making sure to flip halfway through cooking.

Chapter 6 Catfish

Catfish Filled with Veggies and Rice

Prep time: 10 minutes | Cook time: 10 minutes | Serves 4

1 cup halved grape tomatoes	Freshly ground black pepper
1 medium zucchini, cut into ½-inch rounds	4 catfish fillets (1½ pounds / 680 g), patted dry
½ medium red onion, cut into ¼-inch strips	Zest and juice of 1 lemon
4 tablespoons extra-virgin olive oil, divided	1½ cups cooked wild rice
Kosher salt	3 handfuls baby kale

1. Preheat the oven to 400°F (205°C). Line a baking sheet with parchment paper or aluminum foil.
2. Toss the tomatoes, zucchini, onion, and 2 tablespoons of olive oil together on the prepared baking sheet. Generously season with salt and pepper. Spread the vegetables in a single layer, leaving a space in the center for the fish, and roast for 10 minutes.
3. Drizzle 1 tablespoon of olive oil over the catfish and season both sides with salt and pepper.
4. Remove the baking sheet from the oven and place the fish in the center of the pan. Drizzle the lemon juice over the fish and return to the oven. Roast for 10 minutes, or until the fish is tender and flaky.
5. While the fish is roasting, in a large bowl, toss the lemon zest, wild rice, and kale together with the remaining 1 tablespoon of olive oil.
6. Transfer the roasted vegetables to the wild rice salad and toss gently to combine. Divide the salad among serving plates. Gently lift the catfish from the pan and place on top of each salad. Drizzle the juices from the baking sheet over the fish and serve immediately.

Delicious Catfish Hush Puppies

Prep time: 10 minutes | Cook time: 3 minutes | Serves 4

4 cups vegetable oil, for frying	Freshly ground black pepper
1 cup cornmeal (preferably stone-ground)	1 cup plus 2 tablespoons buttermilk
¾ cup all-purpose flour	8 ounces (227 g) catfish
1 teaspoon baking powder	2 large eggs, beaten
¼ teaspoon cayenne pepper	1 garlic clove, minced
Kosher salt	2 scallions, finely chopped (white and green parts)

1. In a Dutch oven, heat the oil over medium-high heat to 375°F (190°C), or when the end of a wooden spoon dipped into the oil causes bubbling and sizzling. Set a wire rack over a baking sheet and set aside.
2. While the oil is heating, in a medium bowl, whisk together the cornmeal, flour, baking powder, and cayenne. Season with salt and pepper.
3. In another bowl, stir together the buttermilk, catfish, eggs, garlic, and scallions. Fold the buttermilk mixture into the flour mixture until just incorporated.
4. Working in batches, scoop rounded tablespoonfuls of the batter and, using a second spoon, gently nudge the batter off the spoon into the oil. Using a slotted spoon or wire skimmer, turn the hush puppies and fry until golden brown, about 3 minutes.
5. Transfer to the wire rack and lightly season with salt while still hot. Transfer to a platter and serve.

Chili-Lime Catfish with Corn Salad

Prep time: 15 minutes | Cook time: 16 minutes | Serves 4

¼ cup extra-virgin olive oil, divided
1 pasilla pepper, cut into ¼-inch dice
Kosher salt
Freshly ground black pepper
1 large shallot, thinly sliced
2 large garlic cloves, minced
2 cups frozen yellow corn kernels, thawed
Zest of 2 limes
Juice of 3 limes, divided
4 (6-ounce / 170-g) catfish fillets
1 tablespoon chili powder
¼ cup coarsely chopped fresh cilantro leaves, divided
2 large handfuls baby arugula

1. Preheat the broiler. Line a baking sheet with aluminum foil.
2. To make the salad, in a cast iron skillet, heat 2 tablespoons of olive oil over medium-high heat. When shimmery wavy lines run through the oil, add the pasilla pepper and season with salt and pepper. Cook until the peppers become soft, about 4 minutes. Add the shallot and garlic and sauté for 1 minute, until the garlic is fragrant.
3. Add the corn and lightly season with salt and pepper. Continue to cook, stirring occasionally, until the corn begins to char slightly, 5 to 7 minutes. Some of the kernels may actually pop. Remove from the heat and stir in the lime zest and the juice of two limes.
4. To make the catfish, while the corn is charring, season the fillets on both sides with chili powder, salt, and pepper, then drizzle with the remaining 2 tablespoons of olive oil.
5. Place the fillets on the prepared baking sheet and broil for 6 to 7 minutes, or until an instant-read thermometer inserted into the thickest part of the fish reads 145°F. Remove from the oven and let the fish rest for 1 minute.
6. Toss 3 tablespoons of cilantro and the arugula with the corn salad, then divide evenly among plates. Place a piece of catfish on each salad. Squeeze the juice of the remaining lime over each plate and garnish with the remaining 1 tablespoon of cilantro. Serve immediately.

Cornmeal-Fried Catfish Fillets Sandwich

Prep time: 15 minutes | Cook time: 10 minutes | Serves 4

½ cup mayonnaise
Zest and juice of 1 lemon
2 teaspoons finely chopped capers
1 teaspoon Old Bay seasoning
½ teaspoon hot sauce (such as Tabasco or Crystal)
Kosher salt
Freshly ground black pepper
Vegetable oil, for frying
2 large eggs, beaten
1½ cups medium-ground cornmeal
½ cup all-purpose flour
¼ cup cornstarch
4 catfish fillets (1½ pounds / 680 g), trimmed to fit the length of the rolls
4 French bread sandwich rolls
4 green leaf lettuce leaves
2 Roma tomatoes, each cut into 6 slices

1. Preheat the oven to 350°F (180°C).
2. In a small mixing bowl, combine the mayonnaise, lemon zest, lemon juice, capers, Old Bay, and hot sauce. Season with salt and pepper. Cover with plastic wrap and refrigerate until ready to use.
3. In a cast iron skillet, heat ½ inch of vegetable oil over medium-high heat to 375°F (190°C), or when the end of a wooden spoon dipped into the oil causes bubbling and sizzling.
4. While the oil is heating, in a wide shallow bowl, beat the eggs. In another wide shallow bowl, combine the cornmeal, flour, and cornstarch.
5. When the oil is ready, season the catfish on both sides with salt and pepper. One at a time, dip the fillets into the egg, then coat in the cornmeal mixture and shake off the excess.
6. Lower the fish into the oil, letting it fall away from you. Fry the fillets for 3 to 4 minutes on each side, or until golden. Transfer the fillets to a plate lined with paper towels and season with kosher salt.
7. Split the rolls horizontally in half and toast lightly in the oven, about 7 to 8 minutes. Remove from the oven and spread the mayonnaise mixture on both sides, top with a fried catfish fillet, then top with the lettuce and tomato. Serve each sandwich sliced in half.

Catfish Curry Fillets with Basmati Rice

Prep time: 15 minutes | Cook time: 24 minutes | Serves 4

1½ cups basmati rice
3 tablespoons coconut oil
1 large yellow onion, cut into ¼-inch dice
Kosher salt
Freshly ground black pepper
1 (½-inch) piece fresh ginger, peeled and minced
2 garlic cloves, minced
2 tablespoons tomato paste
1 (15-ounce / 425-g) can coconut milk
2 tablespoons Madras curry powder
2 cups water
4 (6-ounce / 170-g) catfish fillets, each cut into 4 pieces
2 tablespoons coarsely chopped fresh cilantro, for garnish

1. In a large bowl, rinse the basmati rice several times, swirling the rice in the water each time to loosen any dust and debris. Cover the rice with fresh water and soak for 15 minutes.
2. While the rice is soaking, heat a large sauté pan or skillet over medium heat. Add the coconut oil and swirl to coat the pan. When the oil has melted, and add the onion and sauté for 7 minutes, or until the onion is soft and translucent. Season with salt and pepper.
3. Add the ginger and garlic and sauté for 1 minute, until fragrant. Add the tomato paste and cook for 2 minutes, stirring the tomato paste into the onion. Add the coconut milk and curry powder and stir. Lower the heat to low, lightly season with salt and pepper, and simmer for 5 minutes.
4. While the curry is simmering, drain the rice and transfer to a saucepan. Add a pinch of salt and the water. Cover and bring to a boil over medium-high heat. As soon as the water boils, lower the heat to low and continue to simmer for 10 minutes.
5. While the rice is cooking, slip the catfish pieces into the curry and simmer for 10 to 12 minutes, until an instant-read thermometer inserted into the thickest part of the fish reads 145°F (63ºC) and the flesh is opaque and flakes with a fork.
6. To serve, spoon a portion of rice into shallow bowls and ladle the fish and curry over the rice. Garnish with the cilantro and serve immediately.

Caramel Simmered Catfish Fillets

Prep time: 15 minutes | Cook time: 34 minutes | Serves 4

2 catfish fillets (1½ pounds / 680 g), cut into 4 equal pieces
1 teaspoon Chinese five-spice powder
1 tablespoon fish sauce
Kosher salt
Freshly ground black pepper
2 tablespoons vegetable oil
1 small shallot, thinly sliced
4 garlic cloves, thinly sliced
1 red Fresno pepper, thinly sliced
1 cup coconut water
4 tablespoons sugar
2 tablespoons water
Juice of 1 lime, for garnish
1 tablespoon chopped fresh cilantro, for garnish
Steamed rice, for serving

1. Blot the catfish with paper towels and place in a bowl. Season with the five-spice powder, fish sauce, salt, and pepper. Marinate for 5 to 10 minutes.
2. In a nonstick skillet, heat the oil over medium-high heat. Add the shallot and garlic and sauté until they turn brown, about 1 minute. Add the Fresno pepper and sauté for 1 more minute.
3. Push the vegetables to the side of the pan and sear the catfish on both sides, about 3 minutes per side, until golden brown. Add the coconut water and lower the heat to medium-low. Braise the fish in the simmering coconut water while you prepare the sauce.
4. In a small saucepan or nonstick skillet, heat the sugar and water over medium-high heat until the mixture starts to bubble and begins to caramelize, about 6 to 7 minutes. Immediately pour it over the fish.
5. Simmer the fish in the caramel sauce for 20 minutes, or until the sauce thickens and the fish has taken on a deep caramelized color.
6. Transfer the fish and sauce to bowls. Garnish with the lime juice and cilantro. Serve with steamed rice.

Cajun Catfish Fillets and Shrimp Boil

Prep time: 10 minutes | Cook time: 20 minutes | Serves 4

4 (4-ounce / 113-g) catfish fillets, cut into 2 pieces each
½ pound shrimp, peeled and deveined
1 tablespoon Cajun seasoning
4 russet potatoes, cut into eighths

2 ears of corn, cut into 4 pieces on the cob
½ cup water
Sea salt, for seasoning
Freshly ground black pepper, for seasoning

1. Preheat the oven to 400°F (205ºC). Cut 4 pieces of aluminum foil, each 12 inches square with the edges turned up to form a rough bowl, and set aside.
2. In a medium bowl, toss the catfish, shrimp, and Cajun seasoning together until well combined.
3. Divide the potatoes and corn between the foil pieces and top with the catfish and shrimp.
4. Drizzle the fish and vegetables with water and lightly season with salt and pepper.
5. Fold the foil up to form tightly sealed packets and put them on a baking sheet.
6. Bake until the fish flakes when pressed with a fork and the vegetables are tender, 20 to 25 minutes.

Delicious Catfish and Shrimp Jambalaya

Prep time: 15 minutes | Cook time: 4¹¹/₁₂ hours | Serves 3

4 ounces (113 g) catfish (cut into 1-inch cubes)
4 ounces (113 g) shrimp (peeled and deveined)
1 tablespoon olive oil
1¼ cups vegetable broth
¾ cup sliced celery stalk
¼ teaspoon minced garlic
½ cup chopped onion
1 cup canned diced

tomatoes
1 cup uncooked long-grain white rice
½ tablespoon Cajun seasoning
¼ teaspoon dried thyme
¼ teaspoon cayenne pepper
½ teaspoon dried oregano
Salt and freshly ground black pepper, to taste

1. Select the Sauté function on your Instant Pot and add the oil into it.
2. Put the onion, garlic, celery to the pot and cook for 10 minutes.
3. Add all the remaining ingredients to the pot except seafood.
4. Stir well, then secure the cooker lid.
5. Select the Slow Cook function on a medium mode.
6. Keep the pressure release handle on venting position. Cook for 4 hours.
7. Once done, remove the lid and add the seafood to the gravy.
8. Secure the lid again, keep the pressure handle in the venting position.
9. Cook for another 45 minutes then serve.

Dijon Walnut-Crusted Catfish Fillets

Prep time: 10 minutes | Cook time: 10 minutes | Serves 4

2 large eggs
1 cup panko bread crumbs
¾ cup finely chopped walnuts
½ cup grated Parmesan Cheese
2 tablespoons melted butter
1½ tablespoons Dijon

mustard
1 tablespoon Italian seasoning
Pinch salt
Pinch freshly ground black pepper
4 (6-ounce / 170-g) catfish fillets, skin removed, patted dry

1. Preheat the oven to 425°F (220ºC). Line a baking sheet with parchment paper or aluminum foil.
2. In a medium bowl, lightly beat the eggs to form a simple egg wash. In a large bowl, mix to combine the bread crumbs, walnuts, cheese, butter, Dijon mustard, Italian seasoning, salt, and black pepper for the crust, and place next to the egg wash. The texture should resemble moist crumbles.
3. Dip the fillets into the egg wash, then coat with the crust mixture and place on the baking sheet.
4. Bake for 10 to 12 minutes, or until fully cooked and easily flaked. The crust should appear golden brown and crispy.
5. Serve immediately.

Kung Pao Catfish Fillets

Prep time: 15 minutes | Cook time: 6 minutes | Serves 4

For the Catfish:

1½ pounds (680 g) catfish fillets, cut into 1-inch chunks	1 tablespoon egg white, lightly beaten until frothy
2 tablespoons cornstarch	1 teaspoon soy sauce
	2 cups vegetable oil

For the Kung Pao Sauce:

1 tablespoon Chinese black vinegar	1 teaspoon sesame oil
1 teaspoon light soy sauce	1 teaspoon cornstarch
1 teaspoon hoisin sauce	½ teaspoon ground Sichuan pepper (optional)

For the Stir-Fry:

2 tablespoons vegetable oil	2 garlic cloves, minced
8 to 10 dried red chiles	1 teaspoon grated peeled fresh ginger
3 scallions, thinly sliced, divided (white and green parts)	¼ cup unsalted dry-roasted peanuts
	Steamed rice

1. To make the catfish, in a large bowl, toss the catfish with the cornstarch, egg white, and soy sauce. Make sure the fish is evenly coated with the mixture. Set aside for 10 minutes.
2. In a wok, large sauté pan, or skillet, heat the vegetable oil over medium-high heat to 325°F (163°C), or when the end of a wooden spoon dipped into the oil causes bubbling and sizzling.
3. Working in batches to avoid overcrowding, carefully lower the fish into the oil and gently move it around so it doesn't stick to the sides of the pan. Fry for about 2 minutes on each side, using a fish spatula or slotted spoon to flip the fish over, until golden. Transfer the fish to a plate lines with paper towels. Discard the oil and wipe out the wok.
4. To make the kung pao sauce, in a small bowl, combine the black vinegar, soy sauce, hoisin sauce, sesame oil, cornstarch, and Sichuan pepper (if using). Stir until the cornstarch is blended and set aside.
5. To make the stir-fry, return the wok to medium-high heat until a bead of water sizzles and evaporates on contact. Add the vegetable oil and swirl to coat the bottom. Add the chiles and stir-fry for about 30 seconds, or until the chiles

have just begun to blacken and the oil is slightly fragrant.
6. Add the scallion whites, garlic, and ginger and stir-fry for about 30 seconds. Pour in the sauce and mix to coat the other ingredients. Add the fried fish and gently toss to coat but don't break up the fish too much. Stir in the peanuts and cook for another 1 to 2 minutes. Transfer to a serving plate, sprinkle the scallion greens on top, and serve with steamed rice.

Pecan-Crusted Catfish Fillets

Prep time: 10 minutes | Cook time: 15 minutes | Serves 4

2 tablespoons unsalted butter, melted	½ cup panko bread crumbs
¼ cup all-purpose flour	½ cup finely chopped pecans
½ teaspoon ground nutmeg	Zest and juice of 1 lemon, divided
Kosher salt	4 (6-ounce / 170-g) catfish fillets
Freshly ground black pepper	1 lemon, quartered, for serving
2 large eggs, beaten	

1. Preheat the oven to 425°F (220°C). Line a baking sheet with aluminum foil and brush the bottom of the pan with the butter. Set aside.
2. In a wide shallow bowl, stir together the flour, nutmeg, and a pinch each of salt and pepper.
3. In another wide shallow bowl, beat the eggs. In a third wide shallow bowl or large plate, stir together the bread crumbs, pecans, and lemon zest.
4. Blot the fillets with paper towels and season both sides with salt and pepper. One at time, dredge the fillets in the flour mixture and shake off the excess.
5. Dip the fillets into the egg mixture and coat in the pecan mixture. Place the fillets on the prepared baking sheet.
6. Bake the fish for 15 minutes, rotating the pan halfway through, until an instant-read thermometer inserted into the thickest part of the fish reads 145°F (63°C) and it flakes easily with a fork. Tent with foil to rest for 5 minutes.
7. Serve the fillets hot on plates garnished with the lemon wedges for squeezing.

Catfish Fillets Cakes with Remoulade Sauce

Prep time: 20 minutes | Cook time: 10 minutes | Serves 4

For the Remoulade Sauce:

½ cup mayonnaise
1 scallion, finely chopped (white and green parts)
1 tablespoon prepared horseradish
2 teaspoons whole-grain mustard

2 teaspoons hot sauce (such as Tabasco)
2 teaspoons freshly squeezed lemon juice
Kosher salt
Freshly ground black pepper

For the Catfish Cakes:

2 tablespoons unsalted butter
½ small yellow onion, grated
2 garlic cloves, minced
2 tablespoons all-purpose flour
1 teaspoon Old Bay seasoning
½ cup milk
Kosher salt

Freshly ground black pepper
1 (8-ounce / 227-g) catfish fillet, cooked and flaked
2 cups panko bread crumbs, divided
1 tablespoon minced fresh flat-leaf parsley
2½ cups vegetable oil, for frying
1 large egg, beaten

1. To make the remoulade sauce, in a small bowl, stir together the mayonnaise, scallion, horseradish, mustard, hot sauce, and lemon juice. Season with salt and pepper. Cover with plastic wrap and refrigerate until ready to use.

2. To make the catfish cakes, in a nonstick skillet, melt the butter over medium-low heat. Add the onion and garlic and cook until tender, about 4 minutes. Sprinkle in the flour and Old Bay and cook until a paste forms, about 2 minutes. Whisk in the milk until a thick sauce develops. Lightly season with salt and pepper and remove the pan from the heat.

3. Add the catfish to the pan and fold in gently. Add ¾ cup of bread crumbs and the parsley. Season with salt and pepper. Shape the mixture into 12 equal patties. Transfer the patties to a plate and refrigerate for 15 minutes.

4. In a large Dutch oven, heat the vegetable oil over medium heat to 350°F (180ºC), or when the end of a wooden spoon dipped into the oil causes bubbling and sizzling.

5. While the oil is heating, set up a dredging station. Beat the egg in a shallow bowl. In another shallow bowl, add the remaining 1¼ cups of bread crumbs. Working in batches, dip the patties in the egg, then dredge in the bread crumbs. Press the bread crumbs gently into the patties and place on another plate.

6. Working in batches, lower 3 or 4 cakes into the oil and cook for about 2 minutes. Flip the patties over and cook for another 2 minutes, until golden brown. Transfer the cakes to a plate lined with paper towels to drain. Season with salt and serve warm with the remoulade sauce.

Chapter 7 Salmon

Salmon Salad Fillets Wrap

Prep time: 10 minutes | Cook time: 0 minutes | Serves 6

1 pound (454 g) salmon fillets, cooked and flaked
½ cup diced carrots
½ cup diced celery
3 tablespoons diced red onion
3 tablespoons chopped fresh dill
2 tablespoons capers
1½ tablespoons extra-virgin olive oil
1 tablespoon aged balsamic vinegar
¼ teaspoon kosher or sea salt
½ teaspoon freshly ground black pepper
4 whole-wheat flatbread wraps or soft whole-wheat tortillas

1. In a large bowl, stir together all the ingredients, except for the wraps.
2. On a clean work surface, lay the wraps. Divide the salmon mixture evenly among the wraps. Fold up the bottom of the wraps, then roll up the wrap.
3. Serve immediately.

Easy Instant Pot Poached Salmon

Prep time: 5 minutes | Cook time: 3 minutes | Serves 4

1 lemon, sliced ¼ inch thick
4 (6-ounce / 170-g) skinless salmon fillets, 1½ inches
thick
½ teaspoon salt
¼ teaspoon pepper
½ cup water

1. Layer the lemon slices in the bottom of the Instant Pot.
2. Season the salmon with salt and pepper, then arrange the salmon (skin-side down) on top of the lemon slices. Pour in the water.
3. Secure the lid. Select the Manual mode and set the cooking time for 3 minutes at High Pressure.
4. Once cooking is complete, do a quick pressure release. Carefully open the lid.
5. Serve warm.

Baked Salmon Fillets with Greek Veggies

Prep time: 15 minutes | Cook time: 10 minutes | Serves 4

4 (6-ounce / 170-g) salmon fillets
1 tablespoon extra-virgin olive oil, plus more for brushing
Pinch salt
Freshly ground black pepper
1 avocado
½ cup plain, low-fat Greek yogurt
1 tablespoon fresh dill, chopped
Juice of 1 lemon
½ teaspoon garlic powder
1½ cups shredded cucumber
2 cups cucumber, sliced
1 cup halved cherry tomatoes
½ red onion, thinly sliced
12 to 16 Kalamata olives, pitted
1 tablespoon balsamic vinegar
1 teaspoon dried oregano
½ cup feta cheese crumbles

1. Preheat the oven to 400°F (205ºC). Line a baking sheet with parchment paper or aluminum foil.
2. Pat the salmon fillets dry, brush with olive oil, and season with salt and pepper. Place on the baking sheet and bake for 10 to 12 minutes, or until easily flaked with a fork.
3. Meanwhile, in a small bowl, make the tzatziki. Mash the avocado until creamy and smooth. Add the Greek yogurt, dill, lemon juice, garlic powder, and shredded cucumber, season with pepper, and mix well. Cover and chill until ready to serve.
4. In a large bowl, mix to combine the sliced cucumber, cherry tomatoes, onion, and Kalamata olives. Drizzle with 1 tablespoon of olive oil and balsamic vinegar. Sprinkle with the oregano, and top with the feta cheese.
5. When the salmon is finished cooking, remove from the oven and place on four plates. Top with the avocado tzatziki or serve on the side. Evenly divide the Greek veggies onto each plate and serve immediately.

Balsamic-Honey Glazed Salmon Fillets

Prep time: 5 minutes | Cook time: 6 minutes | Serves 4

½ cup balsamic vinegar
1 tablespoon honey
4 (8-ounce / 227-g) salmon fillets

Sea salt and freshly ground pepper, to taste
1 tablespoon olive oil

1. Heat a skillet over medium-high heat. Combine the vinegar and honey in a small bowl.
2. Season the salmon fillets with the sea salt and freshly ground pepper; brush with the honey-balsamic glaze.
3. Add olive oil to the skillet, and sear the salmon fillets, cooking for 3 to 4 minutes on each side until lightly browned and medium rare in the center.
4. Let sit for 5 minutes before serving.

Salmon Fillets Salad with Margarita Dressing

Prep time: 15 minutes | Cook time: 12 minutes | Serves 4

1 pound (454 g) fresh or frozen salmon fillets, cut into 4 pieces
5 tablespoons extra-virgin olive oil, divided
3 tablespoons freshly squeezed lime juice, divided
2 teaspoons Jamaican jerk seasoning
6 cups tightly packed mixed greens or

spring mix lettuce
1 cup fresh strawberries, sliced
1 mango, diced
1 avocado, diced
¼ cup sliced or slivered almonds
1 tablespoon honey
1½ teaspoons ground cumin
⅛ teaspoon salt
Fresh cilantro, for garnish

1. Thaw the fish in cold water if using frozen, and preheat the oven to 400°F (205°C).
2. Place the fillets on a baking sheet, and brush with 1 tablespoon of olive oil, then drizzle with 1 tablespoon of lime juice and sprinkle with the jerk seasoning. Broil the fish on the top rack for 12 to 14 minutes, or until it reaches an internal temperature of 145°F and the salmon flakes easily with a fork. Remove from the oven and allow to cool.
3. Meanwhile, in a large serving bowl, layer the salad greens followed by the strawberries, mango, avocado, and almonds. Toss gently to mix.
4. In a small bowl, prepare the dressing by whisking together the remaining 4 tablespoons of olive oil, the remaining 2 tablespoons of lime juice, and the honey, cumin, and salt.
5. To serve, arrange the salad mix on 4 plates. Top each salad with one salmon fillet, and gently flake apart. Add the dressing, and garnish with fresh cilantro, if desired.

Zucchini Pancakes Topped with Smoked Salmon

Prep time: 10 minutes | Cook time: 4 minutes | Serves 4

2 cups tightly packed shredded zucchini
½ red onion, diced (about ½ cup)
½ cup shredded Pepper Jack Cheese
2 garlic cloves, minced
½ teaspoon dried basil

4 large eggs, lightly beaten
¾ cup all-purpose flour
½ teaspoon baking soda
4 tablespoons low-fat cream cheese
4 ounces (113 g) smoked salmon

1. Squeeze the shredded zucchini tightly over a colander or fine-mesh strainer to remove excess liquid.
2. Heat a large skillet over medium to medium-high heat. In a large mixing bowl, stir together the zucchini, onion, Pepper Jack Cheese, garlic, basil, eggs, flour, and baking soda until a batter forms.
3. Drop the batter into the heated skillet to form 5- to 6-inch pancakes (about ⅓ cup of batter).
4. Cook for 2 to 3 minutes on one side, then flip and cook for 2 to 3 minutes more. The pancake should brown slightly on each side. Repeat with the remaining batter to make eight pancakes total.
5. To serve, spread cream cheese on top of each pancake and top with smoked salmon. Serve immediately.

Cream-Cheese Smoked Salmon Deviled Eggs

Prep time: 10 minutes | Cook time: 0 minutes | Serves 4

6 large hard-boiled eggs	Pinch salt
2 ounces (57 g) low-fat cream cheese	Pinch freshly ground black pepper
2 tablespoons mayonnaise	2 ounces (57 g) smoked salmon
½ teaspoon dried dill	Smoked paprika, for garnish (optional)
¼ teaspoon mustard powder	Fresh dill, for garnish (optional)

1. Halve each egg lengthwise. Remove the yolks and add to a mixing bowl with the cream cheese, mayonnaise, dill, mustard powder, salt, and pepper. Use a fork to mash into a smooth mixture, combining until creamy with no chunks remaining.
2. Spoon the mixture into a zip-top bag and snip a bottom tip off the bag with kitchen shears. Pipe the filling back into the well of each egg white.
3. Flake the smoked salmon apart and layer on top. Garnish with smoked paprika or fresh dill, if desired, and serve.

Savory Old Bay Salmon Patties

Prep time: 10 minutes | Cook time: 10 minutes | Serves 4

1 (14¾-ounce / 418-g) can wild salmon, drained	1 teaspoon dried dill
1 large egg	½ teaspoon freshly ground black pepper
¼ cup diced onion	1 teaspoon salt
½ cup whole wheat bread crumbs	1 teaspoon Old Bay Seasoning

1. Spray the air fryer basket with olive oil.
2. Put the salmon in a medium bowl and remove any bones or skin.
3. Add the egg, onion, bread crumbs, dill, pepper, salt, and Old Bay Seasoning and mix well.
4. Form the salmon mixture into 4 equal patties.
5. Place the patties in the greased air fryer basket.
6. Set the temperature to 370ºF (188ºC). Set the timer and grill for 5 minutes.
7. Flip the patties. Reset the timer and grill the patties for 5 minutes more.
8. Plate, serve, and enjoy!

Salmon Caesar Salad with Bread Crumbs

Prep time: 10 minutes | Cook time: 18 minutes | Serves 4

1 pound (454 g) salmon	inches anchovy paste
Kosher salt	1 large garlic clove, minced
Freshly ground black pepper	1 ½ tablespoons Dijon mustard
Zest of 1 lemon, and 6 tablespoons lemon juice, divided	1/3 cup Parmigiano-Reggiano
½ cup plus 2 tablespoons extra-virgin olive oil, plus more for drizzling	1 ½ cups panko bread crumbs
3 or 4 anchovies or 3	1 bunch kale (about 6 cups), washed, ribs removed

1. Preheat the oven to 425ºF (220ºC).
2. Season the salmon with salt and pepper. Whisk together the lemon zest and 3 tablespoons of lemon juice. While still whisking, stream in the olive oil. Season with salt and pepper. Pour this over the salmon and bake until it reaches an internal temperature of 145ºF (63ºC), 15 to 20 minutes.
3. While the salmon is cooking, in a small bowl, mash the anchovies with the garlic. Whisk in the remaining 3 tablespoons of lemon juice and Dijon mustard. While still whisking, drizzle in the olive oil; then add the Parmigiano-Reggiano. Season with salt and pepper. Set aside.
4. In a skillet over medium-low heat, heat a drizzle of olive oil, and add the panko. Toss until golden brown, about 3 minutes.
5. In a large bowl, tear the kale leaves into bite-size pieces. Massage a little of the anchovy dressing into the leaves to tenderize the kale.
6. Add most of the panko and the rest of the anchovy dressing and toss to combine. Plate the kale, top with the salmon, and sprinkle with panko. Serve.

Egg Wraps with Smoked Salmon

Prep time: 10 minutes | Cook time: 20 minutes | Serves 4

2 tablespoons extra-virgin olive oil
10 large eggs
1 teaspoon salt
½ teaspoon freshly ground black pepper
½ cup sun-dried to-mato cream cheese or store-bought full-fat cream cheese
8 ounces (227 g) smoked salmon
2 avocados, chopped
2 tablespoons capers

1. Preheat the oven to 350°F (180°C).
2. Line a large sheet pan with parchment paper, leaving a 2-inch overhang on each of the short ends. Brush the parchment paper with the olive oil.
3. In a large bowl, whisk the eggs, salt, and pepper until thoroughly combined.
4. Pour the eggs into the prepared sheet pan and bake for 20 minutes, or until the eggs are puffed on the edges and just set. Let cool for 5 minutes.
5. Evenly spread the cream cheese over the baked egg (still on the sheet pan), then cut the egg crosswise into 4 equal portions.
6. Distribute the smoked salmon and avocados evenly over each egg portion. Sprinkle with the capers.
7. Starting on the long side of one of the egg portions, roll the egg up to make a wrap. Repeat with the remaining portions.

Smoked Salmon Eggs Benedict Bowls

Prep time: 10 minutes | Cook time: 7 minutes | Serves 4

3 teaspoons extra-virgin olive oil, divided
2 cups sliced zucchini
½ small onion, chopped
Cauliflower Fried Rice
4 large eggs
8 ounces (227 g) sliced smoked salmon
4 tablespoons crumbled feta cheese
2 tablespoons capers

1. In a large nonstick skillet, heat 1½ teaspoons of olive oil over medium-high heat, until hot. Add the zucchini and onion and sauté for 4 minutes, or until the vegetables begin to soften. Remove from the heat.

2. Spoon 1 cup of the fried cauliflower rice into each of four small serving bowls. Divide the zucchini mixture on top of the cauliflower rice. Wipe the skillet clean with a paper towel and return to the stove.
3. In the skillet, heat the remaining 1½ teaspoons of olive oil over medium-high heat until hot. Crack the eggs into the pan and immediately reduce the heat to low. Cook the eggs for 3 minutes, or until the whites have set.
4. Meanwhile, dividing evenly, arrange the smoked salmon in the bowls next to the zucchini.
5. Place one cooked egg in each bowl next to the smoked salmon. Sprinkle each bowl with 1 tablespoon of feta cheese and ½ tablespoon of capers.

Delicious Salmon Onigiri

Prep time: 10 minutes | Cook time: 5 minutes | Serves 2

2 teaspoons vegetable oil or canola oil
1 (6-ounce / 170-g) can boneless, skinless salmon, drained
2 teaspoons mirin or seasoned rice vinegar
1 teaspoon soy sauce
1 tablespoon furikake
3 cups cooked short-grain rice (sushi rice preferred)
Kosher salt
2 tablespoons toasted sesame seeds
1 sheet nori seaweed, cut into 4 strips

1. In a small skillet, heat the oil over medium heat. When shimmery wavy lines run through the oil, add the salmon, mirin, and soy sauce.
2. Gently sauté, breaking up the salmon and mixing it with the sauce, for 5 minutes, until the sauce has been absorbed and the salmon is slightly crispy.
3. Transfer to a small bowl and set aside to cool. When cooled, fold in the furikake.
4. Lightly season the cooked rice with salt. Fold in the salmon mixture and sesame seeds. Divide the rice mixture into four equal balls. Wet your hands with cold water and roll one of the balls into an egg shape. Wrap one strip of nori around the middle of the egg and place on a serving plate. Repeat the process with the remaining rice and nori.
5. Serve immediately or keep wrapped in plastic wrap at room temperature for up to 2 hours.

Rice Wrap Salmon

Prep time: 10 minutes | Cook time: 10 minutes | Serves 4

For the Cilantro Pesto:

½ cup extra-virgin olive oil
½ bunch cilantro, leaves and stems
½ bunch flat-leaf parsley leaves
2 garlic cloves, coarsely chopped

1 tablespoon seasoned rice vinegar
1 teaspoon kosher salt
1 teaspoon ground coriander
Freshly ground black pepper

For the Salmon:

4 (3-ounce / 85-g) salmon fillets, skin and pin bones removed
Kosher salt
Pinch freshly ground

black pepper
4 (9-inch) rice paper rounds
2 tablespoons vegetable oil

1. To make the cilantro pesto, in a food processor or blender, process the olive oil, cilantro, parsley, garlic, rice vinegar, salt, coriander, and pepper until smooth but thick. Taste and adjust for seasoning with salt and pepper. Set aside.
2. To make the salmon, lightly season the salmon on both sides with salt and pepper. In a wide shallow pan filled with warm water, soak the rice paper rounds one at a time to soften. When the rice paper is soft and pliable, place it on a clean cutting board.
3. Place one piece of salmon on the lower third of a softened rice paper round. Spread 1 tablespoon of cilantro pesto on top of the salmon. Bring the two opposite sides over to the middle of the salmon, then roll the salmon up, as you would roll a burrito. Set aside and cover with a damp towel to keep the rice wraps from drying out. Repeat the process with the remaining salmon and rice wraps.
4. Heat a large nonstick skillet over medium heat. Add the vegetable oil and swirl to coat the pan. When shimmery wavy lines run through the oil, place the salmon packages in the pan and fry on one side for 5 minutes, or until the rice wraps are brown and crispy. Flip the packages over and fry on the other side for another 5 minutes more until brown and crispy. Serve hot.

Gouda Canned-Tuna Noodle Casserole

Prep time: 10 minutes | Cook time: 32 minutes | Serves 6

4 tablespoons butter, divided
1 yellow onion, diced
1 (8-ounce / 227-g) package white or baby bella mushrooms, sliced
3 tablespoons low-sodium soy sauce
2 tablespoons apple cider vinegar
12 ounces rotini pasta
¼ cup all-purpose

flour
2 cups low-sodium vegetable stock
½ cup heavy (whipping) cream
1½ cups frozen green peas, thawed
2 (5-ounce / 142-g) cans tuna, drained
1½ cups shredded Gouda cheese
¾ cup panko bread crumbs

1. Preheat the oven to 350°F (180°C).
2. In a large skillet over medium-high heat, heat 1 tablespoon of butter Add the onion, and sauté for 3 to 5 minutes.
3. Add the mushrooms, and cook for 2 to 3 minutes more. Add the soy sauce and apple cider vinegar, and continue cooking until the liquid is reduced almost completely, about 7 minutes. Remove the mixture from the skillet and set aside.
4. Bring a medium saucepan of water to a boil. Cook the pasta according to package instructions. Then drain, transfer to a large bowl, and set aside.
5. In the same skillet over medium heat, melt the remaining 3 tablespoons of butter. Immediately add the flour, and stir to combine to form a simple roux. Continue cooking, stirring frequently, until the roux becomes a golden brown.
6. Add the stock and cream. Bring to a simmer, stirring to prevent scalding. Once the mixture has thickened to a gravy consistency, remove from the heat and pour over the pasta.
7. Add the peas, tuna, and sauce to the pasta, and stir well to combine. Transfer to a large, lightly greased casserole dish or baking dish. Top with the Gouda cheese, then sprinkle the panko bread crumbs over the cheese. Bake, covered, for 20 to 25 minutes, or until the cheese is bubbling and the topping becomes slightly browned. Allow to cool slightly, and serve hot.

Salmon Fillets Teriyaki

Prep time: 10 minutes | Cook time: 13 minutes | Serves 4

½ cup sake
¼ cup mirin
¼ cup soy sauce
½ teaspoon grated peeled fresh ginger
4 (3-ounce / 85-g) salmon fillets, skin on and pin bones removed
Kosher salt
Freshly ground black pepper

2 tablespoons vegetable oil or canola oil
1½ cups cooked white rice, for serving
1 teaspoon toasted sesame seeds, for garnish
1 scallion, thinly sliced, for garnish (white and green parts)

1. In a small bowl, whisk together the sake, mirin, soy sauce, and ginger. Set aside.
2. Season the salmon on both sides with salt and pepper.
3. Heat a medium nonstick skillet over medium-high heat.
4. Add the vegetable oil and swirl to coat the pan. When shimmery wavy lines run through the oil, place the salmon in the pan, skin-side down, and sear for 6 minutes. Tilt the pan occasionally to redistribute the oil as the salmon cooks. Gently flip the salmon over and cook the other side for 2 minutes.
5. Add more oil, 1 teaspoon at a time, if needed.
6. Transfer the salmon to a clean plate and, using a paper towel, wipe the oil from the skillet. Pour the prepared sauce into the skillet and bring to a boil over medium-high heat. Cook until the sauce has reduced by one-third, about 3 minutes.
7. Return the salmon to the pan, skin-side up, and spoon the reduced sauce over top. Keep cooking for another 2 minutes, until an instant-read thermometer inserted into the thickest part of the fish reads 125°F (52ºC). The flesh should change to opaque pink and, when flaked with a fork, reveal a softer, slightly translucent pink toward the center.
8. Divide the rice between four plates. Place the salmon on top of each. Spoon the excess sauce from the pan over the salmon and rice. Garnish with the sesame seeds and scallions and serve.

Baked Salmon and Veggie Salad

Prep time: 15 minutes | Cook time: 40 minutes | Serves 4

½ cup extra-virgin olive oil, divided, plus more for preparing the baking dish
1 cup dried French green lentils, rinsed and picked over for debris
4 cups water
2 bay leaves
3 tablespoons sherry wine vinegar
2 teaspoons Dijon mustard
1 teaspoon kosher salt plus ¼ teaspoon

3 tablespoons minced shallot
½ cup chopped fresh Italian parsley
4 cups fresh baby spinach
4 (6-ounce / 170-g) wild Alaskan salmon fillets
Pinch freshly ground black pepper
¼ teaspoon ground fennel seed (or fennel pollen)
12 cornichons

1. Preheat the oven to 400°F (205ºC). Brush an ovenproof baking dish large enough to hold the salmon with oil.
2. In a medium saucepan over high heat, combine the lentils, water, and bay leaves. Bring the water to a boil. Lower the heat to maintain a simmer, cover the pan, and simmer for about 20 minutes until the lentils are tender. Drain any excess water, remove and discard the bay leaves, and transfer the lentils to a large bowl.
3. While the lentils cook, in a small bowl, whisk the vinegar, mustard, and 1 teaspoon of salt. While whisking constantly, gradually pour in about 7 tablespoons of oil, whisking to emulsify.
4. Add the shallot, parsley, and three-quarters of the dressing to the lentils and stir until the lentils are coated with the dressing. Add the spinach, working in batches, stirring until it wilts. Keep warm until ready to serve.
5. Wipe the salmon dry with a paper towel. Set the salmon in the prepared baking dish, skin-side down. Brush with the remaining 1 tablespoon of oil, then sprinkle with the remaining ¼ teaspoon of salt, the pepper, and fennel seed.
6. Bake for about 20 minutes until just cooked through.
7. Divide the salmon among 4 plates. Spoon mounds of lentil salad alongside. Offer the remaining dressing and the cornichons on the side for serving.

Mediterranean Canned-Salmon Wraps

Prep time: 15 minutes | Cook time: 0 minutes | Serves 4

2 (6-ounce / 170-g) cans salmon, drained
¼ cup chopped fresh parsley
¼ cup pitted Kalamata olives, chopped
¼ cup diced red onion
1 tablespoon extra-virgin olive oil
½ teaspoon lemon zest
Juice of 1 lemon
⅛ teaspoon coarse sea salt
4 small (6-inch) whole-wheat tortillas
2 cups chopped romaine
½ cup diced red bell pepper
1 Roma tomato, thinly sliced
½ cup feta cheese crumbles

1. In a large bowl, combine the salmon, parsley, olives, onion, olive oil, lemon zest, and lemon juice. Season with salt, and stir to combine.
2. Layer ½ cup chopped romaine in the center of each tortilla. Top with a quarter each of the salmon mixture and bell peppers and two slices of tomato. Sprinkle with the feta cheese.
3. Fold in each tortilla about 1 inch from the end of the filling on each side. Tightly roll, being careful not to break the wrap. Secure the edge of the wrap underneath, then cut in half. Serve immediately.

Salmon Fillets Taco Bowls

Prep time: 15 minutes | Cook time: 8 minutes | Serves 4

1 pound (454 g) salmon fillets, in 4 portions
½ tablespoon chili powder
¾ teaspoon ground cumin
¼ teaspoon paprika
¼ teaspoon garlic powder
¼ teaspoon onion powder
¼ teaspoon dried oregano
1 tablespoon extra-virgin olive oil
1 lime, sliced
Cauliflower Fried Rice
1 avocado, sliced
4 tablespoons keto-friendly salsa
½ cup chopped fresh cilantro (optional)
Lime wedges, for serving (optional)

1. Preheat the oven to 350°F (180°C). Line a baking sheet with parchment paper.
2. Arrange the salmon on the baking sheet.
3. In a small bowl, combine the chili powder, cumin, paprika, garlic powder, onion powder, and oregano. Sprinkle evenly over the salmon fillets. Drizzle with the olive oil.
4. Place the slices of lime over the salmon fillets. Bake for 8 minutes, or until the thickest part of the fish begins to flake but is still slightly translucent in the center.
5. Divide the cauliflower rice among four serving bowls. Place a portion of salmon over the rice. Dividing evenly, top the bowls with avocado and salsa. If desired, sprinkle with cilantro and squeeze a lime wedge on top.

Seattle-Flavor Grilled Salmon

Prep time: 10 minutes | Cook time: 8 minutes | Serves 4

For the Sauce:
3 tablespoons sour cream
1 tablespoon mayonnaise
1 teaspoon freshly squeezed lemon juice
¼ teaspoon kosher salt
2 tablespoons chopped fresh dill

For the Salmon:
1 (2-pound / 907-g) skin-on salmon fillet
Extra-virgin olive oil
Kosher salt
Lemon wedges, for serving

To Make the Sauce
1. In a small bowl, whisk the sour cream, mayonnaise, lemon juice, and salt until smooth. Stir in the dill. Refrigerate until needed.

To Make the Salmon
1. Preheat a grill to high.
2. Rinse the salmon and pat it dry, then brush it with oil and sprinkle with salt.
3. Place the salmon on the grill, flesh-side down, and sear for 4 minutes. Reduce the heat a bit and flip the salmon, continuing to grill for about 4 minutes more, or until the fish is cooked to 145°F (63°C). (The exact cooking time will vary, depending on the thickness of the fish.) Alternatively, you can bake or broil the salmon.
4. Serve the fish on a platter with the sauce and lemon wedges alongside it.

Garlic Skillet Salmon Fillets

Prep time: 10 minutes | Cook time: 16 minutes | Serves 4

1 tablespoon extra-virgin olive oil
2 garlic cloves, minced
1 teaspoon smoked paprika
1½ cups grape or cherry tomatoes, quartered
1 (12-ounce / 340-g) jar roasted red peppers, drained and chopped
1 tablespoon water
¼ teaspoon freshly ground black pepper
¼ teaspoon kosher or sea salt
1 pound (454 g) salmon fillets, skin removed and cut into 8 pieces
1 tablespoon freshly squeezed lemon juice

1. In a large skillet over medium heat, heat the oil. Add the garlic and smoked paprika and cook for 1 minute, stirring often.
2. Add the tomatoes, roasted peppers, water, black pepper, and salt. Turn up the heat to medium-high, bring to a simmer, and cook for 3 minutes, stirring occasionally and smashing the tomatoes with a wooden spoon toward the end of the cooking time.
3. Add the salmon to the skillet, and spoon some of the sauce over the top. Cover and cook for 10 to 12 minutes, or until the salmon is cooked through and just starts to flake.
4. Remove the skillet from the heat, and drizzle lemon juice over the top of the fish. Stir the sauce, then break up the salmon into chunks with a fork. Serve hot.

Delicious Smoke Salmon Scramble

Prep time: 10 minutes | Cook time: 7 minutes | Serves 4

6 large eggs
2 tablespoons low-fat milk
¼ teaspoon salt
⅛ teaspoon freshly ground black pepper
1 tablespoon unsalted butter
4 ounces (113 g) smoked salmon, chopped
Chopped fresh chives, for garnish (optional)
Whole-wheat bread, for serving (optional)

1. In a medium bowl, whisk the eggs, milk, salt, and pepper.
2. In an 8-inch nonstick skillet, heat the butter over low-medium heat.
3. When the butter has melted, add the egg mixture.
4. As the eggs begin to set, using a spatula, gently push the eggs towards the center of the pan, forming soft, fluffy curds. Repeat until the eggs are nearly cooked through and no liquid remains, about 7 minutes. Turn off the heat.
5. Add in the smoked salmon, gently tossing around the pan. Sprinkle with chives (if using) before serving hot with whole-wheat toast (if using).

Salmon Fillets with Balsamic Maple Glaze

Prep time: 5 minutes | Cook time: 10 minutes | Serves 4

4 (6-ounce / 170-g) fillets of salmon
Salt and freshly ground black pepper
Olive oil
¼ cup pure maple syrup
3 tablespoons balsamic vinegar
1 teaspoon Dijon mustard

1. Preheat the air fryer to 400ºF (204ºC).
2. Season the salmon well with salt and freshly ground black pepper. Spray or brush the bottom of the air fryer basket with vegetable oil and place the salmon fillets inside. Air fry the salmon for 5 minutes.
3. While the salmon is air frying, combine the maple syrup, balsamic vinegar and Dijon mustard in a small saucepan over medium heat and stir to blend well. Let the mixture simmer while the fish is cooking. It should start to thicken slightly, but keep your eye on it so it doesn't burn.
4. Brush the glaze on the salmon fillets and air fry for an additional 5 minutes. The salmon should feel firm to the touch when finished and the glaze should be nicely browned on top. Brush a little more glaze on top before removing and serving with rice and vegetables, or a nice green salad.

Lemon-Cream Seared Salmon

Prep time: 10 minutes | Cook time: 8 minutes | Serves 4

4 (5-ounce / 142-g) salmon fillets	Juice and zest of 1 lemon
Sea salt and freshly ground black pepper, to taste	1 teaspoon chopped fresh thyme
1 tablespoon extra-virgin olive oil	½ cup fat-free sour cream
½ cup low-sodium vegetable broth	1 teaspoon honey
	1 tablespoon chopped fresh chives

1. Preheat the oven to 400ºF (205ºC).
2. Season the salmon lightly on both sides with salt and pepper.
3. Place a large ovenproof skillet over medium-high heat and add the olive oil.
4. Sear the salmon fillets on both sides until golden, about 3 minutes per side.
5. Transfer the salmon to a baking dish and bake in the preheated oven until just cooked through, about 10 minutes.
6. Meanwhile, whisk together the vegetable broth, lemon juice and zest, and thyme in a small saucepan over medium-high heat until the liquid reduces by about one-quarter, about 5 minutes.
7. Whisk in the sour cream and honey.
8. Stir in the chives and serve the sauce over the salmon.

Canned-Salmon Burgers

Prep time: 15 minutes | Cook time: 3 minutes | Serves 4

For the Cabbage Slaw:

1½ cups shredded red cabbage	Juice of 1 lime
1½ cups shredded carrots	1½ tablespoons extra-virgin olive oil
½ cup chopped fresh cilantro	¼ teaspoon salt
2 scallions, thinly sliced	¼ teaspoon red pepper flakes
	2 teaspoons honey

For the Salmon Burgers:

2 large eggs	powder
1 (12-ounce / 340-g) can salmon, drained	½ teaspoon Old Bay seasoning
½ cup whole-wheat bread crumbs	¼ teaspoon salt
½ teaspoon garlic	¼ cup canola oil, for frying

To Make the Cabbage Slaw
1. In a large bowl, combine the cabbage, carrots, cilantro, and scallions. Add the lime juice, olive oil, salt, red pepper flakes, and honey, and mix well to combine. Cover and refrigerate until ready to serve.

To Make the Salmon Burgers
1. In another large bowl, lightly beat the eggs. Add the salmon, bread crumbs, garlic powder, Old Bay seasoning, and salt. Stir to combine, then shape into 4 equal-size patties.
2. In a large skillet over medium-high heat, heat the canola oil. Once the oil is heated, place the patties into the skillet and cook for 3 to 4 minutes on each side. If the pan is overcrowded, panfry in two batches.
3. Serve the burgers with the cabbage slaw, and store leftovers for up to 3 days.

Herbed Cream Cheese Smoked Salmon

Prep time: 10 minutes | Cook time: 0 minutes | Serves 2

For the Herbed Crean Cheese:

¼ cup cream cheese, at room temperature	chopped fresh chives or sliced scallion
2 tablespoons chopped fresh flat-leaf parsley	½ teaspoon garlic powder
2 tablespoons	¼ teaspoon kosher salt

For the Toast:

2 slices bread	sprouts
4 ounces (113 g) smoked salmon	1 tablespoon capers, drained and rinsed
Small handful microgreens or	¼ small red onion, very thinly sliced

To Make the Herbed Cream Cheese
1. In a medium bowl, combine the cream cheese, parsley, chives, garlic powder, and salt.
2. Using a fork, mix until combined. Chill until ready to use.

To Make the Toast
1. Toast the bread until golden.
2. Spread the herbed cream cheese over each piece of toast, then top with the smoked salmon.
3. Garnish with the microgreens, capers, and red onion.

Norwegian Salmon Salad

Prep time: 15 minutes | Cook time: 1 minutes | Serves 4

For the Vinaigrette:
3 tablespoons walnut oil

2 tablespoons champagne vinegar

1 tablespoon chopped fresh dill

½ teaspoon kosher salt

¼ teaspoon ground mustard

Freshly ground black pepper

For the Salad:
Handful green beans, trimmed

1 (3- to 4-ounce / 85- to 113-g) package spring greens

12 spears pickled asparagus

4 large soft-boiled eggs, halved

8 ounces smoked salmon, thinly sliced

1 cucumber, thinly sliced

1 lemon, quartered

To Make the Dressing
1. In a small bowl, whisk the oil, vinegar, dill, salt, ground mustard, and a few grinds of pepper until emulsified. Set aside.

To Make the Salad
1. Start by blanching the green beans: Bring a pot of salted water to a boil.
2. Drop in the beans. Cook 1 to 2 minutes until they turn bright green, then immediately drain and rinse under cold water. Set aside.
3. Divide the spring greens among 4 plates.
4. Toss each serving with dressing to taste. Arrange 3 asparagus spears, 1 egg, 2 ounces of salmon, one-fourth of the cucumber slices, and a lemon wedge on each plate. Serve immediately.

Salmon Fillets Baked in Foil

Prep time: 10 minutes | Cook time: 25 minutes | Serves 4

2 cups cherry tomatoes

3 tablespoons extra-virgin olive oil

3 tablespoons lemon juice

3 tablespoons almond butter

1 teaspoon oregano

½ teaspoon salt

4 (5-ounce / 142-g) salmon fillets

1. Preheat the oven to 400ºF (205ºC).
2. Cut the tomatoes in half and put them in a bowl.
3. Add the olive oil, lemon juice, butter, oregano, and salt to the tomatoes and gently toss to combine.
4. Cut 4 pieces of foil, about 12-by-12 inches each.
5. Place the salmon fillets in the middle of each piece of foil.
6. Divide the tomato mixture evenly over the 4 pieces of salmon. Bring the ends of the foil together and seal to form a closed pocket.
7. Place the 4 pockets on a baking sheet. Bake in the preheated oven for 25 minutes.
8. Remove from the oven and serve on a plate.

Lemon Salmon Fillets with Parsley

Prep time: 10 minutes | Cook time: 10¾ minutes | Serves 4

3 tablespoons cashew butter

1 garlic clove, minced, or ½ teaspoon garlic powder

1 teaspoon salt

2 tablespoons freshly squeezed lemon juice

1 tablespoon minced

fresh parsley

1 teaspoon minced fresh dill

1 teaspoon salt

½ teaspoon freshly ground black pepper

4 (4-ounce / 113-g) salmon fillets

1. Line the air fryer basket with parchment paper.
2. In a small microwave-safe mixing bowl, combine the cashew butter, garlic, salt, lemon juice, parsley, dill, salt, and pepper.
3. Place the bowl in the microwave and cook on low for about 45 seconds.
4. Meanwhile, place the salmon fillets in the parchment-lined air fryer basket.
5. Spoon the sauce over the salmon.
6. Set the temperature to 400ºF (204ºC). Set the timer and bake for 10 minutes. Since you don't want to overcook the salmon, begin checking for doneness at about 8 minutes. Salmon is done when the flesh is opaque and flakes easily when tested with a fork.

Delicious Mini Smoked Salmon Tartines

Prep time: 15 minutes | Cook time: 7 minutes | Serves 4 to 6

1 baguette, cut into ½-inch-thick slices
Extra-virgin olive oil
8 ounces (227 g) cream cheese, at room temperature
1 celery stalk, finely diced
1 carrot, peeled and finely diced
3 scallions, sliced
½ cup Italian flat-leaf parsley, leaves removed from stems
Fronds from 2 dill sprigs
1 large garlic clove, minced
Zest of 1 lemon and 2 tablespoons juice
Kosher salt
Freshly ground black pepper
8 ounces (227 g) smoked salmon

1. Preheat the oven to 425°F (220°C).
2. Place the baguette slices on a baking sheet. Drizzle with olive oil. Bake for about 7 minutes until lightly golden brown. Set aside to cool.
3. In a food processor, combine the cream cheese, celery, carrot, scallions, parsley, dill, garlic, lemon zest and juice, and a pinch of salt and pepper. Pulse to combine, and then blend until smooth. Spoon into a bowl, place plastic wrap directly on top of the mixture, and refrigerate until ready to use.
4. To serve, add a shmear of cream cheese to each slice of bread, and top with flaked smoked salmon. Finish with another pinch of salt and pepper, if desired.

Salmon Fillets Fattoush with Tahini Vinaigrette

Prep time: 10 minutes | Cook time: 15 minutes | Serves 4

Zest of 2 lemons, and ¼ cup plus 2 tablespoons juice, divided
Kosher salt
Freshly ground black pepper
½ cup plus 2 tablespoons extra-virgin olive oil, divided
1 pound (454 g) salmon fillet
2 tablespoons tahini
1 large garlic clove, minced
4 cups torn romaine lettuce leaves
2 Persian cucumbers, halved lengthwise and diced
2 scallions, thinly sliced
1 avocado, diced
Pita chips, lightly crushed

1. Preheat the oven to 400°F (205°C). Line a baking sheet with parchment paper.
2. In a small bowl, whisk together half the lemon zest and 2 tablespoons of lemon juice with a good pinch of salt and pepper. While still whisking, stream in 2 tablespoons of olive oil.
3. Place the salmon on the prepared baking sheet and brush with the lemon mixture. Bake for 15 to 17 minutes, until the salmon is firm but still juicy.
4. In a small bowl, whisk together the tahini, garlic, remaining lemon zest, and the remaining ¼ cup of lemon juice. Add a pinch of salt and pepper. While still whisking, slowly stream in the remaining ½ cup of olive oil.
5. In a large bowl, combine the lettuce, cucumbers, and scallions, and toss with 2 tablespoons of dressing.
6. Divide the veggies evenly among 4 plates. Top each plate with the diced avocado, the salmon, and a generous amount of pita chips. Finish with the remaining dressing.

Chapter 8 Cod

Cod Fillets with Cilantro-Lime Butter

Prep time: 10 minutes | Cook time: 3 minutes | Serves 4

For the Cod
¼ teaspoon salt
¼ teaspoon ground cumin
⅛ teaspoon cayenne pepper
4 (6 ounces / 170 g) cod fillets
1 tablespoon extra-virgin olive oil

For the Cilantro-Lime Butter
2 tablespoons unsalted butter, at room temperature
2 tablespoons finely chopped fresh cilantro
½ teaspoon grated
lime zest
¼ teaspoon paprika
⅛ teaspoon salt
Lime wedges, for serving (optional)

To Prepare the Cod
1. In a small bowl, combine the salt, cumin, and cayenne. Sprinkle evenly over both sides of the cod fillets.
2. In a large nonstick skillet, heat the oil over medium-high heat until hot. Place the seasoned cod in the skillet and cook for 3 minutes on each side, or until the fish flakes easily when tested with a fork.

To Make the Cilantro-Lime Butter
1. In a small bowl, mix together the butter, cilantro, lime zest, paprika, and salt.
2. Dividing evenly, top each fillet with cilantro-lime butter. If desired, squeeze lime juice over the fish before serving.

Scandi-Style Cod Cakes with Rémoulade

Prep time: 15 minutes | Cook time: 5 minutes | Serves 4

For the Rémoulade:
1 cup mayonnaise
½ cup minced dill pickles or cornichons
¼ cup lightly packed chopped fresh herbs (e.g., parsley and dill)
2 tablespoons capers, drained and rinsed
1 teaspoon Dijon mustard
1 tablespoon freshly squeezed lemon juice
¼ teaspoon kosher salt

For the Fish Cakes:
1½ pounds (680 g) cod fillets, cut into small pieces
1 teaspoon kosher salt
1 small onion, roughly chopped
3 tablespoons melted butter plus 2 tablespoons at room temperature
2 large eggs
2 scallions, white and
light-green parts only, chopped
¼ cup finely chopped fresh parsley
¼ cup finely chopped fresh dill
2 tablespoons freshly squeezed lemon juice
2 tablespoons all-purpose flour
2 tablespoons vegetable oil

To Make the Rémoulade
1. In a medium bowl, stir together the mayonnaise, pickles, herbs, capers, mustard, lemon juice, and salt. Cover and refrigerate until ready to serve.

To Make the Fish Cakes
1. Put the cod on a paper-towel-lined plate and lightly sprinkle with salt. Let sit for 10 minutes. Using a paper towel, wipe away the moisture and any excess salt. You're drawing out the moisture here rather than seasoning the fish.
2. In a food processor, finely chop the onion. Add the cod and pulse to break down the fish a bit. Add 3 tablespoons of melted butter, the eggs, scallions, parsley, dill, and lemon juice. Process until almost smooth. Add the flour and process until smooth and combined. (You can make the fish cakes up to this point, 1 to 2 hours in advance, just keep the mixture refrigerated.)
3. Wet your hands and form the fish mixture into 12 balls. Slightly flatten each and place the cakes on a paper-towel-lined plate while you work so they continue to release excess moisture.
4. In a large skillet over medium heat, heat the oil and remaining 2 tablespoons of butter. Carefully place the patties into the pan, working in batches if needed. Cook for about 5 minutes per side until golden outside and cooked through. Serve with the rémoulade.

Cod Piccata Fillets with Spaghetti Squash

Prep time: 15 minutes | Cook time: 58 minutes | Serves 4

1 large spaghetti squash (about 4 pounds / 1.8 kg)
1 tablespoon extra-virgin olive oil, plus more for brushing
Pinch salt
Pinch freshly ground black pepper
2 tablespoons butter, divided
4 (6-ounce / 170 g) cod fillets
3 garlic cloves, minced

¼ cup white wine
1 cup low-sodium vegetable stock
Juice of 2 lemons
3 tablespoons capers, drained, plus more for garnish
2 teaspoons cornstarch
2 tablespoons cold water
½ cup half-and-half
Fresh parsley, for garnish

1. Preheat the oven to 400°F (205°C). Line a baking sheet with parchment paper or aluminum foil.
2. Use a very sharp knife to carefully cut the spaghetti squash in half. Scoop out the seeds. Brush with olive oil and season with salt and black pepper, then place flat-side down on the prepared baking sheet. Cover with foil and seal, then bake for 50 minutes.
3. Meanwhile, in a large nonstick skillet, heat the 1 tablespoon olive oil and 1 tablespoon of butter. Pat the cod fillets dry and place in the pan once heated. Cook for about 4 minutes on each side, or until easily flaked. Once finished, transfer to a plate and cover to hold warm.
4. In the same skillet, add the remaining 1 tablespoon of butter and the garlic. Cook for 1 minute, then add the white wine to deglaze the pan, scraping up any browned bits from the bottom. Add the vegetable stock, lemon juice, and capers, and stir.
5. In a small bowl, whisk the cornstarch and cold water together to create a slurry. Add it to the skillet, and bring to a simmer. Stir in the half-and-half and allow to thicken to a gravy-like consistency.
6. To serve, shred the spaghetti squash into noodles with a fork and divide evenly among four plates. Place the cooked cod on top, and add the sauce. Garnish with fresh parsley and additional capers.

Savory Creamy Scandinavian Cod Soup

Prep time: 15 minutes | Cook time: 35 minutes | Serves 4 to 6

2 Yukon Gold potatoes, peeled and cut into 1-inch pieces
Kosher salt
3 tablespoons olive oil
1 leek, white part only, rinsed well and thinly sliced
4 to 6 cups fish stock
1 cup diced carrot
1 cup diced parsnip or celeriac
¼ cup dry white wine
1½ pounds (680 g)

cod, cut into 1½-inch pieces
8 ounces (227 g) shrimp, peeled and deveined
8 ounces (227 g) clams, cleaned and scrubbed
2 to 3 tablespoons red wine vinegar
1½ teaspoons sugar
Chopped fresh curly-leaf parsley, for garnish

1. In a medium pot, combine the potatoes and enough water to cover. Salt the water. Bring to a boil over high heat. Cook for about 20 minutes, or until the potatoes are soft. Reserve ½ cup of the cooking water, drain the potatoes, and set aside to cool a bit.
2. In a large pot over medium-high heat, heat the oil. Add the leek and sauté for about 3 minutes until it starts to lightly brown. Add the fish stock, carrot, and parsnip. Simmer the soup for 10 to 15 minutes until the vegetables are tender but not fully cooked.
3. While the vegetables cook, in a blender, combine the cooked potatoes and reserved cooking liquid. Whirl until creamy. Pour the potatoes into the soup, along with the white wine.
4. Add the cod. Gently simmer for approximately 5 minutes, until the fish is cooked through (it will be opaque and flaky), adding the shrimp and clams a couple minutes before the cod is done cooking.
5. Add the vinegar, sugar, and a little salt, adjusting each of these to your taste—the soup should have a subtle sweet-and-sour flavor.
6. Ladle the soup into bowls and garnish with parsley.

Mediterranean Cod with Veggies

Prep time: 10 minutes | Cook time: 15½ minutes | Serves 2

1 tablespoon olive oil
½ medium onion, minced
2 garlic cloves, minced
1 teaspoon oregano
1 (15-ounce / 425-g) can artichoke hearts in water, drained and halved
1 (15-ounce / 425-g) can diced tomatoes with basil
¼ cup pitted Greek olives, drained
10 ounces (284 g) wild cod
Salt and freshly ground black pepper, to taste

1. In a skillet, heat the olive oil over medium-high heat.
2. Sauté the onion for about 5 minutes, stirring occasionally, or until tender.
3. Stir in the garlic and oregano and cook for 30 seconds more until fragrant.
4. Add the artichoke hearts, tomatoes, and olives and stir to combine. Top with the cod.
5. Cover and cook for 10 minutes, or until the fish flakes easily with a fork and juices run clean.
6. Sprinkle with the salt and pepper. Serve warm.

Steamed Cod Fillets

Prep time: 10 minutes | Cook time: 7 minutes | Serves 4

1 pound (454 g) cherry tomatoes, halved
1 bunch fresh thyme sprigs
4 cod fillets
1 teaspoon olive oil
1 clove garlic, pressed
3 pinches salt
2 cups water
1 cup white rice
1 cup Kalamata olives
2 tablespoons pickled capers
1 tablespoon olive oil
1 pinch ground black pepper

1. Line a parchment paper on the basket of your instant pot. Place about half the tomatoes in a single layer on the paper. Sprinkle with thyme, reserving some for garnish.
2. Arrange cod fillets on top. Sprinkle with a little bit of olive oil.
3. Spread the garlic, pepper, salt, and remaining tomatoes over the fish. In the pot, mix rice and water.

4. Lay a trivet over the rice and water. Lower steamer basket onto the trivet.
5. Seal the lid, and cook for 7 minutes on Low Pressure. Release the pressure quickly.
6. Remove the steamer basket and trivet from the pot. Use a fork to fluff rice.
7. Plate the fish fillets and apply a garnish of olives, reserved thyme, pepper, remaining olive oil, and capers. Serve with rice.

Curry Cod Fillets

Prep time: 15 minutes | Cook time: 12 minutes | Serves 8

3 pounds (1.4 kg) cod fillets, cut into bite-sized pieces
2 tablespoons olive oil
4 curry leaves
4 medium onions, chopped
2 tablespoons fresh ginger, grated finely
4 garlic cloves, minced
4 tablespoons curry powder
4 teaspoons ground cumin
4 teaspoons ground coriander
2 teaspoons red chili powder
1 teaspoon ground turmeric
4 cups unsweetened coconut milk
2½ cups tomatoes, chopped
2 Serrano peppers, seeded and chopped
2 tablespoons fresh lemon juice

1. Add the oil to the Instant Pot and select Sauté function for cooking.
2. Add the curry leaves and cook for 30 seconds. Stir the onion, garlic, and ginger into the pot and cook 5 minutes.
3. Add all the spices to the mixture and cook for another 1½ minutes.
4. Hit Cancel then add the coconut milk, Serrano pepper, tomatoes, and fish to the pot.
5. Secure the lid and select the Manual settings with Low Pressure and 5 minutes cooking time.
6. After the beep, do a Quick release and remove the lid.
7. Drizzle lemon juice over the curry then stir.
8. Serve immediately.

Air-Fried Cod Fillets with Lemon

Prep time: 5 minutes | Cook time: 8 minutes | Serves 2

4 tablespoons cashew butter
8 to 10 Ritz crackers, crushed into crumbs
2 (6-ounce / 170-g) cod fillets
Salt and freshly ground black pepper
1 lemon

1. Preheat the air fryer to 380ºF (193ºC).
2. Heat the butter in a small saucepan on the stovetop or in a microwavable dish in the microwave, and then transfer the butter to a shallow dish. Place the crushed RITZ® crackers into a second shallow dish.
3. Season the fish fillets with salt and freshly ground black pepper. Dip them into the butter and then coat both sides with the Ritz crackers.
4. Place the fish into the air fryer basket and air fry at 380ºF (193ºC) for 8 to 10 minutes, flipping the fish over halfway through the cooking time.
5. Serve with a wedge of lemon to squeeze over the top.

Rosemary Cod Fillets with Cherry Tomato

Prep time: 5 minutes | Cook time: 5 minutes | Serves 6

1½ pounds (680 g) cherry tomatoes, halved
2½ tablespoons fresh rosemary, chopped
6 (4-ounce / 113-g) cod fillets
3 garlic cloves, minced
2 tablespoons olive oil
Salt and freshly ground black pepper, to taste

1. Add the olive oil, half of the tomatoes and rosemary to the insert of the Instant Pot.
2. Place the cod fillets over these tomatoes. Then add more tomatoes to the pot.
3. Add the garlic to the pot. Then secure the lid.
4. Select the Manual function with High Pressure for 5 minutes.
5. After the beep, use the quick release to discharge all the steam.
6. Serve cod fillets with tomatoes and sprinkle a pinch of salt and pepper on top.

Baked Cod with Veggies

Prep time: 20 minutes | Cook time: 30 minutes | Serves 2

1 pound (454 g) thick cod fillet, cut into 4 even portions
¼ teaspoon onion powder (optional)
¼ teaspoon paprika
3 tablespoons extra-virgin olive oil
4 medium scallions
½ cup fresh chopped basil, divided
3 tablespoons minced garlic (optional)
2 teaspoons salt
2 teaspoons freshly ground black pepper
¼ teaspoon dry
marjoram (optional)
6 sun-dried tomato slices
½ cup dry white wine
½ cup crumbled feta cheese
1 (15-ounce / 425-g) can oil-packed artichoke hearts, drained
1 lemon, sliced
1 cup pitted kalamata olives
1 teaspoon capers (optional)
4 small red potatoes, quartered

1. Preheat the oven to 375ºF (190ºC).
2. Season the fish with paprika and onion powder (if desired).
3. Heat an ovenproof skillet over medium heat and sear the top side of the cod for about 1 minute until golden. Set aside.
4. Heat the olive oil in the same skillet over medium heat.
5. Add the scallions, ¼ cup of basil, garlic (if desired), salt, pepper, marjoram (if desired), tomato slices, and white wine and stir to combine. Bring to a boil and remove from heat.
6. Evenly spread the sauce on the bottom of skillet. Place the cod on top of the tomato basil sauce and scatter with feta cheese. Place the artichokes in the skillet and top with the lemon slices.
7. Scatter with the olives, capers (if desired), and the remaining ¼ cup of basil. Remove from the heat and transfer to the preheated oven. Bake for 15 to 20 minutes, or until it flakes easily with a fork.
8. Meanwhile, place the quartered potatoes on a baking sheet or wrapped in aluminum foil. Bake in the oven for 15 minutes until fork-tender.
9. Cool for 5 minutes before serving.

Cod Fillets with Parsley Piston

Prep time: 5 minutes | Cook time: 8 minutes | Serves 4

1 cup packed roughly chopped fresh flat-leaf Italian parsley
Zest and juice of 1 lemon
1 to 2 small garlic cloves, minced
1 teaspoon salt

½ teaspoon freshly ground black pepper
1 cup extra-virgin olive oil, divided
1 pound (454 g) cod fillets, cut into 4 equal-sized pieces

1. Make the pistou: Place the parsley, lemon zest and juice, garlic, salt, and pepper in a food processor until finely chopped.
2. With the food processor running, slowly drizzle in ¾ cup of olive oil until a thick sauce forms. Set aside.
3. Heat the remaining ¼ cup of olive oil in a large skillet over medium-high heat.
4. Add the cod fillets, cover, and cook each side for 4 to 5 minutes, until browned and cooked through.
5. Remove the cod fillets from the heat to a plate and top each with generous spoonfuls of the prepared pistou. Serve immediately.

Buttery Roasted Cod

Prep time: 10 minutes | Cook time: 15 minutes | Serves 4

12 tablespoons (1 ½ sticks) unsalted butter, at room temperature
4 scallions (white and green parts), thinly sliced
3 lemons, 1 for zest and juice, 1 thinly sliced, 1 cut into

wedges
¼ cup chopped flat-leaf parsley
Leaves from 2 thyme sprigs, chopped
Kosher salt
Freshly ground black pepper
2 pounds (907 g) cod fillets

1. Preheat the oven to 425°F (220°C). Line a baking sheet with parchment paper.
2. In the bowl of a food processor, combine the butter, scallions, lemon zest, 2 tablespoons of lemon juice, parsley, thyme, and a pinch of salt and pepper. Pulse into a green mixture of buttery aromatic goodness.

3. Place the cod fillets on the prepared baking sheet. Season with salt and pepper and spread about 6 tablespoons of scallion butter in an even layer on top. Add a few lemon slices and wrap the cod in the parchment paper, making a parcel. Bake for 15 to 20 minutes, until the fish is opaque and slightly firm to the touch. Serve with the lemon wedges.

Cod Fillets with Pepita Pesto

Prep time: 10 minutes | Cook time: 20 minutes | Serves 4

For the Pepita Pesto:
½ cup pepitas
4 cups fresh basil
2 cups arugula
⅓ cup extra-virgin olive oil

3 garlic cloves, peeled
¾ teaspoon sea salt
¼ cup whole-wheat bread crumbs

For the Cod:
4 (6-ounce / 170-g) cod fillets, about 1-inch thick

Salt
Freshly ground black pepper

To Make the Pepita Pesto
1. Heat a small skillet over medium heat. Toast the pepitas for 5 to 7 minutes, constantly moving them around the pan to prevent burning.
2. Add the toasted pepitas, basil, arugula, olive oil, garlic, and salt to a food processor. Pulse until combined. Mix in the bread crumbs.

To Make the Cod
1. Preheat the oven to 350°F (180°C). Line a large sheet pan with parchment paper.
2. Place the fish on the sheet pan. Sprinkle with salt and pepper. Divide the pesto among the cod fillets and spread in an even layer.
3. Bake for 15 to 20 minutes, until the fish is opaque and the flesh flakes easily with a fork.

Crispy Cod and Veggies

Prep time: 15 minutes | Cook time: 38 minutes | Serves 2

Vegetable oil
All-purpose flour, for dredging
2 large eggs, lightly beaten
1½ cups plain bread crumbs
Kosher salt
Freshly ground black pepper
1 pound (454 g) cod, cut into 1.5-by-3-inch sticks
1 dozen baby
potatoes, halved
5 tablespoons extra-virgin olive oil, divided
2 tablespoons apple cider vinegar
¼ cup plus 1 tablespoon chopped fresh dill, divided
1 cup mayonnaise
1 tablespoon capers, drained
Zest of 1 lemon and 1 tablespoon juice

1. Preheat the oven to 425°F (220°C). Line a large baking sheet with parchment paper and brush the entire surface with vegetable oil.
2. In 3 separate shallow bowls, place the flour, eggs, and bread crumbs. Season each with salt and pepper. Season the cod with salt and pepper. Dredge the cod first in flour, tapping off any excess, then in the eggs, and then in the bread crumbs. Shake off any excess and place on the prepared baking sheet. Drizzle with vegetable oil. Bake until golden brown, about 15 minutes.
3. In a large bowl, toss together the potatoes, 3 tablespoons of olive oil, the vinegar, and a pinch of salt and pepper.
4. In a large cast-iron skillet over medium-high heat, heat the remaining 2 tablespoons of olive oil. Arrange the potatoes cut-side down in a single layer in the skillet. Cook until golden brown on one side, about 5 minutes; then flip and drizzle with more olive oil. Cook for 3 to 4 minutes more before transferring to the oven and cooking until fork-tender, about 15 minutes. Top with ¼ cup of dill.
5. In a small bowl, combine the mayonnaise, capers, lemon zest, lemon juice, and the remaining 1 tablespoon of dill. Season with salt and plenty of pepper. Mix to combine.
6. Serve the cod with the warm crispy potatoes and a side of the cool sauce.

Oven-Baked Cod and Chips

Prep time: 10 minutes | Cook time: 38 minutes | Serves 4

2 pounds (907 g) russet potatoes, cut lengthwise into ½-inch wedges
¼ cup olive oil
2 tablespoons kosher salt, plus more for seasoning
1 cup all-purpose flour
2 large egg whites, lightly beaten
1½ cups panko bread crumbs
2 pounds (907 g) cod fillets
1 recipe Coleslaw Worth a Second Helping
Tartar sauce or Rémoulade, for serving
Malt vinegar, for serving
Lemon wedges, for serving
Ketchup, for serving

1. Put the potato wedges in a large bowl and cover with water. Let them soak for about 30 minutes, then drain and pat dry with a paper towel.
2. While the potatoes soak, preheat the oven to 400°F (205°C). Line a large baking sheet with parchment paper.
3. Put the potatoes on the prepared baking sheet and toss them with the oil and salt. Arrange the potatoes in a single layer.
4. Roast for 10 minutes. Flip the potatoes and roast for 10 minutes more until golden and crisp.
5. While the potatoes roast, put the flour in one shallow bowl. In a second shallow bowl, whisk the egg whites and put the panko in a third bowl.
6. Pat the fish dry and season with salt. Dredge the fish in the flour, the egg whites, and the panko.
7. Remove the baking sheet from the oven. Using a heatproof spatula, scoot the potatoes off to the side and make room for the fish. Arrange the fish next to the potatoes in a single layer. Roast for about 18 minutes, depending on the thickness of the fish, flipping the fish once, until golden and crispy and the internal temperature reaches 145°F (63°C).
8. Serve with the coleslaw, tartar sauce, vinegar, lemon wedges, and ketchup.

Mediterranean Cod Fillets Stew

Prep time: 10 minutes | Cook time: 15 minutes | Serves 6

2 tablespoons extra-virgin olive oil
2 cups chopped onion
2 garlic cloves, minced
¾ teaspoon smoked paprika
1 (14½-ounce / 411-g) can diced tomatoes, undrained
1 (12-ounce / 340-g) jar roasted red peppers, drained and chopped
1 cup sliced olives, green or black
⅓ cup dry red wine
¼ teaspoon kosher or sea salt
¼ teaspoon freshly ground black pepper
1½ pounds (680 g) cod fillets, cut into 1-inch pieces
3 cups sliced mushrooms

1. In a large stockpot over medium heat, heat the oil. Add the onion and cook for 4 minutes, stirring occasionally.
2. Add the garlic and smoked paprika and cook for 1 minute, stirring often.
3. Mix in the tomatoes with their juices, roasted peppers, olives, wine, pepper, and salt, and turn the heat to medium-high. Bring the mixture to a boil.
4. Add the cod fillets and mushrooms, and reduce the heat to medium.
5. Cover and cook for about 10 minutes, stirring a few times, until the cod is cooked through and flakes easily, and serve.

Poached Cod with Fennel and Tomatoes

Prep time: 10 minutes | Cook time: 18 minutes | Serves 4

1 tablespoon olive oil
1 cup thinly sliced fennel
½ cup thinly sliced onion
1 tablespoon minced garlic
1 (15-ounce / 425-g) can diced tomatoes
2 cups chicken broth
½ cup white wine
Juice and zest of 1 orange
1 pinch red pepper flakes
1 bay leaf
1 pound (454 g) cod

1. Heat the olive oil in a large skillet. Add the onion and fennel and cook for 6 minutes, stirring occasionally, or until translucent.

2. Add the garlic and cook for 1 minute more.
3. Add the tomatoes, chicken broth, wine, orange juice and zest, red pepper flakes, and bay leaf, and simmer for 5 minutes to meld the flavors.
4. Carefully add the cod in a single layer, cover, and simmer for 6 to 7 minutes.
5. Transfer fish to a serving dish, ladle the remaining sauce over the fish, and serve.

Baked Cod with Pistachio Crust

Prep time: 10 minutes | Cook time: 15 minutes | Serves 4

½ cup extra-virgin olive oil, divided
1 pound (454 g) flaky cod, skin removed
½ cup shelled finely chopped pistachios
½ cup ground flaxseed
Zest and juice of 1 lemon, divided
1 teaspoon ground cumin
1 teaspoon ground allspice
½ teaspoon salt
¼ teaspoon freshly ground black pepper

1. Preheat the oven to 400ºF (205ºC).
2. Line a baking sheet with parchment paper or aluminum foil and drizzle 2 tablespoons of olive oil over the sheet, spreading to evenly coat the bottom.
3. Cut the fish into 4 equal pieces and place on the prepared baking sheet.
4. In a small bowl, combine the pistachios, flaxseed, lemon zest, cumin, allspice, salt, and pepper. Drizzle in ¼ cup of olive oil and stir well.
5. Divide the nut mixture evenly on top of the fish pieces. Drizzle the lemon juice and remaining 2 tablespoons of olive oil over the fish and bake until cooked through, 15 to 20 minutes, depending on the thickness of the fish.
6. Cool for 5 minutes before serving.

Pan-Seared Cod with Special Salad

Prep time: 15 minutes | Cook time: 10 minutes | Serves 4

For the Fish:

1½ pounds (680 g) black cod, skin on, halved as needed to fit in the pan	Kosher salt 1 to 2 tablespoons olive oil

For the Salad:

1 fennel bulb with greens	¼ teaspoon kosher salt
2 tablespoons best-quality extra-virgin olive oil	4 radishes, cut into eighths
2 tablespoons freshly squeezed lemon juice	6 ounces (170 g) fresh blackberries

For the Cucumber Puree:

1 cucumber, peeled and halved lengthwise	squeezed lemon juice
6 tablespoons extra-virgin olive oil	1 tablespoon garlic oil
¼ cup fresh parsley	½ teaspoon kosher salt, plus more for seasoning
2 tablespoons freshly	

For the Mayonnaise:

3 large egg yolks	1 teaspoon kosher salt, plus more for seasoning
1 teaspoon ground mustard	
1 cup extra-virgin olive oil	Dash freshly ground black pepper, plus more for seasoning
2 tablespoons freshly squeezed lemon juice	

To Start the Fish

1. Rinse the black cod and pat it dry. Season with salt and let sit while you prepare the salad and sauces.

To Make the Salad

1. Cut the stalks from the fennel bulb and remove the wispy fronds, roughly chopping them and setting them aside. Cut the bulb as thinly as possible, ideally using a mandoline.
2. In a medium bowl, whisk the oil, lemon juice, and salt to combine.
3. Add the sliced fennel and the chopped fronds, and toss to coat.
4. Add the radishes and blackberries. Set aside.

To Make the Cucumber Puree

1. Using the tip of a spoon, scrape the seeds from the cucumber and cut the flesh into 1-inch pieces. Transfer to a high-powered blender and add the oil, parsley, lemon juice, garlic oil, and salt. Blend until

smooth. Taste and adjust the seasoning, as needed.

To Make the Mayonnaise

1. In a food processor, whirl together the egg yolks and ground mustard.
2. With the machine running, add the oil, a little at a time, letting the oil slowly drip into the egg yolks to emulsify (if your food processor has a pusher with a small hole in the bottom, use this to help moderate the speed, but still take care not to add too much oil at once).
3. Once the oil is incorporated and emulsified, add the lemon juice, salt, and pepper and give it another quick whirl. Taste and adjust the seasonings, as needed. Refrigerate while you prepare the fish.

To Finish the Fish

1. In a large skillet over medium-high heat, heat the oil. Add the cod, flesh-side down, and cook for about 5 minutes until golden brown. Gently flip the fish—it will be very delicate at this point—and cook on the skin side for about 5 minutes more until the fish is opaque and cooked through.
2. Arrange the fennel salad on each of 4 plates. Arrange the cod in the middle. Spoon a dollop of mayonnaise on top and drizzle the cucumber sauce around.

Quick Fried Cod Fillets

Prep time: 5 minutes | Cook time: 6 minutes | Serves 4

½ cup all-purpose flour	4 (4- to 5-ounce / 113- to 142-g) cod fillets
1 teaspoon garlic powder	1 tablespoon extra-virgin olive oil
1 teaspoon salt	

1. Mix together the flour, garlic powder, and salt in a shallow dish.
2. Dredge each piece of fish in the seasoned flour until they are evenly coated.
3. Heat the olive oil in a medium skillet over medium-high heat.
4. Once hot, add the cod fillets and fry for 6 to 8 minutes, flipping the fish halfway through, or until the fish is opaque and flakes easily.
5. Remove from the heat and serve on plates.

Tomato-Sauce Cast-Iron Cod

Prep time: 15 minutes | Cook time: 18 minutes | Serves 2 to 4

2 tablespoons extra-virgin olive oil, plus more for drizzling
1 yellow onion, halved, then cut into ¼-inch-thick slices
Kosher salt
Freshly ground black pepper
6 garlic cloves, chopped
3 tablespoons chopped fresh thyme, divided
1 tablespoon chopped fresh rosemary
¼ teaspoon red pepper flakes
4 cups diced Roma tomatoes
¾ cup dry white wine
2 cups panko bread crumbs
1 pound (454 g) cod, cut into 4 portions
1 lemon, cut into wedges

1. Preheat the oven to 425°F (220ºC).
2. In a cast-iron skillet over medium heat, heat the olive oil. Once hot, add the onion and season with salt and pepper. Sauté until translucent; then add the garlic, 2 tablespoons of thyme, the rosemary, and the red pepper flakes. Sauté until the garlic is fragrant, about 30 seconds.
3. Add the tomatoes and a pinch more salt. Stir to combine, and simmer for 2 minutes.
4. Add the wine and deglaze the pan by scraping the bottom with a spoon. Increase the heat to medium-high and simmer for 30 seconds. Gently crush the tomatoes with the back of a wooden spoon to help release their juices as they are cooking.
5. In a small bowl, mix together the panko and remaining 1 tablespoon of thyme. Season with salt and pepper and drizzle with olive oil so the mixture resembles slightly damp sand.
6. Season the cod with salt and pepper. Nestle the cod into the sauce, and sprinkle with the panko. Bake until the fish is opaque, 15 to 20 minutes. Serve with the lemon wedges.

Easy Coconut Tangy Cod Curry

Prep time: 15 minutes | Cook time: 3 minutes | Serves 6

1 (28-ounce / 794-g) can coconut milk
Juice of 2 lemons
2 tablespoons red curry paste
2 teaspoons fish sauce
2 teaspoons honey
4 teaspoons Sriracha
4 garlic cloves, minced
2 teaspoons ground turmeric
2 teaspoons ground ginger
1 teaspoon sea salt
1 teaspoon white pepper
2 pounds (907 g) cod, cut into 1-inch cubes
½ cup chopped fresh cilantro, for garnish
4 lime wedges, for garnish

1. Add all the ingredients, except the cod cubes and garnish, to a large bowl and whisk them well.
2. Arrange the cod cube at the base of the Instant Pot and pour the coconut milk mixture over it.
3. Secure the lid and hit the Manual key, select High Pressure with 3 minutes cooking time.
4. After the beep, do a Quick release then remove the lid.
5. Garnish with fresh cilantro and lemon wedges then serve.

Poached Cod with Creamy Dill Sauce

Prep time: 10 minutes | Cook time: 7 minutes | Serves 4

For the Sauce:
¼ cup crème fraîche
¼ cup chopped fresh dill
½ teaspoon freshly squeezed lemon
juice, plus more for seasoning
⅛ teaspoon kosher salt, plus more for seasoning

For the Fish:
3 cups water
2 tablespoons fresh rosemary leaves
1 bay leaf
1 teaspoon kosher
salt
1½ pounds (680 g) cod fillets, rinsed, cut to fit in a large skillet

To Make the Sauce
1. In a small bowl, stir together the crème fraîche, dill, lemon juice, and salt. Taste and adjust seasonings, as needed. Set aside.

To Make the Fish
1. In a large skillet over medium-high heat, combine the water, rosemary, bay leaf, and salt. Bring to a low boil.
2. Add the cod and adjust the heat to maintain a simmer. Cook for about 7 minutes, depending on thickness, until the cod is cooked through and begins to flake.
3. Carefully transfer the fish to a platter. Serve the fish with the sauce drizzled over top or in a ramekin on the side.

Healthy Baked Cod and Chip

Prep time: 10 minutes | Cook time: 50 minutes | Serves 4

2 pounds (907 g) baby gold potatoes, halved
2 tablespoons avocado oil
½ teaspoon Old Bay Seasoning, divided
1 teaspoon salt, divided
4 (6-ounce / 170-g) cod fillets, cut into
strips
¼ teaspoon freshly ground black pepper, divided
½ cup all-purpose flour
2 large eggs
1 cup seasoned whole-wheat bread crumbs

1. Preheat the oven to 375°F (190°C).
2. In a large bowl, toss the potatoes in avocado oil, ¼ teaspoon of Old Bay, and ½ teaspoon of salt. Transfer to a large sheet pan. Be careful not to overcrowd the pan.
3. Roast the potatoes for 35 minutes, tossing halfway through.
4. While the potatoes are roasting, season the cod with ¼ teaspoon of salt and ⅛ teaspoon of pepper.
5. Set up a breading workspace. Pour the flour on a plate and season with the remaining ¼ teaspoon of salt. In a medium, shallow bowl, whisk the eggs with the remaining ⅛ teaspoon of pepper. Last, on a second plate, mix the bread crumbs with the remaining ¼ teaspoon of Old Bay.
6. To bread the fish, dredge in flour, then dip the fish in egg, allowing the excess to drip off. Last, coat the fish in bread crumbs. Place on a sheet pan and repeat with the remaining fish.
7. Bake for 15 minutes, flipping halfway through, until the fish flakes with a fork. Serve with the crispy potatoes.

Chapter 9 Halibut

Herb-Poached Halibut Fillets

Prep time: 10 minutes | Cook time: 8 minutes | Serves 4

1 cup vegetable broth
2 garlic cloves, minced
2 thyme sprigs
¼ teaspoon freshly ground black pepper
4 (1 to 1½ inches thick, 6-ounce / 170-

g) halibut fillets
1 teaspoon salt
3 tablespoons unsalted butter
3 tablespoons minced shallot
1 tablespoon fresh lemon juice

1. In a large skillet, combine the vegetable broth, garlic, thyme, and pepper and bring to a boil.
2. Evenly season the halibut with the salt.
3. Add the fish to the skillet, reduce the heat to a simmer, cover, and cook for 5 minutes, or until the fish flakes easily with a fork.
4. Remove the fish from the liquid and set aside. Cover loosely to keep warm.
5. Add the butter and shallot to the skillet and cook for 2 minutes, until the shallots are softened.
6. Add the lemon juice, bring to a boil, then reduce the heat and simmer for 1 minute until the liquid has reduced slightly.
7. Serve the fish with the butter herb sauce spooned on top.

Savory Halibut with Lemon Caper Sauce

Prep time: 10 minutes | Cook time: 4½ minutes | Serves 2

1 pound (454 g) fresh halibut, skinned, and cut into two equal portions
4 tablespoons butter, divided
1 tablespoon extra-virgin olive oil
½ teaspoon kosher salt
Few grinds black pepper

3 to 4 slices lemon
2 teaspoons fresh garlic, finely chopped
¼ cup white wine such as Chardonnay
2 tablespoons lemon juice
2 tablespoon capers drained
2 tablespoons fresh flat leaf parsley chopped

1. Salt the top of the fish with just a small sprinkle of kosher or sea salt.
2. Place two tablespoons of butter and the olive oil in a medium to large skillet or sauté pan and heat over medium heat.
3. Swirl the butter and oil around and once it starts to slightly brown, add the fish top side down. Sprinkle the side facing up with the rest of the salt and the pepper.
4. Cook for five minutes then using one or two long fish spatulas, gently flip over being careful not to splash hot fat.
5. Add the lemon slices to the pan as the fish cooks and cook the fish about 3 to 5 more minutes. Poke the fish to test for doneness or insert a small knife in the side of the center to see if the fish flakes. You want to stop the cooking just before it fully cooks so a little undercooked in the center is fine. It will continue to cook outside of the pan.
6. Using one or two fish turners, remove the fish fillets to a platter along with the cooked lemon slices.
7. Pour off all but two tablespoons of the fat left in the pan. Best to pour it all into a bowl, let the burned bits sink to the bottom then skim off a few tablespoons of the fat at the top and place back into the pan.
8. Keep the heat at medium and add the garlic and cook one minute. Add the wine and cook to evaporate. Then add the lemon juice, capers and parsley. Cook for 1 minute then remove from heat and stir in the remaining 2 tablespoons of butter and stir to make the sauce.
9. Put the fish back into the pan along with any liquid from the platter, bring heat back to medium and use a spoon to spoon the sauce over the top and cook for 30 seconds then remove to a platter and serve.
10. Serve each portion with a cooked lemon slice and some of the pan sauce.

Crispy Herb Crusted Halibut Fillets

Prep time: 10 minutes | Cook time: 20 minutes | Serves 4

4 (5-ounce / 142-g) halibut fillets, patted dry
Extra-virgin olive oil, for brushing
½ cup coarsely ground unsalted pistachios
1 tablespoon chopped

fresh parsley
1 teaspoon chopped fresh basil
1 teaspoon chopped fresh thyme
Pinch sea salt
Pinch freshly ground black pepper

1. Preheat the oven to 350ºF (180ºC). Line a baking sheet with parchment paper.
2. Place the fillets on the baking sheet and brush them generously with olive oil.
3. In a small bowl, stir together the pistachios, parsley, basil, thyme, salt, and pepper.
4. Spoon the nut mixture evenly on the fish, spreading it out so the tops of the fillets are covered.
5. Bake in the preheated oven until it flakes when pressed with a fork, about 20 minutes.
6. Serve immediately.

Cast-Iron Halibut Fillets with Veggies

Prep time: 15 minutes | Cook time: 16½ minutes | Serves 2

1 pound (454 g) halibut fillet
Kosher salt
Freshly ground black pepper
2 tablespoons extra-virgin olive oil, plus more for drizzling
2 shallots, thinly sliced
4 garlic cloves, chopped
½ teaspoon red pepper flakes
1 (15-ounce / 425-g)

can cannellini beans, drained and rinsed
½ cup dry white wine
¼ cup Castelvetrano olives, pitted and chopped
2 tablespoons chopped fresh thyme
1 teaspoon chopped fresh rosemary
1 cup vegetable stock
2 lemons, 1 thinly sliced, 1 cut into wedges

1. Preheat the oven to 400ºF (205ºC).
2. Season the fish with salt and pepper. In a large cast-iron skillet, heat 2 tablespoons of olive oil. Add the shallots and sauté until translucent.
3. Add the garlic and red pepper flakes and sauté until fragrant, about 30 seconds. Stir in the beans, wine, olives, thyme, and rosemary. Let simmer for 1 minute, stirring regularly.
4. Add the stock. Season with salt and pepper.
5. Nestle the fish in the center of the pan, top with the lemon slices, and give everything a healthy drizzle of olive oil.
6. Bake for 15 to 20 minutes, until the fish is opaque. Serve with the lemon wedges.

Halibut Tomato Stew

Prep time: 15 minutes | Cook time: 20 minutes | Serves 2

2 tablespoons olive oil
½ small onion, diced
½ green pepper, diced
2 teaspoons dried basil
2 teaspoons dried oregano
½ cup dry white wine
1 (14½-ounce / 411-g) can diced tomatoes with basil
1 (8-ounce / 227-g) can no-salt-added tomato sauce

1 (6½-ounce / 184-g) can minced clams with their juice
8 ounces (227 g) peeled, deveined raw shrimp
4 ounces (113 g) halibut (a thick piece works best)
3 tablespoons fresh parsley
Salt and freshly ground black pepper, to taste

1. In a Dutch oven, heat the olive oil over medium heat.
2. Sauté the onion and green pepper for 5 minutes, or until tender.
3. Stir in the basil, oregano, wine, diced tomatoes, and tomato sauce and bring to a boil.
4. Once boiling, reduce the heat to low and bring to a simmer for 5 minutes.
5. Add the clams, shrimp, and fish and cook for about 10 minutes, or until the shrimp are pink and cooked through.
6. Scatter with the parsley and add the salt and black pepper to taste.
7. Remove from the heat and serve warm.

Simple Broiled Halibut and Salad

Prep time: 10 minutes | Cook time: 7 minutes | Serves 4

1 pound (454 g) halibut fillets, rinsed and patted dry
¼ cup olive oil, plus more for brushing the fish
Kosher salt
4 ears fresh corn, kernels cut from the cob
1 pint cherry tomatoes, halved crosswise

½ shallot, minced
¼ cup chopped fresh cilantro leaves, plus a few leaves for garnish
¼ cup freshly squeezed lime juice
1 teaspoon ground cumin
½ teaspoon ground coriander
2 avocados, peeled, halved, pitted, and cut into slices

1. Preheat the broiler.
2. Place the halibut on a broiler pan, skin-side down, and brush the top with oil. Sprinkle salt evenly over the top.
3. Roast for about 7 minutes, or until the fish reaches 145°F (63°C), depending on the thickness of the fish. When done, it should flake easily with a fork and be opaque inside.
4. While the fish cooks, in a large bowl, stir together the corn, tomatoes, shallot, cilantro, oil, lime juice, cumin, and coriander to combine. Season with salt. Distribute the salad among 4 plates and arrange the avocado slices attractively over each salad.
5. Divide the halibut into 4 portions and nestle them against the salad.

Easy Miso Halibut Soup with Chard

Prep time: 5 minutes | Cook time: 13 minutes | Serves 4

6 cups low-sodium vegetable stock
2 tablespoons white miso paste
1 tablespoon grated fresh ginger

1 pound (454 g) halibut, thinly sliced
2 cups roughly chopped Swiss chard, thoroughly washed

1. In a large saucepan, bring the vegetable stock to a boil over medium-high heat.
2. Stir in the miso paste and ginger and simmer for 5 minutes.

3. Add the halibut and simmer until just cooked through, about 5 minutes.
4. Stir in the chard and simmer until wilted, about 3 minutes.
5. Serve immediately.

Broiled Halibut Fillets with Orzo Risotto

Prep time: 15 minutes | Cook time: 25 minutes | Serves 4

Nonstick cooking spray (optional)
4 (4-ounce / 113-g) halibut fillets
1 tablespoon Italian seasoning
1 tablespoon extra-virgin olive oil
1⅓ cups uncooked orzo pasta
3½ cups water
3 garlic cloves,

minced
2 cups cherry tomatoes, quartered
1 tablespoon capers, drained and rinsed, plus more for garnish
1 teaspoon salt
1 teaspoon freshly ground black pepper
1 tablespoon butter
1 tablespoon fresh parsley, chopped

1. Position the top oven rack 6 to 8 inches from the heating element. Preheat the oven to broil for at least 10 minutes.
2. Prepare a baking sheet with nonstick cooking spray. Evenly space the fillets on top and coat with the Italian seasoning, saving the excess. Broil until the fish is fully cooked and easily flaked, 8 to 10 minutes. Remove from the oven. Tent with foil to keep warm while the orzo finishes cooking.
3. Meanwhile, in a large skillet over medium heat, toast the orzo until the color becomes a light golden brown, about 2 minutes.
4. Add the water and bring to a simmer. Stir frequently. Once most of the liquid is absorbed, after about 15 minutes, add the garlic, cherry tomatoes, capers, remaining Italian seasoning, salt, and black pepper. Continue cooking until all liquid is absorbed. Remove from the heat, and stir in the butter.
5. Plate a quarter of the orzo risotto and top with one fillet.
6. Garnish with the parsley and additional capers, repeat with the remaining orzo risotto and fish, and serve.

Blackened Halibut Tacos with Corn Salsa

Prep time: 20 minutes | Cook time: 6 minutes | Serves 4

For the Fish and Tacos:
1 pound (454 g) halibut fillets, thawed
1½ tablespoons extra-virgin olive oil
2 tablespoons Jamaican jerk seasoning
¼ teaspoon freshly ground black pepper
Pinch salt
8 small (6-inch) flour tortillas

For the Corn Salsa:
1 cup sweet corn kernels
1 cup canned black beans, drained and rinsed
1 cup jicama, peeled and diced or cut into matchsticks
½ red onion, finely diced
½ red bell pepper, diced
½ cup chopped fresh cilantro
Juice of 1 lime

For the Sauce:
¼ cup plain, low-fat Greek yogurt
¼ cup chopped fresh cilantro
½ jalapeño pepper, minced
½ teaspoon ground cumin
½ teaspoon garlic powder

To Make the Fish
1. Preheat the oven to broil. Line a baking sheet with aluminum foil.
2. Place the halibut fillets on the baking sheet and brush with the olive oil. Generously coat with jerk seasoning and black pepper. Season with salt. Broil for 6 to 8 minutes, depending on the thickness. Once fully cooked and flaky, remove from oven and allow to cool slightly.

To Make the Corn Salsa
1. In a large bowl, mix the sweet corn, black beans, jicama, onion, bell pepper, cilantro, and lime juice. Set aside.

To Make the Sauce
1. In another large bowl, combine the Greek yogurt, cilantro, jalapeño pepper, cumin, and garlic powder. Set aside.

To Prepare the Tacos
1. When ready to serve, flake the fish apart with a fork and place inside the toasted flour tortillas. Top with the corn salsa and sauce. Serve immediately.

Red-Wine Poached Halibut with Mushrooms

Prep time: 10 minutes | Cook time: 11 minutes | Serves 2

$^4/_5$ cup red wine
½ cup fresh chicken stock
3 thyme sprigs
3 black peppercorns
2 (150 g) portions halibut
1 tablespoon
rapeseed oil
1 to 2 tablespoon butter
100 g wild mushrooms
½ lemon, juiced
115 g spinach

1. Heat oven to 160ºF (71ºC).
2. Put the wine, stock, thyme, peppercorns and a pinch of salt in a deep-sided frying pan and bring to just below the boil. Drop in the halibut, turn down the heat and poach for 8 minutes or until flaking apart.
3. In the same frying pan, heat the oil and 1 tablespoon butter until foaming.
4. Add the mushrooms and cook until you get a lovely golden colour. (If using a king oyster mushroom, turn over to get an even colour on both sides.) Once cooked, add the lemon juice to taste and sprinkle with a little salt.
5. Lift the cooked fish from the pan, lay on a plate, cover with foil and keep warm in the oven. Turn the heat up on the poaching liquid, reduce by two-thirds, then pour through a fine sieve.
6. Wash the spinach in cold water and add to the mushrooms. Season, add more butter if needed, and cook for about 3 minutes, stirring until wilted. Divide the spinach and mushrooms between two plates and serve the halibut on top. Spoon over the reduced sauce.

Dijon Walnut-Crusted Halibut Fillets

Prep time: 10 minutes | Cook time: 10 minutes | Serves 4

2 large eggs
1 cup panko bread crumbs
¾ cup finely chopped walnuts
½ cup grated Parmesan Cheese
2 tablespoons melted butter
1½ tablespoons Dijon mustard
1 tablespoon Italian seasoning
Pinch salt
Pinch freshly ground black pepper
4 (6-ounce / 170-g) halibut fillets, skin removed, patted dry

1. Preheat the oven to 425°F (220°C). Line a baking sheet with parchment paper or aluminum foil.
2. In a medium bowl, lightly beat the eggs to form a simple egg wash. In a large bowl, mix to combine the bread crumbs, walnuts, cheese, butter, Dijon mustard, Italian seasoning, salt, and black pepper for the crust, and place next to the egg wash. The texture should resemble moist crumbles. Dip the fillets into the egg wash, then coat with the crust mixture and place on the baking sheet.
3. Bake for 10 to 12 minutes, or until fully cooked and easily flaked. The crust should appear golden brown and crispy. Serve immediately.

Baked Halibut Steaks wtih Veggies

Prep time: 10 minutes | Cook time: 20 minutes | Serves 4

2 teaspoon olive oil, divided
1 clove garlic, peeled and minced
½ cup minced onion
1 cup diced zucchini
2 cups diced fresh tomatoes
2 tablespoons
chopped fresh basil
¼ teaspoon salt
¼ teaspoon ground black pepper
4 (6-ounce / 170-g) halibut steaks
⅓ cup crumbled feta cheese

1. Preheat oven to 450°F (235°C). Coat a shallow baking dish lightly with 1 teaspoon of olive oil.
2. In a medium saucepan, heat the remaining 1 teaspoon of olive oil.
3. Add the garlic, onion, and zucchini and mix well. Cook for 5 minutes, stirring occasionally, or until the zucchini is softened.
4. Remove the saucepan from the heat and stir in the tomatoes, basil, salt, and pepper.
5. Place the halibut steaks in the coated baking dish in a single layer. Spread the zucchini mixture evenly over the steaks. Scatter the top with feta cheese.
6. Bake in the preheated oven for about 15 minutes, or until the fish flakes when pressed lightly with a fork. Serve hot.

Chapter 10 Snapper

Baked Red Snapper Fillets

Prep time: 10 minutes | Cook time: 12 minutes | Serves 4

4 tablespoons butter, melted, divided
1 pound red snapper fillets
2 teaspoons minced fresh parsley
1 teaspoon snipped fresh chives (optional)
1 garlic clove, minced
½ teaspoon Cajun seasoning
⅛ teaspoon freshly ground black pepper
4 tablespoons almond meal
2 tablespoons vegan Parmesan Cheese, store-bought or homemade

1. Preheat the oven to 400°F (205°C). Lightly coat a 9-inch by 13-inch baking dish with 1 tablespoon of melted butter.
2. Place the fillets in the baking dish.
3. In a small bowl, whisk the remaining 3 tablespoons of melted butter, the parsley, chives (if using), garlic, Cajun seasoning, and pepper. Brush both sides of the red snapper fillets with the butter and herb mixture.
4. In a small bowl, toss the almond meal and vegan Parmesan together and sprinkle evenly over the fish fillets.
5. Bake for 12 minutes, or until the fish flakes easily and is opaque.

Easy Oven-Roasted Snapper Parcels

Prep time: 5 minutes | Cook time: 12 minutes | Serves 4

1 teaspoon Lemon infused olive oil or regular olive oil
4 snapper fillets
4 tablespoons parsley
1 lemon
2 tablespoons capers
Salt and pepper

1. Preheat the oven to 170°F (77°C).
2. Cut 4 pieces of tin foil big enough to hold a fillet and lightly brush them with lemon oil (or olive oil).
3. Place a snapper fillet in the middle of each piece of tin foil.
4. Chop the parsley and divide it between the fillets. Zest the lemon and sprinkle this over the fish. Squeeze a little lemon juice over each fillet.
5. Sprinkle over the capers and season with pepper and a small amount of salt.
6. Fold and scrunch the foil up to make a secure parcel around each fillet and slide the parcels onto a baking sheet.
7. Bake the parcels for 12 to 14 minutes until just cooked.

Snapper Fillets and Veggie En Papillote

Prep time: 10 minutes | Cook time: 13 minutes | Serves 4

1 pound (454 g) haricot verts
4 (6-ounce / 170-g) snapper fillets, about ½-inch thick
½ teaspoon salt
½ teaspoon freshly ground black pepper
½ teaspoon garlic
powder
4 teaspoons unsalted butter
4 teaspoons capers
1 cup chopped fresh parsley
2 lemons, thinly sliced

1. Preheat the oven to 400°F (205°C).
2. Prepare four large pieces of parchment paper that are each large enough to fold over your fish fillet, with a couple of inches of a border.
3. To assemble one packet, place one-quarter of the green beans in a single layer on the lower half of each piece of parchment paper. Place each fish fillet on top of each layer of green beans. Season each with ⅛ teaspoon of salt, pepper, and garlic powder. Top the fish with a pat of butter (about 1 teaspoon), 1 teaspoon of capers, ¼ cup of parsley, and 3 or 4 lemon slices.
4. Fold the parchment paper over the fish and fold down the edges, sealing the fish and veggies in a packet. Place on a sheet pan. Repeat with the remaining ingredients to create four packets.
5. Bake for 13 to 15 minutes, until the fish is cooked through and flakes with a fork. Cooking time varies with the thickness of the fish; adjust as necessary.
6. Remove from the oven and let sit for a couple of minutes, until cool to the touch.
7. Carefully open the parchment paper packets, allowing the steam to escape.

Delicious Citrusy Red Snapper Ceviche

Prep time: 15 minutes | Cook time: 20 minutes | Serves 2 to 4

2 tablespoons freshly squeezed orange juice
5 tablespoons freshly squeezed lime juice
1 large garlic clove, minced
Kosher salt
1 pound red snapper, cut into ½-inch pieces
1 cup heirloom cherry tomatoes, cut into thin rounds
½ small red onion, minced
½ small serrano pepper, seeded and minced
1 ½ tablespoons extra-virgin olive oil
1 avocado, cut into ½-inch dice
¾ cup chopped cilantro
¼ cup toasted pepitas
Tortilla chips, for serving

1. In a medium bowl, whisk together the orange juice, lime juice, garlic, and a pinch of salt. Add the snapper, gently tossing to combine. Let sit, stirring occasionally, so all the fish is getting contact with the marinade, until the fish has firmed up a bit, about 15 minutes.
2. Add the tomatoes, onion, serrano pepper, and olive oil, and gently toss to combine. Let sit for 5 minutes.
3. Gently fold in the avocado and cilantro and sprinkle with the pepitas. Serve with tortilla chips.

Grilled Snapper Fillets with Butter

Prep time: 10 minutes | Cook time: 8 minutes | Serves 4

4 (6-ounce / 170-g) skinless snapper fillets
1 tablespoon olive oil
3 tablespoons lemon juice, divided
½ teaspoon dried basil
Pinch salt
Freshly ground black pepper
2 tablespoons cashew butter
2 garlic cloves, minced

1. Rub the fish fillets with olive oil and 1 tablespoon of the lemon juice. Sprinkle with the basil, salt, and pepper, and place in the air fryer basket.

2. Grill the fish at 380ºF (193ºC) for 7 to 8 minutes or until the fish just flakes when tested with a fork. Remove the fish from the basket and put on a serving plate. Cover to keep warm.
3. In a 6-by-6-by-2-inch pan, combine the cashew butter, remaining 2 tablespoons lemon juice, and garlic. Cook in the air fryer for 1 to 2 minutes or until the garlic is sizzling. Pour this mixture over the fish and serve.

Grilled Lemon Garlic Red Snapper Fillets

Prep time: 10 minutes | Cook time: 14 minutes | Serves 4

1½ pounds (680 g) red snapper fillet
1 tablespoon olive oil
½ teaspoon salt
⅛ teaspoon black pepper
¼ teaspoon garlic powder
⅛ teaspoon paprika
¼ teaspoon dried parsley
1 lemon juiced and sliced

1. Preheat the grill to high heat.
2. While the grill heats begin seasoning the fish. Pour the olive oil over the red snapper. Then sprinkle half the salt, black pepper, garlic powder and paprika over the finish. Massage into the fish. Flip over and repeat. Flip the fish back over and sprinkle the dried parsley on top.
3. Cut the lemon in half. Juice one half of the lemon and drizzle over, then slice the other half of the lemon and place on top of the fish. Reduce the heat on the grill to low. Spray the grill grates with non-stick cooking spray. Carefully, place the fish on top of the grill grates.
4. Grill with lid closed for 7 minutes. Using tongs, remove the lemon slices from the top of the fish and place on the grill grate. Carefully, using a spatula, flip the fish.
5. Place the lemon slices back on the fish, close the lid and grill for an additional 7 minutes or until internal temperature reaches 165ºF (74ºC) and the fish is cooked through.
6. Cut fish into slices (if whole fillet), divide among plates, and enjoy immediately.

Cajun-Spiced Snapper with Salsa

Prep time: 15 minutes | Cook time: 5 minutes | Serves 4

For the Cajun Seasoning:

2 tablespoons smoked paprika
1 tablespoon sea salt
1 tablespoon garlic powder
1 tablespoon freshly ground black pepper
1 teaspoon Italian seasoning
1 teaspoon ground cayenne pepper
½ tablespoon dried thyme

For the Snapper:

4 (6-ounce / 170-g) snapper fillets, about ¼- to ½-inch thick
2 cups chopped pineapple
¼ cup finely chopped red onion
¼ cup roughly chopped fresh cilantro
¼ teaspoon chili powder

To Make the Cajun Seasoning

1. In a small container or jar, combine the smoked paprika, salt, garlic powder, pepper, Italian seasoning, cayenne, and thyme. Mix well.

To Make the Snapper

1. Place the fish skin-side down on a large sheet pan. Generously rub about 1 tablespoon of the spice mixture on top, until the fish is completely coated. You will have leftover seasoning.
2. Broil for 5 to 7 minutes, until the fish flakes with a fork. Cooking time may vary slightly depending on the thickness of the fish.
3. While the fish cooks, in a medium bowl, toss together the pineapple, red onion, cilantro, and chili powder.
4. When the fish is done cooking, top with pineapple salsa and serve warm.

Savory Sun-Dried Tomato Pesto Snapper

Prep time: 5 minutes | Cook time: 12 minutes | Serves 4

1 sweet onion, cut into ¼-inch slices
4 (5-ounce / 142-g) snapper fillets
Freshly ground black
pepper, for seasoning
¼ cup sun-dried tomato pesto
2 tablespoons finely chopped fresh basil

1. Preheat the oven to 400°F (205°C). Line a baking dish with parchment paper and arrange the onion slices on the bottom.
2. Pat the snapper fillets dry with a paper towel and season them lightly with pepper.
3. Place the fillets on the onions and spread 1 tablespoon of pesto on each fillet.
4. Bake until the fish flakes easily with a fork, 12 to 15 minutes.
5. Serve topped with basil.

Red Snapper Fillets with Orange Salsa

Prep time: 10 minutes | Cook time: 8 minutes | Serves 2

2 oranges, peeled, segmented and chopped
1 tablespoon minced shallot
1 to 3 teaspoons minced red Jalapeño or Serrano pepper
1 tablespoon chopped fresh cilantro
Lime juice, to taste
Salt, to taste
2 (5- to 6-ounce / 142- to 170-g) red snapper fillets
½ teaspoon Chinese five spice powder
Salt and freshly ground black pepper
Olive oil, in a spray bottle
4 green onions, cut into 2-inch lengths

1. Start by making the salsa. Cut the peel off the oranges, slicing around the oranges to expose the flesh. Segment the oranges by cutting in between the membranes of the orange. Chop the segments roughly and combine in a bowl with the shallot, Jalapeño or Serrano pepper, cilantro, lime juice and salt. Set the salsa aside.
2. Preheat the air fryer to 400°F (204°C).
3. Season the fish fillets with the five-spice powder, salt and freshly ground black pepper. Spray both sides of the fish fillets with oil. Toss the green onions with a little oil.
4. Transfer the fish to the air fryer basket and scatter the green onions around the fish. Air fry at 400°F (204°C) for 8 minutes.
5. Remove the fish from the air fryer, along with the fried green onions. Serve with white rice and a spoonful of the salsa on top.

Garlic-Herb Snapper Bake

Prep time: 10 minutes | Cook time: 14 minutes | Serves 4 to 5

2 (6- to 8-ounce / 170- to 227-g) red snapper fillets
4 tablespoons butter
1 medium clove garlic, minced
3 to 4 drops Worcestershire sauce
½ teaspoon Creole seasoning
⅛ teaspoon freshly ground black pepper
1 to 2 teaspoons chopped fresh parsley
1 teaspoon snipped chives, optional
3 to 4 tablespoons plain dry breadcrumbs (or seasoned breadcrumbs)
2 tablespoons freshly grated Parmesan Cheese, optional

1. Gather the ingredients. Preheat the oven to 400°F (205°C).
2. Place the snapper fillets in a baking dish that has been sprayed with a nonstick cooking spray.
3. In a skillet, melt the butter with the garlic, Worcestershire sauce, Creole seasoning blend, pepper, parsley, and chives, if using. Cook over low heat for 2 minutes just to blend flavors.
4. Brush both sides of the fish fillets with the butter and herb mixture.
5. Toss the breadcrumbs with the remaining butter mixture and Parmesan Cheese, if using.
6. Spread the breadcrumb mixture over the fillets, adding an equal amount to each. Use your hands to spread it out evenly and press onto the tops of the fillets.
7. Bake in the preheated oven for about 12 minutes, depending on the thickness of the red snapper fillets. The fish will be opaque and flake easily with a fork when done.

Mediterranean Roasted Red Snapper

Prep time: 10 minutes | Cook time: 25 minutes | Serves 4 to 5

2 large whole snapper fish, cleaned and gutted
15 large garlic cloves, minced and combined with a pinch of salt
2 teaspoons ground cumin
2 teaspoons ground coriander salt
1 teaspoon black pepper
1 teaspoon ground sumac
½ cup chopped fresh dill
3 bell peppers, different colors, sliced in rounds
1 large tomato, sliced into rounds
1 medium red onion, sliced into rounds
Greek extra virgin olive oil
2 lemons

6. Preheat the oven to 425°F (220°C).
7. Pat the snapper fish dry. With a large knife, make two slits on each side of the fish. Fill the slits and coat the gut cavity of each fish with the minced garlic.
8. To make the spice mix, combine the cumin, coriander, salt, pepper and sumac in a small bowl. Use ¾ of the spice mix to season the snapper on both sides; pat the spices into the fish pushing into the slits you made earlier. Keep the remainder ¼ of the spice mix aside for now.
9. Stuff each gut cavity with the chopped dill, and as much of the sliced peppers, tomatoes and onions as possible. Place the stuffed fish in a lightly oiled baking sheet.
10. Add the remaining sliced vegetables to form a frame around the fish. Sprinkle the vegetables with a pinch of salt and the remaining ¼ of the spice mix. Drizzle everything generously with olive oil.
11. Place the baking sheet on the lower rack of your 425°F (220°C) heated oven.
12. Roast for 25 minutes until the fish flakes. Transfer the fish to a serving platter and squeeze juice of one lemon all over it. Use the slits you made earlier to cut through and portion the fish. Serve it with wedges of the remaining lemon.

Chapter 11 Trout

Lemon-Pepper Roasted Trout Fillets

Prep time: 10 minutes | Cook time: 15 minutes | Serves 4

Olive oil cooking spray
1½ pounds (680 g) trout fillets, skin removed
1 tablespoon extra-virgin olive oil
1 teaspoon freshly

ground black pepper
½ teaspoon salt
4 lemon slices
2 teaspoons grated lemon zest
2 tablespoons fresh lemon juice

1. Preheat the oven to 400°F (205ºC). Lightly mist a 9-inch by 13-inch baking dish with cooking spray.
2. Rub the trout fillets with the olive oil and season with the pepper and salt. Place in the prepared baking dish. Lay the lemon slices over the trout and sprinkle with lemon zest and lemon juice.
3. Tightly cover the dish with aluminum foil. Bake for 15 minutes, or until the fish flakes easily and is cooked through.

Salt Baked Whole Trout

Prep time: 10 minutes | Cook time: 25 minutes | Serves 4

2 whole trout (2 pounds / 907 g), butterflied and boned
2 tablespoons dry white wine (such as Sauvignon blanc)
Freshly ground black

pepper
6 tarragon sprigs, plus more for garnish
1 lemon, thinly sliced
6 cups kosher salt
4 large egg whites, beaten until frothy

1. Preheat the oven to 475°F (245ºC). Line a baking sheet with parchment paper or aluminum foil.
2. Open the trout, drizzle with the wine, and lightly season with pepper. Stuff each fish with the tarragon and lemon slices and fold them closed. Secure each trout closed with toothpicks.
3. In a bowl, mix the salt and egg whites together until it resembles the texture of wet sand.

4. On the baking sheet, spread 2 cups of the salt mixture in a thick even layer. Place the fish on the salt bed, side by side, with a 2-inch space between them.
5. Cover each trout with 1 cup of the salt mixture, packing the salt to cover the fish entirely. Use the remaining salt to cover in any gaps.
6. Bake the fish for 25 to 30 minutes, or until the salt begins to turn golden brown. Remove the pan from the oven and let it cool for 10 minutes.
7. Carefully break the salt crust around the top half of each fish and lift the "lid" off the fish. Lift each trout from the salt bed and transfer to a plate, removing the toothpicks and scraping away the tarragon and lemon.
8. Garnish with more pepper and tarragon. Serve hot.

Easy Trout Breakfast Salad

Prep time: 5 minutes | Cook time: 5 minutes | Serves 4

8 cups baby arugula
1½ tablespoons extra-virgin olive oil
Pinch salt
4 large eggs
1 teaspoon white

vinegar
8 ounces (227 g) smoked trout
Freshly ground black pepper

1. In a large bowl, toss the arugula, olive oil, and salt. Set aside.
2. Crack an egg into a ramekin or small saucer and set aside.
3. Bring a small saucepan of water to a boil, then reduce the heat to a simmer. Add the vinegar to the water. Swirl the water with a knife, creating a vortex. Slip the egg into the water. Let cook, without touching the egg or water, for about 5 minutes, until the egg white is set.
4. Using a slotted spoon, remove the egg from the water and drain on a paper towel. Be sure the water remains at a simmer as you repeat with the remaining eggs.
5. Distribute the arugula among four bowls. Divide the smoked trout among the bowls. Top each with a poached egg and pepper to taste.

Trout Fillets with Edamame Succotash

Prep time: 10 minutes | Cook time: 10 minutes | Serves 4

1 tablespoon butter
1½ cups sweet corn kernels
1½ cups shelled edamame, thawed
1 zucchini, diced
1 cup halved cherry tomatoes
Pinch salt
Pinch freshly ground black pepper
6 to 8 fresh basil leaves
1 tablespoon canola oil
4 trout fillets, skin on
2 lemons, cut into wedges

1. In a large skillet, over medium-high heat, melt the butter.
2. Add the corn, edamame, and zucchini, and cook for 3 to 5 minutes, then stir in tomatoes, salt, and pepper. Remove from the skillet and transfer to a serving bowl. Chop or chiffonade the fresh basil, and sprinkle on top.
3. Return the pan to medium-high heat, and add the canola oil. Once heated, lay the trout, skin-side down, in the heated pan. Season the top with salt and pepper, if desired. Sear for about 6 minutes, then carefully flip the fillets and cook for 1 to 2 minutes more.
4. To serve, plate each trout fillet over a quarter of the vegetable mixture and squeeze the lemon wedges over the top.

Pan-Fried Trout Fillets and Fingerlings

Prep time: 5 minutes | Cook time: 38 minutes | Serves 4

4 (5-ounce / 142-g) trout fillets, skinned
Sea salt, for seasoning
Freshly ground black pepper, for seasoning
1 pound fingerling
potatoes, halved
3 tablespoons olive oil, divided
½ teaspoon paprika
2 teaspoons finely chopped fresh dill

1. Preheat the oven to 400°F (205°C).
2. Line a baking sheet with parchment paper and set aside.
3. Pat the trout fillets dry with paper towels and season them with salt and pepper.
4. In a large bowl, toss the potatoes with 2 tablespoons of olive oil and the paprika. Season the potatoes with salt and pepper.
5. Spread the potatoes on the prepared baking sheet and roast until golden brown and fork-tender, about 30 minutes.
6. When the potatoes have been in the oven for 20 minutes, place a large skillet over medium-high heat and heat the remaining 1 tablespoon of olive oil.
7. Pan sear the fish for 4 minutes per side, or until just cooked through and golden brown.
8. Sprinkle the fish with dill and serve with roasted potatoes.

Fried Trout and Rosemary Broth

Prep time: 10 minutes | Cook time: 9 minutes | Serves 2

1 whole trout, cleaned
Kosher salt
2 tablespoons olive oil
1 cup dry white wine
Juice of ½ large lemon
4 thin lemon slices
3 garlic cloves, crushed
3 rosemary sprigs
1 (14-ounce / 397-g) can butter beans, drained and rinsed
3 tablespoons butter

1. Rinse the trout and pat it dry. Halve it lengthwise and sprinkle salt over the flesh of each portion.
2. In a large pan over medium heat, heat the oil. Add the trout, flesh-side down. Cook for about 4 minutes until the flesh is turning golden. Carefully flip the fish skin-side down.
3. Pour in the white wine and lemon juice and nestle the lemon slices, garlic cloves, and rosemary sprigs in with the fish. Cook for 3 minutes, or until the fish is cooked through. Using a slotted spoon, gently remove the trout and set aside.
4. Add the beans and butter to the pan and bring to a simmer. Cook for about 2 minutes until the beans are heated through and the butter is melted.
5. Spoon the beans into 2 large bowls and pour the cooking liquid over. Top with the trout and garnish with the rosemary sprigs and lemon slices from the pan.

Garlic-Butter Trout Fillets in Foil

Prep time: 10 minutes | Cook time: 15 minutes | Serves 2

1 pound (454 g) steelhead trout fillet, skin removed
2 tablespoons butter
½ a lemon, juice squeezed

1 to 2 garlic cloves, minced
1 teaspoon parsley, minced (optional)
Salt and pepper, to taste

1. Preheat oven to 375ºF (190ºC).
2. Spray a sheet of aluminum foil with cooking spray and place the trout fillet in the center.
3. Fold up all 4 sides of the foil. Season trout with salt and pepper and then squeeze juice from half a lemon over the fish until covered.
4. Melt butter in microwave safe bowl, stir in fresh minced garlic, and drizzle over the trout until evenly coated. Top with fresh minced parsley.
5. Fold the sides of the foil over the trout, covering completely, and seal into a closed packet.
6. Place directly on oven rack and bake until cooked through, about 15 to 20 minutes.

Trout Meunière with Spice

Prep time: 10 minutes | Cook time: 4½ minutes | Serves 4

4 (6- to 8-ounce / 170- to 227-g) rainbow trout fillets, skin on
¾ cup flour
¾ teaspoon salt
½ teaspoon paprika
¼ teaspoon onion powder
Freshly ground black pepper
1 tablespoon olive oil

6 tablespoons butter, divided
1 to ½ tablespoons shallots, very finely chopped
1½ to 2 tablespoons freshly squeezed lemon juice
3 to 4 tablespoons fresh parsley, finely chopped
4 lemon wedges

1. Combine the flour, salt, paprika, onion powder and a few grinds of black pepper in a shallow dish. Dredge the fillets in the flour mixture, shaking off the excess.
2. Heat the olive oil along with 2 tablespoons of the butter in a large skillet over medium-high heat.

3. Add 2 of the trout fillets, skin side up and cook until golden on the first side, 1½ to 2 minutes. Turn carefully and finish cooking, 1½ to 2 minutes longer. Transfer to a serving platter and repeat with the remaining 2 fillets.
4. Keeping the pan over medium-high heat, add 1 tablespoon of the remaining butter. Add the shallots and sauté until soft and translucent, about 1½ minutes.
5. Add the remaining butter and cook, stirring constantly, until the butter begins to foam and the color starts to darken. Quickly whisk in the lemon juice, add the parsley, combine well, drizzle over the trout fillets and serve immediately.
6. Garnish with lemon wedges.

Spicy Grilled Trout Fillets

Prep time: 5 minutes | Cook time: 20 minutes | Serves 6

2 (½-pound / 227-g) trout fillet, about one-inch thick at the thickest portion
½ tablespoon olive oil
4 garlic cloves, minced
2 teaspoons brown

sugar
1 teaspoon crushed red pepper flakes
½ teaspoon kosher salt
½ teaspoon black pepper

1. Preheat the grill to medium high heat, you want to be cooking at a temperature of 400ºF (205ºC) to 450ºF (235ºC).
2. Place the trout fillet, skin side down, on a foil grilling pan. If you don't have one you could also use a double layer of tin foil.
3. In a small bowl, whisk together the olive oil, garlic, brown sugar, red pepper flakes, salt and pepper. Spread the mixture all over the trout fillet, coating the entire top of the fish.
4. Place the foil pan on the grill and close the lid. Grill the trout for 20 to 25 minutes, or until it flakes easily with a fork at the thickest portion.

Almond-Crusted Trout Fillet

Prep time: 10 minutes | Cook time: 9 minutes | Serves 4

2 large eggs
½ cup almond meal
⅓ cup vegan Parmesan Cheese, store-bought or homemade
3 tablespoons chopped fresh dill, divided

½ teaspoon salt
¼ teaspoon freshly ground black pepper
2 tablespoons extra-virgin olive oil
4 (6 ounces / 170 g) skin-on trout fillets
1 lemon, cut into wedges

1. In a shallow bowl, whisk the eggs until combined. In another shallow bowl, stir together the almond meal, vegan Parmesan, 2 tablespoons of dill, the salt, and pepper.
2. In a large nonstick skillet, heat the olive oil over medium heat.
3. Dip each fillet in the egg, then dip in the almond meal mixture, coating both sides.
4. Lay the fillets in the skillet and cook for 6 minutes. Turn the fillets over and cook another 3 minutes, or until the fish flakes easily and is cooked through.
5. Serve garnished with the remaining 1 tablespoon of dill and lemon wedges for squeezing.

Pan-Seared Rainbow Trout

Prep time: 10 minutes | Cook time: 8 minutes | Serves 4

4 (5-ounce / 142-g) rainbow trout fillets
Kosher salt
Freshly ground black pepper
2 tablespoons extra-virgin olive oil
3 tablespoons unsalted butter, divided
4 large garlic cloves,

thinly sliced
¼ cup dry white wine (such as Sauvignon blanc)
Zest and juice of 1 lemon
2 teaspoons chopped fresh thyme leaves
2 tablespoons coarsely chopped fresh flat-leaf parsley

1. Heat a 12-inch nonstick skillet over medium-high heat. While the pan is heating, generously season both sides of the fillets with salt and pepper.

2. When the pan is just barely smoking, heat the olive oil and 2 tablespoons of butter and swirl the pan to combine. Lower the heat to medium and place the fish, flesh-side down, in the pan. Cook for 4 to 5 minutes, or until the fish develops a golden crust.
3. Carefully flip the fish over and sear the skin for another 2 minutes.
4. Transfer the fish to a plate and tent with aluminum foil.
5. In the same pan, still over medium heat, add the garlic and sauté for 1 minute, or until fragrant.
6. Add the wine, lemon zest and juice, and thyme, stirring with a wooden spoon to scrape up any brown bits stuck to the pan. Simmer the wine mixture for about 2 minutes, until the liquid reduces by half.
7. Remove from the heat and swirl in the remaining 1 tablespoon of butter until it melts and creates a velvety sauce. Return the fish to the pan and spoon the sauce over it.
8. To serve, drizzle the sauce over the top of the fillets. Garnish with the parsley and serve hot.

Lemon-Pepper Roasted Trout Fillets

Prep time: 10 minutes | Cook time: 15 minutes | Serves 4

Olive oil cooking spray
1½ pounds (680 g) trout fillets, skin removed
1 tablespoon extra-virgin olive oil
1 teaspoon freshly

ground black pepper
½ teaspoon salt
4 lemon slices
2 teaspoons grated lemon zest
2 tablespoons fresh lemon juice

1. Preheat the oven to 400°F (205°C). Lightly mist a 9-inch by 13-inch baking dish with cooking spray.
2. Rub the trout fillets with the olive oil and season with the pepper and salt. Place in the prepared baking dish. Lay the lemon slices over the trout and sprinkle with lemon zest and lemon juice.
3. Tightly cover the dish with aluminum foil. Bake for 15 minutes, or until the fish flakes easily and is cooked through.

Smoked Trout and Potato Frittata

Prep time: 10 minutes | Cook time: 22 minutes | Serves 6

2 yellow potatoes, peeled and cut into 3- to 4-inch pieces
1½ cups chopped asparagus (1-inch pieces)
1 tablespoon extra-virgin olive oil, divided
8 large eggs
1½ tablespoons 2% milk
Pinch salt
Pinch freshly ground black pepper
8 ounces (227 g) smoked trout
1 tablespoon chopped fresh dill, divided
¼ cup feta cheese
4 cups loosely packed mixed salad greens
Freshly squeezed lemon juice (optional)

1. Preheat the oven to 450°F (235°C).
2. Bring a large saucepan of water to a boil and cook the potatoes for 10 minutes, or until tender. Place in a colander.
3. Add the asparagus to the pot and boil for about 1 minute, or until crisp-tender, then transfer with a slotted spoon to the colander. Rinse the potatoes and asparagus under cold water to cool.
4. Add ½ tablespoon of oil to a large cast iron or oven-safe skillet. Coat the surface and heat over medium-high heat. Meanwhile, in a large mixing bowl, whisk the eggs and milk together. Season with salt and pepper.
5. Cut the potatoes into thin slices. Flake the smoked trout with a fork, then layer in the skillet along with the potatoes and asparagus. Pour the egg mixture on top. Sprinkle ½ tablespoon of dill on top, along with the feta cheese.
6. Cook for 7 to 8 minutes on the stove top, or until the frittata is set along the edges and wobbly in the middle.
7. Transfer the skillet to the preheated oven and bake for 5 to 8 minutes more, or until the edges begin to brown and pull away from the pan. Remove, then cut into six wedges. Lightly dress the salad greens with the remaining ½ tablespoon of olive oil and the lemon juice, if using. Garnish with the remaining ½ tablespoon of dill, and serve immediately. Store leftovers, refrigerated, for up to 4 days.

Trout Fillets Topped with Cilantro

Prep time: 10 minutes | Cook time: 20 minutes | Serves 4

4 cups cauliflower florets
2 red bell peppers, seeded and thinly sliced into strips
2 cups snow peas, stringed
4 (5-ounce / 142-g)
trout fillets
Sea salt, for seasoning
Freshly ground black pepper, for seasoning
2 tablespoons olive oil
2 tablespoons finely chopped cilantro

1. Preheat the oven to 400°F (205°C). Cut 4 pieces of aluminum foil, each 12 inches square.
2. Evenly divide the cauliflower, bell peppers, and snow peas between the pieces of foil.
3. Pat the trout fillets dry with paper towels and season them with salt and pepper.
4. Place a fillet on each foil square and drizzle the olive oil over the fish.
5. Fold the foil up to form tightly sealed packets and put them on a baking sheet.
6. Bake until the fish flakes when pressed with a fork, about 20 minutes.
7. Serve topped with cilantro.

Milk-Poached Trout Fillets

Prep time: 10 minutes | Cook time: 16 minutes | Serves 4

1 tablespoon olive oil
3 leeks, white and greens parts, washed, halved lengthwise, and thinly sliced
1 teaspoon minced garlic
2 cups 2 percent milk
Juice and zest of 1
lemon
2 teaspoons finely chopped fresh thyme
4 (5-ounce / 142-g) skinless trout fillets
Sea salt, for seasoning
Freshly ground black pepper, for seasoning

1. In a large skillet, heat the olive oil over medium-high heat.
2. Sauté the leeks until softened, about 5 minutes.
3. Add the garlic and sauté 1 minute more.
4. Stir in the milk, lemon juice, lemon zest, and thyme.
5. Bring the milk mixture to a boil and then reduce the heat to low so the liquid just simmers.
6. Add the trout and poach until the fish is cooked through and flakes, about 10 minutes.
7. Season with salt and pepper and serve.

Savory Trout Amandine

Prep time: 10 minutes | Cook time: 4 minutes | Serves 4

4 tablespoons (½ stick) unsalted butter, divided
¼ cup sliced almonds
4 small rainbow trout (1½ pounds / 680 g), skin on, butterflied, and boned
Kosher salt
Freshly ground black pepper

½ cup all-purpose flour
½ cup almond flour
3 tablespoons vegetable oil
¼ cup finely chopped fresh flat-leaf parsley
Juice of 1 large lemon (about 2 to 3 tablespoons)

1. Preheat the oven to 300°F (150°C).
2. In a nonstick skillet, melt 2 tablespoons of butter over medium-high heat. Add the almonds and cook, stirring occasionally, until the almonds begin to look toasty brown. Transfer to a bowl and set aside.
3. Blot the fish with paper towels and season both sides with salt and pepper. In a wide shallow bowl, combine the all-purpose and almond flours, then dredge the fish on all sides, making sure it is completely coated.
4. In a skillet over medium-high heat, add the vegetable oil and swirl to coat the pan. When the oil reaches its smoke point, place the fish, flesh-side down, in the skillet and tilt the pan a few times to run the oil underneath the fish. Cook until the fish develops a golden crust, about 3 minutes. Carefully flip and cook for 1 minute on the skin side.
5. Transfer the fish to a plate and place in in the oven to keep warm. Pour the oil into a glass bowl and set aside to cool completely before discarding. Do not wipe out the pan, but let the pan cool for about 5 minutes before moving on.
6. Return the pan to medium heat and melt the remaining 2 tablespoons of butter. Continue to cook the butter until the milk solids begin to turn golden brown and smell nutty.
7. Remove from the heat and add the parsley. Let it sizzle before adding the lemon juice. Season the brown butter with salt and pepper and stir in the almonds.

8. Transfer the fish to serving plates and spoon the brown butter, parsley, and almonds over the fish. Serve hot.

Foil-Broiled Trout Recipe

Prep time: 10 minutes | Cook time: 15 minutes | Serves 4

4 whole trout (2 pounds / 907 g), butterflied
Kosher salt
Freshly ground black pepper
Nonstick cooking spray
2 carrots, peeled and cut into ¼-inch-thick

coins
1 leek, trimmed and thinly sliced
1 lemon, cut into ¼-inch-thick slices (about 6 slices)
4 dill or thyme sprigs
4 tablespoons (½ stick) unsalted butter

1. Preheat the broiler.
2. Season the fish on both sides with salt and pepper.
3. Place two sheets of aluminum foil on top of each other and lightly spray the center with nonstick cooking spray. Make a bed from one-quarter of the carrots and leeks and lightly season with salt and pepper. Place one fish, opened and skin-side down, on the vegetables.
4. Top with a slice of lemon and a sprig of dill. Place 1 tablespoon of butter on the fish and close the fish. Fold and seal the foil into an airtight package. Repeat the process with the remaining fish, carrots, leek, lemon, dill, and butter.
5. Place the fish packets on a baking sheet and cook, turning once, for 15 to 20 minutes, or until the skin peels away from the fish and the flesh is flaky.
6. Open the packets carefully, as the steam can burn you, and place the entire foil packet on a plate.
7. Serve hot.

Chapter 12 Swordfish

Tandoori Swordfish Fillets

Prep time: 10 minutes | Cook time: 8 minutes | Serves 4

4 (6-ounce / 170-g) Swordfish fillets
1 cup Greek whole milk yogurt
2 tablespoons fresh minced ginger
1 tablespoon minced garlic

Juice of 1 lemon
½ tablespoon Urban Accents Punjab Red Tandoori
2 tablespoons Urban Accents Kashmir Garam Masala

1. Combine all Ingredients, except fish, in flat glass or ceramic baking dish; whisk well.
2. Add fish fillets; refrigerate and marinade for up to two hours.
3. Prepare grill or stovetop grill pan for high heat.
4. Remove excess marinade and grill fillets for about 3 to 4 minutes on each side, getting good grill marks on each side.
5. Remove and let fish rest for 5 minutes. Serve with Basmati rice.

Mediterranean Stuffed Swordfish Steak

Prep time: 5 minutes | Cook time: 8 minutes | Serves 2

1 (8 ounce / 227 g) swordfish steak, about 2-inch thick
1 tablespoon olive oil
1 tablespoon fresh lemon juice

2 cups fresh spinach - rinsed, dried and torn into bite size pieces
1 teaspoon olive oil
1 clove garlic, minced
¼ cup crumbled feta

1. Preheat an outdoor grill for high heat, and lightly oil grate.
2. Cut a slit in steak to create a pocket that is open on one side only. In a cup, mix together 1 tablespoon olive oil and lemon juice; brush over both sides of fish. Set aside.
3. In a small skillet, heat 1 teaspoon olive oil and garlic over medium heat. Cook spinach in oil until wilted. Remove from heat, and stuff into pocket. Place feta in pocket over spinach.

4. Arrange fish on grill, and cook for 8 minutes. Turn over, and continue cooking until cooked through.

Swordfish Steaks with Chimichurri

Prep time: 15 minutes | Cook time: 20 minutes | Serves 4

½ cup tightly packed chopped fresh parsley
¼ cup coarsely chopped fresh oregano
1 cup diced red onion, divided
4 garlic cloves, peeled
¼ cup red wine vinegar
½ cup extra-virgin olive oil plus 1½ tablespoons, divided, and more for brushing
1 tablespoon red

pepper flakes
Salt
Freshly ground black pepper
1 zucchini, halved lengthwise and sliced
1 small head cauliflower, cut into florets
1 large carrot, trimmed and peeled, then sliced
4 (6-ounce / 170-g) swordfish steaks

1. For the chimichurri sauce, add the herbs to a food processor along with ½ cup of red onion, the garlic, red wine vinegar, ½ cup of olive oil, red pepper flakes, salt, and black pepper. Pulse several times, until combined, leaving some chunks in the mixture. Transfer to a ramekin or serving bowl to allow the flavors to combine.
2. Preheat the oven to 400°F (205°C).
3. In a large bowl, toss the zucchini, cauliflower, carrot, the remaining ½ cup of red onion, and 1½ tablespoons of olive oil. Season with salt and black pepper. Arrange in a single layer on a large baking sheet, and roast for 15 to 20 minutes, to your preferred doneness.
4. Meanwhile, heat the grill or a stove-top grill pan to medium-high heat. Brush the swordfish steaks with olive oil, and season with salt and pepper. Grill for 5 to 6 minutes on each side, depending on thickness.
5. Put one swordfish steak on each plate with a quarter of the vegetables. Top with the chimichurri sauce and serve immediately.

Lemon-Parsley Swordfish Steaks

Prep time: 10 minutes | Cook time: 17 minutes | Serves 4

1 cup fresh Italian parsley
¼ cup lemon juice
¼ cup extra-virgin olive oil
¼ cup fresh thyme
2 cloves garlic
½ teaspoon salt
4 swordfish steaks
Olive oil spray

1. Preheat the oven to 450ºF (235ºC).
2. Grease a large baking dish generously with olive oil spray.
3. Place the parsley, lemon juice, olive oil, thyme, garlic, and salt in a food processor and pulse until smoothly blended.
4. Arrange the swordfish steaks in the greased baking dish and spoon the parsley mixture over the top.
5. Bake in the preheated oven for 17 to 20 minutes until flaky.
6. Divide the fish among four plates and serve hot.

Basic Lemon-Butter Swordfish

Prep time: 10 minutes | Cook time: 17 minutes | Serves 4

1 pound (454 g) swordfish
1 tablespoon olive oil
1 tablespoon butter
¼ cup chicken stock or dry white wine
Leaves of fresh mixed herbs (such as rosemary, thyme, or sage), minced
1 garlic clove, peeled and minced
1 Meyer lemon one half juiced, one half sliced into rounds
Salt and pepper, to taste

1. Pat the swordfish dry and season with salt and pepper.
2. Heat olive oil in a skillet over medium high until shimmering and very hot.
3. Add the swordfish and cook for 6 minutes. Flip and cook an additional 6 minutes. The swordfish should be at about 135ºF (57ºC) at this point.
4. Add the butter to the skillet with the swordfish and cook until melted and frothy. Add the chicken stock, lemon juice, herbs, and minced garlic.
5. Reduce heat to medium and cook until reduced slightly, about 5 minutes. Once the fish reaches 145ºF (63ºC), turn off the heat.

6. Add the fish to a serving plate and spoon the sauce over top. Garnish with two slices of lemon. Serve.

Savory Swordfish with Lemon and Garlic

Prep time: 10 minutes | Cook time: 8 minutes | Serves 4

For the Lemon Garlic Mixture:
2 tablespoons salted butter, softened to room temp
1 tablespoon freshly chopped chives
2 tablespoons garlic cloves, minced
⅛ teaspoon kosher
salt
¼ teaspoon freshly ground black pepper
1 tablespoon juice from fresh lemon
1 tablespoon grated lemon peel
For the Fish:
2 tablespoon olive oil
2 (6- to 7-ounce / 170- to 198-g) swordfish fillets, each
1-inch thick
kosher salt and freshly ground black pepper

1. Preheat oven to 400ºF (205ºC) with rack on middle position. In a small pan, combine all Lemon Garlic Mixture ingredients and stir to fully combine. Set aside.
2. Use paper towels to pat-dry all excess moisture from the swordfish fillets. Evenly sprinkle both sides of fillets with pinches of kosher salt and freshly ground black pepper. Set aside.
3. In a large, oven-proof pan, heat the olive oil over medium high heat. Once oil is hot, add the swordfish fillets to pan and let cook until browned on one side, about 3 minutes (do not move fish around much.) Carefully flip fish fillets over to the other side, turn stove off, and immediately transfer pan into hot oven.
4. Let fish roast about 5-6 minutes or just until the top is golden and center is just cooked through. Take care not to overcook. A minute before fish is done cooking in oven, cook small pan of prepared lemon-garlic mixture over medium high heat, constantly stirring, just until melted and bubbly. Immediately turn heat off and pour mixture over the cooked fish. Be sure to pour on any juices from the swordfish pan as well.

Citrus Glazed Swordfish Steaks with Almondine

Prep time: 15 minutes | Cook time: 16 minutes | Serves 4

Citrus Glaze:

¼ cup orange juice
½ cup mirin
1 tablespoon grated

fresh ginger
1 tablespoon honey

Almondine Sauce:

2 (12-ounce / 340-g) swordfish steaks, about 1-inch thick, cut in half portions
3 shallots, sliced
Sea salt and freshly ground black pepper
½ cup toasted almonds
2 teaspoons toasted

sesame oil
1 tablespoon extra-virgin olive oil
2 scallions, thinly sliced
1 tablespoon chopped fresh cilantro
1 tablespoon toasted sesame seeds

1. Place orange juice, mirin, ginger, and honey in a small saucepan. Bring to a boil and simmer, uncovered, until reduced by half and a light syrup forms. Pour the citrus glaze into a measuring cup.
2. Heat olive oil in a large skillet over medium-high heat. Season swordfish on both sides with sea salt and pepper.
3. Add the swordfish and sear for 3-4 minutes. Pour some of the citrus glaze onto the swordfish and spread with the back of a spoon. Flip over the fish and coat with more of the citrus glaze.
4. Sear for 3-4 minutes. Total cooking time should only be 7 to 8 minutes until browned and almost opaque in the center. Be careful not to overcook the swordfish. Transfer swordfish from the skillet to a platter.
5. Lower the heat to medium, add 1 tablespoon of olive oil and sesame oil to the same skillet. Add the shallots and scallions and sauté until softened and lightly golden, about 3 minutes.
6. Season with salt and pepper. Add almonds, cilantro, and 3 tablespoons of citrus glaze, gently stirring the sauce until heated through.
7. Top swordfish steaks with almondine sauce and drizzle with remaining citrus glaze. Sprinkle with toasted sesame seeds and serve.

Sicilian Swordfish Steak Stew

Prep time: 15 minutes | Cook time: 6½ minutes | Serves 4 to 6

2 tablespoons extra-virgin olive oil
2 onions, chopped fine
1 teaspoon table salt
½ teaspoon pepper
1 teaspoon minced fresh thyme or ¼ teaspoon dried
Pinch red pepper flakes
4 garlic cloves, minced, divided
1 (28-ounce / 794-g) can whole peeled tomatoes, drained with juice reserved, chopped coarse

1 (8-ounce / 227-g) bottle clam juice
¼ cup dry white wine
¼ cup golden raisins
2 tablespoons capers, rinsed
1½ pounds (680 g) skinless swordfish steak, 1 to 1½ inches thick, cut into 1-inch pieces
¼ cup pine nuts, toasted
¼ cup minced fresh mint
1 teaspoon grated orange zest

1. Using highest Sauté function, heat oil in Instant Pot until shimmering.
2. Add onions, salt, and pepper and cook until onions are softened, about 5 minutes. Stir in thyme, pepper flakes, and three-quarters of garlic and cook until fragrant, about 30 seconds. Stir in tomatoes and reserved juice, clam juice, wine, raisins, and capers. Nestle swordfish into pot and spoon some cooking liquid over top.
3. Lock lid in place and close pressure release valve. Select Manual function and cook for 1 minute. Turn off Instant Pot and quick release pressure. Carefully remove lid, allowing steam to escape away from you.
4. Combine pine nuts, mint, orange zest, and remaining garlic in bowl. Season stew with salt and pepper to taste. Sprinkle individual portions with pine nut mixture before serving.

Mixed-Peppercorn Buttery Swordfish

Prep time: 10 minutes | Cook time: 13 minutes | Serves 4

¼ cup (½ stick) butter, room temperature
2 teaspoons chopped fresh parsley
1 garlic clove, minced
½ teaspoon ground mixed peppercorns, plus more for sprinkling
½ teaspoon (packed) grated lemon peel
1 tablespoon olive oil
4 (6 ounces / 170 g) swordfish fillets, each 1-inch-thick

1. Preheat oven to 400°F (205ºC). Mash butter, parsley, garlic, ½ teaspoon ground mixed peppercorns, and lemon peel in small bowl. Season to taste with salt.
2. Heat oil in heavy large ovenproof skillet over medium-high heat. Sprinkle swordfish with salt and ground mixed peppercorns.
3. Add swordfish to skillet. Cook until browned, about 3 minutes.
4. Turn swordfish over and transfer to oven.
5. Roast until just cooked through, about 10 minutes longer.
6. Transfer swordfish to plates. Add seasoned butter to same skillet. Cook over medium-high heat, scraping up browned bits, until melted and bubbling.
7. Pour butter sauce over swordfish and serve.

Delicious Marinated Swordfish

Prep time: 10 minutes | Cook time: 22 minutes | Serves 4

4 (6-ounce / 170-g) center-cut swordfish steaks, 1-inch thick
Salt and freshly ground pepper, to taste
3 tablespoons olive oil
2 teaspoons soy sauce
1 tablespoon red-wine vinegar
4 sprigs rosemary or
1 teaspoon dried
1 tablespoon finely chopped garlic
2 teaspoons ground coriander
1 teaspoon ground cumin
2 teaspoons grated lemon rind
¼ teaspoon red pepper flakes

1. Preheat a charcoal grill or broiler, or heat a grill pan.
2. Sprinkle fish with salt and pepper on both sides. Place oil in a flat dish, and add soy sauce, vinegar, rosemary, garlic, coriander, cumin, lemon rind and pepper flakes. Blend well.
3. Place fish steaks in marinade, coat well on both sides, cover with plastic wrap and let stand for 10 to 15 minutes.
4. If the swordfish is to be cooked on a grill (or grill pan), place fish on grill and cook for 3 to 4 minutes. Turn and cook for 3 minutes more.
5. Cook longer if desired. If it is to be cooked under a broiler, place fish on a rack and cook for 3 to 4 minutes on each side. Serve with a string bean salad.

Grilled Swordfish Steaks with Butter

Prep time: 10 minutes | Cook time: 7 minutes | Serves 4

2 (about 2 pounds / 907 g) swordfish steaks, 1-inch thick
Juice of ½ lemon

Extra virgin olive oil
Kosher salt and freshly ground black pepper

For the Lemon-Basil Butter:

4 tablespoons unsalted butter, softened
1 teaspoon freshly squeezed lemon juice
Zest of 1 lemon

½ teaspoon garlic, minced
¼ teaspoon salt
2 tablespoons minced fresh basil

1. Preheat a gas or charcoal grill to high heat.
2. Cut each swordfish steak in half, drizzle with lemon juice and let stand for 1 minute.
3. Rub both sides of each steak with olive oil, salt and pepper and set aside.
4. Place the butter, lemon juice, lemon zest, garlic, salt and basil in a small bowl and combine well. Set aside until ready to serve.
5. Oil the grill grates and add the fish.
6. Grill the swordfish steaks until opaque throughout, 3½ to 4½ minutes per side. To avoid drying out the fish, do not leave unattended.
7. Top each piece of fish with about 1 tablespoon of the lemon-basil butter just as it comes off the grill.
8. Allow to rest for 2 to 3 minutes before serving.

Pan-Roasted Swordfish Steaks

Prep time: 10 minutes | Cook time: 6 minutes | Serves 4

2 pounds (907 g) swordfish steaks
2 tablespoons olive oil
2 cloves garlic, finely minced
Juice of 1 lemon
1 tablespoon unsalted

butter
1 tablespoon fresh chives, chopped
1 tablespoon fresh parsley, chopped
Salt and pepper, to taste

1. Season the swordfish on both sides with salt and pepper.
2. Pour the olive oil into a large frying pan over high heat.
3. When the oil begins to lightly smoke, add the swordfish. Turn the heat down to medium-high and cook for 3 to 4 minutes per side, or until it reaches 145°F (63ºC).
4. Remove the swordfish from the pan and add the garlic. Stir and cook for 1 minute, then add the lemon juice.
5. Turn off the heat. Melt in the butter and add the herbs.
6. Serve the sauce with the cooked swordfish.

Chapter 13 Arctic Char

Slow-Roasted Dijon Arctic Char Fillets

Prep time: 5 minutes | Cook time: 20 minutes | Serves 4

4 (6-ounce / 170-g) arctic char fillets
1 teaspoon smoked paprika
¼ teaspoon salt

¼ teaspoon freshly ground black pepper
¼ cup Dijon mustard
1 teaspoon light or dark brown sugar

1. Preheat the oven to 300ºF (150ºC).
2. Place the arctic char fillets on a sheet pan. Season with smoked paprika, salt, and pepper. Spread the mustard on top of the fish. Sprinkle the brown sugar on top.
3. Bake the fish for 20 minutes, until it flakes easily with a fork.

Cherry-Tomato Arctic Char Fillets

Prep time: 10 minutes | Cook time: 9 minutes | Serves 4

3 tablespoons extra-virgin olive oil, divided
4 (6-ounce / 170-g) arctic char fillets
¾ teaspoon coarse salt, divided
½ teaspoon black pepper, divided

4 garlic cloves, halved
3 pints multicolored cherry tomatoes
¼ cup thinly sliced fresh basil
2 shallots, thinly sliced

1. Preheat oven to 400ºF (205ºC).
2. Heat a large ovenproof skillet over high heat. Add 1 tablespoon oil to pan; swirl to coat. Sprinkle fillets with ½ teaspoon salt and ¼ teaspoon pepper.
3. Add fillets, flesh side down, to pan, and sauté for 2 minutes. Place pan in oven; cook at 400ºF (205ºC) for 3 minutes or until desired degree of doneness.
4. Heat a large cast-iron skillet over medium heat. Add remaining 2 tablespoons oil to pan; swirl to coat. Add garlic, and cook 2 minutes or until lightly browned, stirring occasionally.
5. Increase heat to medium-high. Add tomatoes to pan; sauté for 2 minutes or until skins blister, stirring frequently.
6. Remove pan from heat. Sprinkle tomato mixture with the remaining ¼ teaspoon salt, remaining ¼ teaspoon black pepper, basil, and shallots; toss to combine.
7. Serve with fish.

Citrus Arctic Char Bake with Asparagus

Prep time: 10 minutes | Cook time: 12 minutes | Serves 2 to 3

1 large fillet of arctic char
1 pound (454 g) asparagus, woody ends trimmed off
2 to 3 tablespoons olive oil

1 meyer lemon, cut into thin slices
1 blood orange, cut into thin slices
A few sprigs fresh thyme
Salt and pepper

1. Preheat oven to 400ºF (205ºC), and line a rimmed baking sheet with parchment.
2. Spread the asparagus on the baking sheet, drizzle with 1 to 2 tablespoons olive oil, season well with salt and pepper, and toss around the pan to coat evenly.
3. Spread the asparagus into an even layer around the edges of the pan, and lay the fish in the middle, skin-side down.
4. Drizzle the fish with the remaining tablespoon olive oil, and season evenly with salt and pepper. Arrange the slices of citrus on top of the fish, alternating lemon and blood orange slices. scatter the fresh thyme on top.
5. Roast on the middle rack for about 12 to 15 minutes. To test the fish, prod it gently with a fork in the thickest part. If it flakes and is opaque all the way through, it's done. If necessary, you can remove the fish to a serving patter and return the asparagus to the oven for another minute or two, or vice versa, if the asparagus is done before the fish. They should be done at about the same time, but again, it will vary depending on the size of your fillet.
6. Remove from the oven and serve immediately. Serve it over a salad (I like arugula here, with it's mild peppery flavor) or with a side of rice or other grain for a more filling meal.

Charmoula Arctic Char

Prep time: 10 minutes | Cook time: 12 minutes | Serves 4

3 unpeeled garlic cloves
⅓ cup plus 2 table-spoons extra-virgin olive oil
¼ cup cilantro leaves
2 tablespoons chopped green olives
1 tablespoons fresh

lemon juice
¼ teaspoon ground cumin
¼ teaspoon paprika
Kosher salt
4 (5-ounce / 142-g) skin-on arctic char
Pepper

1. In a small skillet, toast the garlic over moderate heat, stirring occasionally, until the skins blacken, 7 to 8 minutes. Let cool slightly; discard the skins.
2. In a food processor, puree ⅓ cup of the oil, the garlic, parsley, cilantro, olives, lemon juice, cumin and paprika until smooth.
3. Transfer the charmoula to a bowl and season with salt.
4. In a large nonstick skillet, heat the remaining 2 tablespoons of oil. Season the fish with salt and pepper and place it skin side down in the skillet.
5. Cook the fish over moderately high heat until the skin is golden, about 3 minutes. Flip the fish and cook just until it flakes easily, 2 to 3 minutes.
6. Drain briefly on paper towels.
7. Serve the fish with the charmoula.

Arctic Char Fillets with Mush-rooms

Prep time: 10 minutes | Cook time: 8 minutes | Serves 4

4(6-ounce / 170-g) skinless arctic char fillets, each about 1-inch thick
Kosher salt and freshly ground pepper
4 tablespoons extra-virgin olive oil, plus more for drizzling
8 ounces (227 g) white button

mushrooms, sliced
2 shallots, finely chopped
2 tablespoons red wine vinegar, plus more for drizzling
2 teaspoons whole-grain mustard
1 tablespoon chopped chives

1. Preheat the oven to350ºF (180ºC). Season the fish with salt and pepper.
2. Heat 1 tablespoon olive oil in a large non-stick skillet over medium-high heat until shimmering.
3. Add the fish and sear until golden on the bottom and cooked halfway through, about 3 minutes. Flip onto a baking sheet and bake until cooked through, 3 to 5 more minutes.
4. Meanwhile, wipe out the skillet, return to medium-high heat and add the remaining 3 tablespoons oil. Add the mushrooms and cook, without stirring, until browned on one side, about 1 minute. Stir and cook until browned all over, about 3 more minutes.
5. Add the shallots and cook until soft, stir-ring, about 2 minutes. Whisk in 2 ta-blespoons vinegar and the mustard and bring to a boil. Remove from the heat and stir in the chives and parsley.
6. Drizzle the arugula with oil and vinegar in a bowl, season with salt and pepper and toss. Divide among plates and serve with the fish. Spoon the mushrooms and pan juices on top.

Easy Crispy Arctic Char

Prep time: 5 minutes | Cook time: 7 minutes | Serves 4

2 to 3 tablespoons olive oil
4 (5-ounce / 142-g) skin-on arctic char fillets

Kosher salt and freshly ground black pepper
4 lemon wedges, for serving

1. Heat the oil in a 12-inch cast-iron skillet or nonstick pan over medium-low heat. Season the fish well with salt and pepper.
2. Cook, skin side down and undisturbed, for 7 minutes.
3. The fillets will cook from the bottom up so that the flesh stays moist while the skin gets so crisp that it crackles; if the skin becomes crisp before the top of the fish finishes cooking (it should look just opaque), flip it over and cook very briefly to finish.
4. Serve with a lemon wedge.

Spinach-Butter Arctic Char

Prep time: 10 minutes | Cook time: 31 minutes | Serves 4

10 ounces (283 g) baby spinach
1 (2-pound / 907-g) arctic char, cleaned and left whole
Salt and pepper
1 teaspoon chopped fresh tarragon, plus a few sprigs for inside the fish
2 tablespoons unsalted butter at room temperature, plus 6 chilled tablespoons for sauce
½ cup crème fraîche
½ teaspoon grated lemon zest
1 teaspoon finely sliced chives
1 pound (454 g) boiled new potatoes, for serving (optional)

1. Put spinach in a mixing bowl and pour boiling water over to wilt it. Drain in a colander, rinse with cool water and squeeze completely dry. Chop the spinach as finely as you can and set aside.
2. Heat oven to 375ºF (190ºC). Rinse fish and pat dry. Season fish inside and out with salt and pepper. Put a few tarragon springs in the belly cavity.
3. Line a roasting pan with a big piece of foil slightly longer than the fish, leaving ends hanging over. Smear middle section of foil lengthwise with 1 tablespoon soft butter and set fish on top. Smear top of fish with remaining tablespoon soft butter. Fold the sides of foil to the center and press against fish. Twist both ends of foil to make a tight package. Bake for 30 minutes. Remove pan from oven and let fish rest 5 to 10 minutes, still in the foil package, while you make the sauce.
4. Put crème fraîche in a wide saucepan or skillet over medium high heat and bring to a simmer. Cook for a minute or so, until slightly reduced.
5. Add cooked spinach, stirring to coat. Season with salt and pepper and turn heat to low. Quickly stir in 1 tablespoon chilled butter at a time. Each spoonful should be just melted before adding the next, to make a creamy sauce. Remove from heat. Stir in lemon zest, tarragon and chives.
6. Transfer fish to a warm serving platter. Carefully remove foil. (Fish should be cooked through but moist.) Peel away and discard skin from top of fish. Pour any collected pan juices into the sauce, then spoon sauce over fish.
7. Serve with boiled new potatoes if desired.

Baked Arctic Char Fillets

Prep time: 5 minutes | Cook time: 15 minutes | Serves 4

1 pound (454 g) arctic char fillet
3 tablespoons minced fresh dill
1 to 2 garlic cloves, minced
½ to 1 teaspoon kosher salt, to taste
½ teaspoon pepper
1 lemon, quartered

1. Preheat the oven to 375ºF (190ºC).
2. Line a baking sheet with nonstick aluminum foil. Place the arctic char on the baking sheet, with the skin facing down.
3. In a small bowl, stir together the dill, garlic, salt and pepper. Rub on the top of the arctic char (the flesh, only). You want to distribute it as evenly as you can.
4. Bake for 15 to 20 minutes until it flakes easily with a fork. Cut into four pieces and serve with a lemon wedge.

Easy Arctic Char Fillets

Prep time: 5 minutes | Cook time: 7 minutes | Serves 4

2 (6-ounce / 170-g) arctic char fillets
¼ teaspoon Salt
¼ teaspoon Pepper
1 tablespoon Clarified butter Ghee

1. Preheat oven to 350ºF (180ºC)
2. Salt and pepper arctic char fillets.
3. In an oven proof frying pan over medium high heat, add clarified butter and when hot add the Arctic Char fillets flesh side down.
4. Allow to cook 3 minutes until well browned.
5. Turn fillets over and immediately place in oven for 4 to 5 minutes, just until fillets are firm.

Honey-Dijon Arctic Char

Prep time: 10 minutes | Cook time: 38 minutes | Serves 4

4 arctic char fillets, 1½-inch thick
¼ cup Dijon mustard
¼ cup honey
2 tablespoons olive oil
3 garlic cloves, minced
2 teaspoons fresh thyme
1 teaspoon sea salt
½ teaspoon white pepper
Juice of 1 small lemon

1. Rinse fish off in cold water and pat dry with paper towels. Place into a deep glass baking dish. Combine mustard, honey, oil, garlic, thyme, lemon juice, salt, and white pepper.
2. Using a spoon, coat fillets with mixture. Cover dish with plastic wrap and place into refrigerator for 30 to 40 minutes.
3. Preheat grill for medium-high heat. Right before placing the fish onto the grill, oil grill grates.
4. This can be done by using a large pair of tongs, folded paper towels, and a high smoke point oil like grapeseed or avocado oils.
5. Make 3 to 4 passes across the grates to endure a good non-stick surface. This will help to keep the fish intact during the grilling process.
6. Place fish onto grill, skin side down, and cook for 5 minutes. Carefully, turn fish and cook for an additional 3 to 5 minutes. It is sometimes easier to use two heat-resistant spatulas to turn the fish. One to get underneath and the other to assist with turning.
7. When the flesh of the fish no longer appears shiny, flakes easily and reaches an internal temperature of 145ºF (63ºC), it is done. Carefully remove from grill, plate and serve with your favorite sides.

Arctic Char Fillets with Gribiche Dressing

Prep time: 10 minutes | Cook time: 7 minutes | Serves 4

4 (5- to 6-ounce / 142- to 170-g) skin-on arctic char fillets
Kosher salt, freshly ground pepper
1 tablespoon olive oil
4 cups mixed greens, such as watercress, mizuna
Kosher salt, freshly ground pepper
4 (6-ounce / 170-g) arctic char fillets
1 teaspoon smoked paprika
¼ teaspoon salt
¼ teaspoon freshly ground black pepper
¼ cup Dijon mustard
1 teaspoon light or dark brown sugar
Gribiche Dressing, for serving

1. Season fish with salt and pepper.
2. Swirl oil in a cold large nonstick skillet to coat; lay in fish in pan, skin side down. Set over medium heat and cook fish, occasionally pressing down lightly on fillets to ensure skin is in even contact with pan, until skin is deep golden brown and flesh is opaque around the edges, 6 to 8 minutes.
3. Turn fillets and cook just until opaque on flesh side, about 1 minute longer. Transfer to a platter.
4. Gently toss greens in a medium bowl with enough dressing to lightly coat; season with salt and pepper.
5. Scatter over fish and spoon some additional dressing on top.

Sesame Arctic Char Fillet Donabe

Prep time: 5 minutes | Cook time: 40 minutes | Serves 4

Dashi and Noodles:

2 (5x4") pieces kombu

6 ounces (170 g) dried soba noodles

2 teaspoons toasted sesame oil

1 ounce (28 g) bonito flakes

Fish and Assembly:

1 bunch scallions

⅓ cup mirin (sweet Japanese rice wine)

2 tablespoon. soy sauce

Kosher salt

1 (1 pound / 454 g) skinless arctic char fillet

2 small turnips,

trimmed, scrubbed, thinly sliced

1 small daikon, peeled, thinly sliced

6 ounces (170 g) enoki mushrooms, trimmed

Toasted sesame seeds and toasted sesame oil, for serving

To Make Dashi and Noodles

1. Combine kombu and 4½ cups cold water in a medium saucepan. Let sit until kombu is pliable, 25 to 30 minutes.

2. Meanwhile, cook noodles according to package directions. Drain and rinse under cold water. Shake off excess water and toss noodles in a medium bowl with oil. Divide among serving bowls and set aside.

3. Bring kombu mixture to a boil over medium heat, then immediately remove pan from heat. Lift out kombu from broth with tongs and discard.

4. Add bonito flakes to broth and stir once to moisten. Bring mixture to a simmer over medium, then reduce heat and simmer very gently 5 minutes. Let sit off heat 15 minutes. Strain dashi through a fine-mesh sieve into a large heatproof measuring glass or a medium bowl; discard solids. (You should have about 4 cups.)

5. Do Ahead: Dashi can be made 1 day ahead. Cover and chill.

6. To make Fish and Assembly

7. While dashi is infusing, remove the dark green tops of the scallions from the white bulbs. Thinly slice tops and set aside for serving. Slice bulbs on a diagonal into ½" pieces; set aside.

8. Pour dashi into a large donabe or skillet and add mirin and soy sauce; season with salt. Place fish in the center of the skillet and arrange turnips, daikon, mushrooms, and reserved scallion bulbs around fish. Heat over low until liquid is steaming but not bubbling (simmering will make the liquid cloudy; reduce the heat if needed). Cook until fish looks opaque all across the surface, 10 to 15 minutes. Remove donabe from heat and let rest 5 minutes.

9. To serve, sprinkle sesame seeds and reserved scallion tops over fish and vegetables and drizzle with more oil. Break fish into smaller pieces and divide among reserved noodle bowls. Ladle vegetables and dashi over.

Chapter 14 Flounder

Flounder Fillets Piccata with Veggies

Prep time: 15 minutes | Cook time: 7 minutes | Serves 4

4 (6 ounces / 170 g) flounder fillets
1 teaspoon salt, divided
½ teaspoon freshly ground black pepper, divided
2 large eggs
¾ cup almond meal
1 teaspoon Italian seasoning
2 tablespoons extra-
virgin olive oil
2 tablespoons unsalted butter
¾ cup vegetable broth
1 lemon, sliced
1 tablespoon fresh lemon juice
1 tablespoon capers
2 tablespoons chopped fresh parsley

1. Season the flounder with ½ teaspoon of salt and ¼ teaspoon of pepper.
2. In a shallow bowl, beat the eggs until combined. In another shallow bowl, mix the almond meal, Italian seasoning, and the remaining ½ teaspoon of salt and ¼ teaspoon of pepper.
3. Dip both sides of each fillet in the egg mixture, then in the almond meal mixture.
4. In a large skillet, heat the olive oil over medium heat.
5. Add the flounder and cook for 4 minutes on each side, until the fish is opaque. Remove from the skillet and set aside.
6. In the same skillet, melt the butter over medium heat. Add the vegetable broth, lemon slices, and lemon juice and simmer for 3 minutes. Return the fish to the skillet and spoon the sauce over the top.
7. Serve topped with capers and parsley.

Confetti Jerk Fish Tacos

Prep time: 15 minutes | Cook time: 10 minutes | Serves 4

For the Jamican Jerk Seasoning:
2 teaspoons garlic powder
2 teaspoons onion powder
2 teaspoons dried parsley
2 teaspoons dried thyme
2 teaspoons light brown sugar
1 teaspoon smoked
paprika
1 teaspoon red pepper flakes
1 teaspoon salt
½ teaspoon freshly ground black pepper
½ teaspoon ground allspice
¼ teaspoon ground cinnamon

For the Fish Tacos:
4 (6-ounce / 170-g) flounder fillets
2 cups sliced yellow onion
1 teaspoon avocado oil
8 corn or whole-wheat tortillas
¼ cup roughly chopped fresh cilantro
Juice from ½ lime

To Make the Jamican Jerk Seasoning
1. In a small bowl, combine the garlic powder, onion powder, parsley, thyme, brown sugar, paprika, red pepper flakes, salt, pepper, allspice, and cinnamon.

To Make the Fish Tacos
1. Preheat the oven to 375°F (190ºC). Line a sheet pan with parchment paper.
2. Place the flounder fillets on the prepared sheet pan. Sprinkle about 1 tablespoon of the seasoning on top of each of the fish fillets. The fish should be completely covered with the seasoning.
3. Toss the onion slices in avocado oil and 2 teaspoons of the jerk seasoning. Place on the sheet pan next to the fish.
4. Bake the fish and onions for 10 minutes, or until the fish flakes with a fork.
5. While the fish bakes, in a dry skillet, heat the tortillas over medium-high heat until warm.
6. To assemble the tacos, divide the fish and onions among the tortillas. Top with cilantro and a squeeze of lime.

Spiced Fried Flounder

Prep time: 10 minutes | Cook time: 2 minutes | Serves 10

6 cups vegetable oil, avocado or canola
½ cup yellow corn-meal
½ cup white cornmeal
1½ teaspoons garlic powder
1½ teaspoons lemon pepper
¾ teaspoon ground pepper
¾ teaspoon paprika
½ teaspoon seasoned salt
3 pounds (1.4 kg) flounder fillets

1. Clip a deep-fry or candy thermometer to the edge of a large pot.
2. Add oil to the pot and heat over medium-high heat until it reaches 350ºF (180ºC). Place a wire rack on a baking sheet.
3. Meanwhile, whisk yellow and white cornmeal, garlic powder, lemon pepper, ground pepper, paprika and seasoned salt in a large bowl.
4. Pat fish dry. Working with 4 pieces at a time, dredge the fish in the cornmeal mixture, shaking off excess. Using tongs, carefully add the fish to the hot oil and adjust the heat to maintain a temperature of 350ºF (180ºC).
5. Fry the fish, flipping occasionally, until golden brown and cooked through, 2 to 3 minutes total. Transfer to the rack to drain. Repeat with the remaining fish, letting the oil return to 350ºF (180ºC) between batches.

Lemon Butter Flounder Bake

Prep time: 10 minutes | Cook time: 15 minutes | Serves 4

For The Flounder:
1(½ pound / 227 g) flounder fillets
1 teaspoon salt, to taste
⅛ teaspoon black pepper
4 tablespoons butter, melted
2 tablespoons fresh lemon juice
2 teaspoons finely minced onion
1 teaspoon paprika
Fresh parsley and lemon wedges, to serve

1. Gather the ingredients.
2. Grease a shallow baking dish. Preheat oven to 325ºF (163ºC).
3. Cut the flounder fillets into serving-size portions.
4. Arrange the pieces in the prepared baking dish, and sprinkle fish with salt and the freshly ground black pepper.
5. In a small bowl or measuring cup, combine melted butter, 2 tablespoons lemon juice, and minced onion.
6. Pour the lemon-butter mixture over fish.
7. Sprinkle the fish with paprika.
8. Bake in the preheated oven for about 15 to 25 minutes, depending on thickness of the fillets, or until fish is cooked through and flakes easily with a fork.
9. Garnish with chopped parsley, lemon wedges, and serve with garlic aioli (if desired).

Browned Flounder Au Gratin

Prep time: 10 minutes | Cook time: 12 minutes | Serves 4

4 (6-ounce / 170-g) flounder fillets
¼ cup melted butter
1 cup panko crumbs
⅔ cups freshly grated Parmigiano Reggiano cheese
½ teaspoon kosher salt
Cracked black pepper, to taste
1 teaspoon dried thyme
Chopped fresh parsley, for garnish (optional)

1. Preheat the oven to 400ºF (205ºC).
2. Place the flounder fillets on a lightly oiled baking dish. Brush the tops of the fillets with 1 tablespoon of melted butter.
3. In a small bowl, combine the panko bread crumbs, grated cheese, kosher salt, ground black pepper, and thyme.
4. Add the rest of the melted butter to the crumb mixture and mix it until the crumb mixture becomes buttery, crumbly, and golden in color.
5. Sprinkle the crumb mixture over the fillets and lightly press the crumb mixture down into the fillets.
6. Bake the fish for 12 to 15 minutes, or until the fish is opaque, flakes easily with a fork, and reaches an internal temperature of 145ºF (63ºC).
7. serve.

Bread-Crumbs Flounder Parmesan Bake

Prep time: 5 minutes | Cook time: 15 minutes | Serves 4

4 (2-pound / 907-g) flounder fillets	bread crumbs
Salt and freshly ground pepper	4 tablespoons unsalted butter (melted)
¾ cup freshly grated Parmesan Cheese	2 tablespoons extra-virgin olive oil
½ cup coarse fresh	

1. Preheat the oven to 425ºF (220ºC).
2. In a large baking dish, season the fish fillets with salt and pepper. Mix the Parmesan with the bread crumbs, melted butter and olive oil and sprinkle over the fillets.
3. Bake for 15 minutes, or until the fish is cooked and the topping is golden. Let stand for 5 minutes before serving.

Lemon-Cream Broiled Flounder Fillets

Prep time: 10 minutes | Cook time: 8 minutes | Serves 2

2 tablespoons butter melted	2 garlic cloves, minced
2 flounder fillets	2 tablespoons lemon juice
1 teaspoon Old Bay Seasoning	2 tablespoons butter
⅓ cup heavy cream	Salt and pepper

1. Line a baking sheet with aluminum foil. Preheat broiler.
2. Brush a little melted butter on foil. Place flounder on top, skin side down.
3. Sprinkle with Old Bay and drizzle with remaining butter.
4. Broil for about 8 minutes, or until cooked through.
5. In a small saucepan, bring cream and garlic to a simmer.
6. Remove from heat and whisk in lemon and butter until the butter is melted.
7. Season to taste with salt and pepper. Serve sauce with fish

Golden Flounder Bake

Prep time: 5 minutes | Cook time: 5 minutes | Serves 2

2 (6-ounce / 170-g) flounder fillets	2 teaspoons soy sauce
1 garlic clove	½ teaspoon sugar
2 tablespoons fresh lemon juice	½ teaspoon salt
	2 tablespoons olive oil

1. Preheat oven to 450ºF (235ºC).
2. Arrange fillets in a ceramic or glass baking dish just large enough to hold them in one layer.
3. Mince garlic and in a small bowl combine with lemon juice, soy sauce, sugar, and salt. Whisk in oil until emulsified and pour vinaigrette over fish.
4. Bake fish in middle of oven until just cooked through and no longer translucent, 5 to 7 minutes.

Easy Pan-Fried Flounder

Prep time: 10 minutes | Cook time: 6 minutes | Serves 4

4 skinless flounder fillets	2 tablespoons vegetable oil
Salt and pepper, to taste	3 tablespoons butter, divided
Flour, for dredging fish	1 lemon, juiced
	1 small bottle capers

1. Wash fillets in cold water and pat dry. Sprinkle with salt and pepper. Dredge fillets in flour.
2. Place oil and 2 tablespoons butter in flat, heavy-bottomed skillet and heat on medium-high until butter melts.
3. Keeping heat at medium-high, cook fish on 1 side about 3 minutes (more or less, depending on size of fillets), until deep brown and crispy. Turn fish and cook on second side, about 3 minutes. Turn fish only once.
4. Remove fish to serving platter. Turn off heat. Into hot skillet, whisk in remaining 1 tablespoon butter.
5. Add lemon juice. Pour in capers, liquid and all. Whisk. Pour thin sauce over fish fillets. Serve at once.

Foil-Baked Flounder Fillets

Prep time: 10 minutes | Cook time: 15 minutes | Serves 4

2 pounds (170 g) flounder fillets
1 medium onion, sliced
1 garlic clove, minced
1 lemon, juiced
2 tablespoons butter, melted

1 dash Worcestershire sauce
Salt and pepper, to taste
extra butter, cut in bits
1 tablespoon chopped fresh parsley

1. Preheat oven to 350ºF (180ºC).
2. Place the flounder fillets on a sheet of aluminum foil.
3. Top the fillets with the sliced onion and minced garlic.
4. Combine the lemon juice, melted butter, Worcestershire sauce, salt, and pepper until smooth. Evenly drizzle the sauce over the fish.
5. Dot the fish with small bits of butter and sprinkle with the fresh parsley.
6. Pull up the sides of the aluminum foil and wrap over the fish and seal the edges. Place the foil packet on a baking sheet with rimmed sides and place in the oven. Bake at 350ºF (180ºC) for 15 to 20 minutes or until the fish flakes easily (open one corner of the packet to test).
7. Remove the fish from the oven and serve hot.

Quick Pan-Fried Flounder

Prep time: 10 minutes | Cook time: 4 minutes | Serves 4

1 large egg white, whipped until stiff
¼ cup yellow cornmeal
2 tablespoons grated Parmensan Cheese
1 tablespoon fresh thyme, finely minced (or 1 teaspoon dried thyme)

½ teaspoon table salt, to taste
½ teaspoon black pepper, freshly ground, to taste
2 sprays olive oil cooking spray
1 tablespoon olive oil
½ medium lemon, cut into 4 wedges

1. Rinse fish, pat dry.
2. Place fish on a plate and spread both sides of fish with mustard, dip into egg white and set aside.
3. In a medium bowl, combine cornmeal, Parmesan Cheese, thyme, salt and pepper; dust fish with cornmeal-mixture, making sure to cover both sides.
4. Coat a large oven-proof skillet with cooking spray and set over medium to medium-high heat; heat oil until shimmering.
5. Add fish to skillet and cook for 2 to 3 minutes on one side, flip fish and cook until done on other side, about 2 to 3 minutes more.
6. Serve fish with lemon wedges.

Oven Poached Flounder Fillets

Prep time: 5 minutes | Cook time: 12 minutes | Serves 4

1 pound (454 g) flounder fillets, each ¼ inch thick
¼ cup extra virgin olive oil
2 to 3 garlic cloves,

minced
4 to 5 sprigs fresh thyme
Sea salt
Lemon wedges

1. Preheat oven to 375ºF (190ºC). Spray a 9-inch by 13-inch glass baking dish with cooking oil spray.
2. Rinse the flounder under cool water and arrange in the pan.
3. Whisk together the olive oil and garlic. Then pour over the flounder. Place a spring of thyme on each piece of flounder.
4. Salt, to taste, with sea salt.
5. Slide the baking dish into the preheated oven and bake for 12 to 15 minutes, until the fish flakes easily with a fork.
6. Serve immediately with lemon wedges.

Chapter 15 Sole

Sole Fillets Piccata with Capers

Prep time: 10 minutes | Cook time: 13 minutes | Serves 4

1 teaspoon extra-virgin olive oil
4 (5-ounce / 142-g) sole fillets, patted dry
3 tablespoons almond butter
2 teaspoons minced garlic

2 tablespoons all-purpose flour
2 cups low-sodium chicken broth
Juice and zest of ½ lemon
2 tablespoons capers

1. Place a large skillet over medium-high heat and add the olive oil.
2. Sear the sole fillets until the fish flakes easily when tested with a fork, about 4 minutes on each side. Transfer the fish to a plate and set aside.
3. Return the skillet to the stove and add the butter.
4. Sauté the garlic until translucent, about 3 minutes.
5. Whisk in the flour to make a thick paste and cook, stirring constantly, until the mixture is golden brown, about 2 minutes.
6. Whisk in the chicken broth, lemon juice and zest.
7. Cook for about 4 minutes until the sauce is thickened.
8. Stir in the capers and serve the sauce over the fish.

Creamy Lemon Sole

Prep time: 10 minutes | Cook time: 7 minutes | Serves 4

1 knob of butter
1 garlic clove, peeled and finely chopped
700g of lemon sole, skinned and filleted
1 lemon, juiced

1 cup of double cream
75g of Parmesan, grated
2 tablespoons of fresh parsley, finely chopped

1. Melt the butter in a frying pan until foaming, then add the garlic and fry for 2 to 3 minutes, or until softened.

2. Lay the sole fillets in the pan. Squeeze over the lemon juice and season with salt and freshly ground black pepper
3. Pour the cream over the lemon sole and sprinkle over the Parmesan.
4. Cook gently for 5 to 6 minutes, turning the fish over halfway through cooking, or until the fish is cooked through
5. To serve, place the sole onto a flat serving dish and pour over the creamy cheese sauce. Sprinkle over the chopped parsley and serve with a side of steamed greens

Classic Sole Fillets with Butter

Prep time: 10 minutes | Cook time: 4 minutes | Serves 4

4 boneless sole fillets
Salt and pepper
½ cup flour
8 tablespoons butter
Juice from ½ lemon, cut the rest of the

lemon into slices for garnish
½ cup fresh chopped parsley
2 tablespoons capers

1. Season the fish with salt and pepper on both sides.
2. Put 4 tablespoons of the butter into a large skillet over medium high heat. When the butter is melted and foamy, add the fillets and cook for 2 minutes.
3. Using a fish spatula or other large spatula, carefully turn the fillets over.
4. Cook for another 2 minutes and place each one on a serving plate.
5. Cover with foil to keep warm while you make the sauce.
6. Add the rest of the butter to the skillet, along with the lemon juice and half the parsley. Whisk until the butter is melted.
7. Drizzle the sauce generously over the fillets, sprinkle on the capers, add the lemon slices as a pretty garnish.
8. Serve.

Pan-Fried Lemon-Butter Sole

Prep time: 10 minutes | Cook time: 4 minutes | Serves 4

8 sole fillets
½ cup flour
½ teaspoon seasoning salt, to taste
¼ teaspoon black pepper, to taste

7 tablespoons butter
¼ cup fresh lemon juice
2 tablespoons chopped fresh parsley

1. Mix the flour with seasoned salt and pepper in a shallow dish.
2. Dredge the fish fillets in the flour mixture.
3. Heat a large skillet over high heat.
4. Add in about 3 tablespoons butter to the hot skillet.
5. Saute the fillets in 2 batches, cooking on each side (on high heat about 2 minutes per side) or until just cooked through; transfer the fish to a plate to keep warm.
6. Add in the remaining 4 tablespoons butter and cook until golden in colour; add in lemon juice, bring to a boil and add in the parsley.
7. Season the sauce with salt and pepper.
8. Pour the warm sauce over the fish.
9. Serve immediately.

Mediterranean Sole Fillet Bake

Prep time: 15 minutes | Cook time: 10 minutes | Serves 6

Juice of 1 lime or lemon
½ cup Private Reserve extra virgin olive oil
3 tablespoons ghee or unsalted melted butter
2 shallots, thinly sliced
3 garlic cloves, thinly-sliced
2 tablespoon capers
1 teaspoon seasoned salt
¾ teaspoon ground black pepper

1 teaspoon ground cumin
1 teaspoon garlic powder
10 to 12 (1½-pound /680-g) thin sole fillets
4-6 green onions, top trimmed, halved length-wise
1 lime or lemon, sliced (optional)
¾ cup roughly chopped fresh dill for garnish

1. In a small bowl, whisk together lime juice, olive oil and melted butter with a dash of seasoned salt. Stir in the shallots, garlic and capers.
2. In a separate small bowl, mix together the seasoned salt, pepper, cumin and garlic powder. Spice fish fillets each on both sides.
3. Place the fish fillets on a lightly-oiled large baking pan or dish. Cover with the buttery lime mixture you prepared earlier. Now arrange the green onion halves and lime slices on top.
4. Bake in 375ºF (190ºC)-heated oven for 10 to 15 minutes. Do not overcook.
5. Remove the fish fillets from the oven and garnish with the chopped fresh dill.
6. Serve next to white rice or roasted Greek potatoes and a simple Mediterranean salad.

Citrus Sole Fillets with Spice

Prep time: 10 minutes | Cook time: 8 minutes | Serves 4

1 teaspoon garlic powder
1 teaspoon chili powder
½ teaspoon lemon zest
½ teaspoon lime zest
¼ teaspoon smoked paprika

¼ teaspoon freshly ground black pepper
Pinch sea salt
4 (6-ounce / 170-g) sole fillets, patted dry
1 tablespoon extra-virgin olive oil
2 teaspoons freshly squeezed lime juice

1. Preheat the oven to 450ºF (235ºC). Line a baking sheet with aluminum foil and set aside.
2. Mix together the garlic powder, chili powder, lemon zest, lime zest, paprika, pepper, and salt in a small bowl until well combined.
3. Arrange the sole fillets on the prepared baking sheet and rub the spice mixture all over the fillets until well coated. Drizzle the olive oil and lime juice over the fillets.
4. Bake in the preheated oven for about 8 minutes until flaky.
5. Remove from the heat to a plate and serve.

Lemon Thyme Sole Fillets with Asparagus

Prep time: 10 minutes | Cook time: 56 minutes | Serves 2

1 pound (454 g) asparagus	1 teaspoon pepper
8 (1 pound / 454 g) thin sole fillets	10 sprigs fresh thyme or a pinch of dried thyme
2 tablespoons olive oil	Zest of one lemon
1 teaspoon salt	

Lemon Dijon Sauce:

3 tablespoons butter	5 tablespoons fish cooking liquid
¼ teaspoon dijon mustard	Generous pinch of salt
1 tablespoon lemon juice	

1. Preheat oven to 350ºF (180ºC)
2. Place asparagus in baking dish. Drizzle with 1½ tablespoons olive oil and sprinkle with ¼ teaspoon salt and pepper, ½ of the lemon zest, and a few sprigs of fresh thyme. Bake at 350ºF (180ºC) for 14 minutes.
3. Season sole with salt and pepper on both sides. Lay sole over asparagus.
4. Place remaining fresh thyme and remaining lemon zest over fish, drizzle with remaining (½ tablespoon) olive oil.
5. Roast in oven for 19 minutes, remove from oven and set aside.
6. In a small saucepan over medium heat melt butter and whisk in mustard. Whisk continuously adding lemon juice and 5 tablespoons of fish cooking liquid (I simply tilt the baking dish and scoop out the 5 tablespoons).
7. Cook for 4 minutes, or until sauce thickens. Season sauce with a pinch of sea salt.
8. Pour sauce over fish and serve immediately.

Pacific Dover Sole Dish

Prep time: 10 minutes | Cook time: 10 minutes | Serves 4

1½ pounds (680 g) Pacific Dover sole fillet	zest (approximately one lemon)
2 stalks celery sliced thinly, diagonally	1 tablespoon ginger minced
2 tablespoons butter	¼ cup dry white wine
½ teaspoon smoked paprika	1 tablespoon brown sugar
1 tablespoon lemon	Black rice

1. Cut each fillet into 4 to 5 portions and set aside.
2. Combine the lemon zest, ginger, wine, and sugar in a bowl. Stir to combine and set aside.
3. Turn on the broiler on the oven and allow it to preheat.
4. Heat a cast iron or other oven-proof skillet on the stove top over high heat for 30 seconds.
5. Add the butter and the smoked paprika and stir together as the butter melts.
6. Once the butter is just beginning to bubble up, add the celery and stir together. Cook for about 30 seconds, then add the wine mixture and cook for an additional 2 minutes, stirring occasionally.
7. Add the fish to the frying pan and gently stir to get some of the sauce onto to the fillets. Immediately transfer the frying pan to the oven (use whatever rack allows you to get the frying pan close to the broiler).
8. Broil for 4 to 5 minutes, or until the sauce, celery, and fish as starting to brown at the edges.
9. Remove from heat and serve with black rice.

Special Sole Cake

Prep time: 10 minutes | Cook time: 16 minutes | Serves 8

1 pound (454 g) skinless sole fillets
1 egg, lightly beaten
1⅓ cups whole-wheat panko breadcrumbs, divided
1 (6-ounce / 170-g) container plain fat-free Greek yogurt, divided
2 tablespoons thinly sliced scallions
2 teaspoons chopped fresh thyme
½ teaspoon lower-sodium seafood seasonin
¼ teaspoon ground pepper
2 teaspoons canola oil
½ teaspoon finely shredded lemon peel

1. Preheat the oven to 450ºF (235ºC). Coat a 15-inch by 10-inch baking pan with cooking spray. Measure thickness of fish and pat the fish dry with paper towels. Arrange the fish in a single layer in the prepared pan. Tuck under any thin edges.
2. Bake, uncovered, for 4 to 6 minutes per ½-inch thickness of fish, or until the fish flakes easily when tested with a fork. Remove the fish from oven. Using a fork, coarsely flake the fish. Set aside to cool.
3. Combine egg, 1 cup panko, 3 tablespoons yogurt, the scallions, thyme, seafood seasoning, and pepper in a medium bowl. Stir in the flaked fish.
4. Wipe the 15-inch by 10-inch baking pan clean and line with foil; coat the foil with cooking spray.
5. Spoon ¼-cup mounds of the fish mixture into the baking pan about 2 inches apart. Pat and shape into 2- to 2½-inch patties. Combine the remaining ⅓ cup panko and the oil in a small bowl.
6. Carefully place each patty into the panko mixture, turning to coat both sides. Return to the baking pan, reshaping as necessary.
7. Bake, uncovered, for 12 to 15 minutes or until light brown and heated through (160ºF / 71ºC).
8. Stir lemon peel into the remaining yogurt.
9. Serve the sole cakes with the yogurt mixture.

Herb-Roasted Sole Fillets

Prep time: 10 minutes | Cook time: 13 minutes | Serves 2

1 shallot, thinly sliced
3 garlic cloves, thinly sliced
3 lemons, 1 for zest and juice, 1 very thinly sliced, 1 cut into wedges
2 tablespoons chopped fresh thyme
1 tablespoon chopped fresh dill, plus more for garnish
3 tablespoons butter, melted
½ cup extra-virgin olive oil, plus 2 tablespoons
Kosher salt
Freshly ground black pepper
1 pound (454 g) sole fillets
2 slices seeded whole-wheat bread, torn

1. Preheat the oven to 375ºF (190ºC). Line a baking sheet with parchment paper. Line a second baking sheet with paper towels.
2. In a medium bowl, whisk together the shallot, garlic, half the lemon zest, 2 tablespoons of lemon juice, thyme, dill, and melted butter. While still whisking, stream in ½ cup of olive oil. Season with a pinch of salt and pepper.
3. Place the sole on the parchment paper–lined baking sheet. Top with the lemon slices. Pour the sauce over the lemons. Bake for 10 to 15 minutes, until the sole is opaque and slightly firm to the touch. Note: Sole is a delicate fish and will cook very quickly.
4. While the fish is cooking, in a food processor, pulse the bread into coarse crumbs. In a large skillet over medium heat, heat the remaining 2 tablespoons of olive oil.
5. Add the bread crumbs and cook, tossing regularly, until golden brown, about 3 minutes. Transfer to the paper towel–lined baking sheet and season with salt, pepper, and the remaining lemon zest.
6. Remove the sole from the oven and top it with the bread crumbs. Serve immediately, with the lemon wedges on the side.

Sole Fillets Meunière

Prep time: 10 minutes | Cook time: 3 minutes | Serves 6

½ cup all-purpose flour
6 (4-ounce / 113-g) skinless, boneless sole, patted dry
Kosher salt, to taste
Freshly ground white or black pepper, to taste

4 tablespoons clarified butter
4 tablespoons unsalted butter, diced, at room temperature
3 tablespoons minced parsley
1 lemon, cut into wedges, for serving

1. Heat oven to 200ºF (93ºC) and place a large oven-safe plate or baking sheet inside.
2. Place flour on a large, shallow plate. Season both sides of fish fillets with salt and pepper to taste. Dredge fish in flour, shaking off excess.
3. In a 12-inch nonstick or enamel-lined skillet over medium-high heat, heat 2 tablespoons clarified butter until bubbling. Place half of the fish fillets in the pan and cook until just done, 2 to 3 minutes per side, then transfer to the plate or baking sheet in the oven to keep warm.
4. Add 2 more tablespoons clarified butter to skillet and heat until bubbling, then cook remaining fillets. Wipe out the skillet.
5. Arrange the fish on a warm serving platter. Top with parsley. In reserved skillet, heat remaining 4 tablespoons unsalted butter until bubbling and golden, 1 to 2 minutes, then pour evenly over fillets. Serve immediately, with lemon wedges on the side.

Sole Fillet with Lemon Cream

Prep time: 10 minutes | Cook time: 6 minutes | Serves 4

2 tablespoons butter
2 pounds (907 g) sole fillets, cut to make 4 pieces
¾ teaspoon salt
¼ teaspoon fresh-ground black pepper
¼ cup flour

¾ cup heavy cream
Grated zest of ½ lemon
1 tablespoon lemon juice
2 tablespoons chopped fresh parsley

1. In a large nonstick frying pan, melt the butter over moderate heat. Sprinkle the sole with ½ teaspoon of the salt and the pepper. Dust the sole with the flour and shake off any excess.
2. Put the sole in the pan and cook for 2 minutes. Turn and cook until just done, about 2 minutes longer. Remove the sole from the pan.
3. Add the cream and lemon zest to the pan. Bring to a simmer and cook until starting to thicken, about 2 minutes. Stir in the remaining ¼ teaspoon salt, the lemon juice, and parsley.
4. Serve the sauce over the fish.

Chapter 16 Herring

Soused Herring Fillets

Prep time: 10 minutes | Cook time: 25 minutes | Serves 4

4 whole herring fillets, scaled, filleted, and trimmed
2 cups water
½ sweet onion, thinly sliced
½ cup white

vinegarsee
2 thyme sprigs
1 tablespoon granulated sugar
1 teaspoon sea salt
¼ teaspoon black peppercorns

1. Preheat the oven to 350°F (180°C).
2. Place the herring fillets in a 9-inch by 13-inch baking dish.
3. Add the water, onion, white vinegar, thyme, sugar, salt, and peppercorns.
4. Cover the baking dish with foil and bake the fish until tender, 25 to 30 minutes.
5. Cool before serving. Leftovers can be stored in the refrigerator in a resealable container for 1 week.

Savory Baked Herring

Prep time: 15 minutes | Cook time: 15 minutes | Serves 2

2 small herrings
¼ teaspoon nigella seeds
¼ teaspoon mustard seeds
¼ teaspoon fenugreek seeds
¼ teaspoon fennel seeds
¼ teaspoon caraway seeds
1 tablespoon oil

groundnut, vegetable or light olive oil
2 tablespoons white wine vinegar
Pinch salt
½ green pepper sliced
1 green chilli pepper (optional)
½ stick of celery sliced
½ onion sliced

1. Put all the spices in a pestle and mortar and grind to a powder.
2. Make a few slashes in the skin of the fish. Put them in the middle of a large square of aluminium foil. Sprinkle the spices over the top and season with salt and pepper. If using also add the sliced chilli pepper.
3. Put the vegetables on top of the fish and pull the edges of the foil up to make a parcel. Drizzle with oil and a good slug of vinegar.
4. Bake in the oven for about 15 minutes.

Gernman Red Herring Fillet Salad

Prep time: 15 minutes | Cook time: 0 minutes | Serves 4

½ pound (226 g) pickled (soused) herring fillets, drained and diced small
2 medium apples, cored and diced small
⅓ pound (151 g)

cooked red beets, diced small
1 medium yellow or red onion, diced small
4 to 5 German pickles, diced small

For the Creamy Dressing:

2 to 3 tablespoons pickle juice from the German pickles
1 tablespoon sunflower oil
1 tablespoon white wine vinegar
1 teaspoon sea salt
1 teaspoon sugar

1 teaspoon German yellow mustard
1 cup sour cream
¼ to ⅓ cup heavy whipping cream
3 tablespoons German mayonnaise
1 to 2 tablespoons fresh chopped dill

For Serving:
boiled potatoes, hard-boiled eggs, crusty bread

1. In a small bowl, whisk together the pickle juice, mustard, oil, vinegar, salt and sugar until emulsified and the salt and sugar are dissolved. Stir in the whipping cream, sour cream, mayonnaise, mustard and dill.
2. Place the diced herring, apples, beets, onions, and pickles in a large bowl. Pour the dressing over the herring mixture and carefully stir until thoroughly combined.
3. Add salt and pepper to taste. If the salad is thicker than you prefer, add a little whipping cream. If you prefer the dressing thicker, add more sour cream and/or mayonnaise.
4. To serve, lay some slices of boiled egg over a mound of herring salad with a sprig of fresh dill. You can also add some onions sliced into rings. Place the potatoes next to the salad. Alternatively, spread the herring salad on crusty bread.

Polish Herring Fillets Salad

Prep time: 15 minutes | Cook time: 0 minutes | Serves 6

6 soused herring fillets
A few teaspoons white vinegar
White pepper, to taste
1 large onion, chopped
3 pickled cucumbers, diced
1 large tart apple, diced
250g soured cream
3 tablespoons mayonnaise
1 tablespoon mustard
1 hard-boiled egg, chopped
1 teaspoon chopped fresh parsley
A pinch of sugar

1. Drain the herring fillets; cut into bite size pieces, drizzle generously with vinegar and season with white pepper. Set aside.
2. In a large bowl, combine the onion, pickles and apple. Mix in cream, mayonnaise, mustard, egg and fresh parsley. Add a pinch of sugar and mix well.
3. Add herring pieces, toss to coat and refrigerate overnight.

Herring Fillet Pasta

Prep time: 10 minutes | Cook time: 2 minutes | Serves 4 to 6

500g dried linguine
Sea salt
Freshly ground black pepper
Olive oil
2 garlic cloves, peeled and finely sliced
1 fresh red chili, finely sliced
1 tablespoon small capers
1 small bunch fresh flat-leaf parsley, leaves picked and finely chopped, stalks finely sliced
4 (40 g) herring fillets, from sustainable sources, ask your fishmonger, skin-on, scaled and pin-boned, cut into 2cm strips
1 small handful vine cherry tomatoes, quartered
1 lemon
1 knob butter, optional

1. Add the linguine to a pan of boiling salted water and cook according to packet instructions.
2. Meanwhile, put a large frying pan on a high heat and add a few good lugs of olive oil. Once hot, add the garlic, chilli, capers and parsley stalks. Cook for a couple of minutes until just starting to colour.

3. Add the herring strips to the pan and cook for 2 minutes. They will start to break up but don't worry. Add the tomatoes and squeeze in the juice of a lemon.
4. Use tongs to transfer the cooked linguine straight into the frying pan, bringing a little of the cooking water with it. Add the butter, if using, and toss everything together in the pan.
5. Have a taste, season with salt and pepper, add most of the parsley leaves and a lug of extra virgin olive oil. Mix again, use tongs if you need to, then transfer to a large platter. Scatter over the remaining parsley leaves and whack it in the centre of the table so everyone can tuck straight in.

Delicious Pickled Herring

Prep time: 15 minutes | Cook time: 0 minutes | Serves 6

3 to 4 whole salted herrings
2 cups milk
1½ cups water
1 cup white sugar
1 cup white vinegar
2 teaspoons ground allspice
2 teaspoons yellow mustard seeds
1 teaspoon caraway seeds
2 teaspoons whole black peppercorns
2 teaspoons whole white peppercorns
1 small red onion, sliced in rings
2 carrots, cut in thin slices
2 handfuls fresh dill
2 bay leaves
inch piece fresh horseradish, cut in big slices

1. Soak the herring in the milk for at least 12 hours or up to 24 to draw out a lot of the excess salt. Drain the herring, rinse, and pat dry. Cut off the fins and fillet the herring, leaving the skin on. Cut the fillets crosswise into 2-inch strips.
2. In a saucepan, combine the water, sugar, vinegar, allspice, mustard seeds, caraway seeds, and peppercorns. Bring the mixture to a boil, stirring to dissolve the sugar. Remove from the heat and cool the pickling mixture completely.
3. Arrange the herring fillets, onion, carrots, dill, bay leaves, and horseradish in a glass dish or funky Mason jar. Pour the cooled pickling mixture into the jar so that all the ingredients are completely covered with the liquid. Cover and refrigerate overnight or up to 2 days before serving.

Herring Fillets in Cream Sauce

Prep time: 10 minutes | Cook time: 1 minutes | Serves 4

8 herring fillets	1 cup sour cream
1 large onion	1 cup of cream
3 tablespoon lemon juice	150 g pickles
2 to 3 (400 g) apples	salt
1 cup yoghurt	pepper
	Sugar

1. Start with cutting the onion into halves and then slice it.
2. Set up a pot of water and add ¼ teaspoon. salt, bring to a boil.
3. Add the onions to the boiling water and let cook for 1 to 3 minutes, then remove them from the pot.
4. Peel and cut the apples into small cubes.
5. Cut the pickles into slices.
6. Mix the cream, yoghurt and sour cream in a large bowl.
7. Add salt, pepper, lemon juice and sugar.
8. Next, add the onion slices, the apples and mix it well.
9. Wash the herring and cut into 1 inch size, then add to the sauce and mix well.
10. Cover the bowl with cling wrap and refrigerate for at least 12 hours.
11. Enjoy cold with fresh boiled hot potatoes.

Fried Herring With Lime Pepper Crust

Prep time: 5 minutes | Cook time: 4 minutes | Serves 2

2 (6- to 7-ounces / 170- to 198-g) herring fillets	peppercorns
2 limes	1 rounded desserteaspoonoon plain flour
1 rounded teaspoon whole mixed	2 tablespoons olive oil
	Maldon sea salt

1. First of all crush the peppercorns with a pestle and mortar, not too fine, so they still have some texture.
2. Then grate the zest of the limes and add half of it to the peppercorns, then add the flour. Mix them all together and spread the mixture out on a flat plate.

3. Wipe the herrings dry with kitchen paper and coat the flesh side with the flour-pepper mixture. Press the fish well in to give it a good coating, anything left on the plate can be used to dust the skin side lightly.
4. Now in your largest frying pan, heat the oil until it is very hot and fry the herrings flesh-side down for about 2 to 3 minutes. Have a peek by lifting up the edge with a fish slice, it should be golden.
5. Then turn the fish over on to the other side and give it another 2 minutes, and drain on crumpled silicone paper (baking parchment) before serving.
6. Serve sprinkled with crushed salt, the rest of the lime zest and the limes cut into quarters to squeeze over.

Herring Fillets with Mustard Basil Dressing

Prep time: 5 minutes | Cook time: 6 minutes | Serves 4

3 ounces (85 g) herring fillets	large bunch basil, roughly torn
4 tablespoons extra-virgin olive oil	1 teaspoon clear honey
2 tablespoons wholegrain mustard	1 lemon, grated zest and juice

1. Heat grill to its highest setting. Rinse the fish under running cold water to dislodge any loose scales. Brush with a little of the oil and season lightly.
2. Grill for 6 to 8 minutes, or until cooked; the eye should be white, the skin well browned and the flesh firm and opaque.
3. Meanwhile, make the dressing: whisk the mustard, basil, honey, lemon zest and juice and remaining oil together in a small bowl, and season.
4. Once the fish is cooked, spoon the dressing over and serve.

Easy Curry Pickled Herring

Prep time: 10 minutes | Cook time: 6 minutes | Serves 6

1 tablespoonolive oil
1 small brown onion, finely chopped
1 tablespoon mild yellow curry powder
500g jar marinated herrings, drained, cut into bite-size pieces and patted dry
½ cup thick mayonnaise
½ cup sour cream or crème frâiche
¼ cup capers, finely diced
1 small green apple, peeled, cored and finely diced
¼ cup finely chopped dill, plus extra to serve
1 soft-boiled egg, cut into small pieces
Sliced rye bread, to serve

1. Heat the oil in a small frying pan over medium heat.
2. Add the onion and a pinch of salt and cook for 5 minutes, or until just soft. Add the curry powder and stir for another 1 minute. Remove from the heat and cool.
3. Place the herrings, mayonnaise, sour cream, capers, apple and dill in a bowl and combine well. Add the curried onion. Season to taste and combine well.
4. Spoon onto small pieces rye bread, then top with a little soft-boiled egg and extra chopped dill. Serve.

Pickled Herring Fillet Marinated in Vinegar

Prep time: 10 minutes | Cook time: 4 minutes | Serves 10

$2\frac{1}{5}$ pounds (997.8 g) herring fillets, fresh
For Vinegar Marinade:
3 cups water
5 tablespoons sugar
2 tablespoons salt
4 bay leaves
5 allspice berries
1 teaspoon white/yellow mustard seeds
1 teaspoon black peppercorns
4 ounces (113 g) small onions, yellow or red
$1\frac{1}{3}$ cups white vinegar (10% acidity)
1 small carrot (optional)

1. Peel onions, slice them thinly into rings. Peel the carrot, slice it into rounds.
2. Pour three cups of water into a cooking pot, add 5 tablespoons of sugar, 2 tablespoons of salt and all the spices. Bring to boil, then reduce the heat to 'low'. Cook for 4 to 5 minutes, allowing the spices to release their flavours.
3. Take the marinade off the heat. Drop raw onions in, and allow the whole thing to cool down.
4. When the marinade has cooled, add in the vinegar and stir.
5. Now we'll be packing our herrings into jars. One large jar or a few smaller jars - the size is up to you. I prefer smaller jars, they fit better in my fridge.
6. Arrange herring fillets in the jar, with pieces of onion and carrot in between the layers. Pour in the marinade, making sure that everything is covered completely.
7. Seal the jar(s) and store in the fridge for a few days.
8. Pickled herrings are ready to eat after 3 to 5 days.

Oatmeal Herring and Potato Salad

Prep time: 15 minutes | Cook time: 14 minutes | Serves 2

For the Potato Salad:
7 ounces (198 g) small new potatoes
2 ounces (57 g) kale, very coarsely chopped
¼ cucumber, cut in half lengthways, seeds scooped out with a spoon, thickly sliced
1 to 2 spring onions, trimmed and sliced

For the Dressing:

1 tablespoon white balsamic vinegar	Squeeze lemon juice
2 tablespoons cold-pressed rapeseed oil	Salt and freshly ground black pepper

For the Herring:

2 handfuls medium oatmeal	A dollop of English mustard
Salt and freshly ground black pepper	1¼ ounces (35 g) butter
6 herring fillets, scales and central line of bones removed	Splash rapeseed oil
	Lemon wedges, to serve

1. For the potato salad, boil the new potatoes in a large saucepan of salted water until tender (about 12 minutes). Add the kale and cucumber to the pan three minutes before the potatoes are ready and boil until all of the ingredients are tender. Drain well and set aside.
2. For the dressing, whisk together the vinegar, rapeseed oil and lemon juice in a jug until well combined. Season, to taste, with salt and freshly ground black pepper. Set aside.
3. For the herring, sprinkle the oatmeal onto a plate and season with salt and freshly ground black pepper.
4. Brush both sides of each herring fillet with a little of the mustard, then roll in the seasoned oatmeal until completely covered.
5. Heat the butter and the oil in a large, heavy-based frying pan over a medium heat. Add the coated herring fillets to the pan, skin-side up (do this in batches if necessary).
6. Gently press down on each of the herring fillets using a fish slice so that they stay flat. Fry for 1 to 2 minutes, or until the oats are golden-brown, then turn over and continue to fry on the other side for a further 1 to 2 minutes, or until the herrings are cooked through and the oats are golden-brown.
7. Remove the herring fillets from the pan using a slotted spoon and set aside to drain on kitchen paper.
8. Place the boiled potatoes, kale and cucumber into a serving bowl, stir in the spring onions, and drizzle over the dressing. Mix well and season, to taste, with salt and freshly ground black pepper.
9. To serve, divide the herring equally between two serving plates. Spoon the potato salad alongside and serve with a wedge of lemon.

Chapter 17 Sea Bass

Easy Sea Bass Bake

Prep time: 10 minutes | Cook time: 10 minutes | Serves 6

¼ cup olive oil
2 pounds (907 g) sea bass
Sea salt and freshly ground pepper, to taste
1 garlic clove, minced
¼ cup dry white wine
3 teaspoons fresh dill
2 teaspoons fresh thyme

1. Preheat the oven to 425ºF (220ºC).
2. Brush the bottom of a roasting pan with the olive oil. Place the fish in the pan and brush the fish with oil.
3. Season the fish with sea salt and freshly ground pepper. Combine the remaining ingredients and pour over the fish.
4. Bake in the preheated oven for 10 to 15 minutes, depending on the size of the fish.
5. Serve hot.

Grilled Sea Bass with Spice

Prep time: 10 minutes | Cook time: 14 minutes | Serves 6

¼ teaspoon garlic powder
¼ teaspoon onion powder
¼ teaspoon paprika lemon pepper, to taste
sea salt, to taste
2 pounds (907 g) sea
bass
3 tablespoons butter
2 large garlic cloves, chopped
1 tablespoon chopped Italian flat leaf parsley
1½ tablespoons extra virgin olive oil

1. Preheat grill for high heat.
2. In a small bowl, stir together the garlic powder, onion powder, paprika, lemon pepper, and sea salt. Sprinkle seasonings onto the fish.
3. In a small saucepan over medium heat, melt the butter with the garlic and parsley. Remove from heat when the butter has melted, and set aside.
4. Lightly oil grill grate. Grill fish for 7 minutes, then turn and drizzle with butter. Continue cooking for 7 minutes, or until easily flaked with a fork. Drizzle with olive oil before serving.

Easy Pan-Seared Chilean Sea Bass

Prep time: 5 minutes | Cook time: 8 minutes | Serves 2

12 ounces (340 g) Chilean sea bass
2 tablespoons olive oil
¼ cup butter
½ tablespoon minced garlic
Salt

1. Let sea bass sit out for 30 minutes before cooking
2. Add butter and garlic to a small sauce pan and shimmer
3. Add olive oil to another pan over medium heat
4. Pat dry sea bass and salt both sides of fish
5. Add fish to pan and cook for 4 minutes on each side
6. Strain garlic from butter and pour over plated fish

Lemony Baked Sea Bass

Prep time: 10 minutes | Cook time: 25 minutes | Serves 2

About 290g jar whole roasted peppers, drained and sliced
1 red onion, sliced into very thin wedges
Drizzle olive oil
4 garlic cloves, unpeeled
3 fat slices lemon,
rest cut into wedges to serve
2 sea bass
15 Kalamata or black olives
25g toasted pine nut
Handful roughly chopped parsley

1. Heat oven to 200ºF (93ºC).
2. Toss the peppers and onions with seasoning plus a small drizzle of olive oil. Spread on a baking tray and cook for 5 minutes.
3. Toss in the garlic and lemon with the onions and peppers, sit on the sea bass, brush fish with a little more oil, season fish and roast for 15 minutes.
4. Stir the olives and pine nuts into the vegetable and roast for 5 minutes more until the fish is just cooked through.
5. Squeeze over some lemon juice and scatter with parsley to serve.

Delicious Mediterranean Grilled Sea Bass

Prep time: 10 minutes | Cook time: 15 minutes | Serves 6

¼ teaspoon onion powder
¼ teaspoon garlic powder
¼ teaspoon paprika
Lemon pepper and sea salt, to taste
2 pounds (907 g) sea bass

3 tablespoons extra-virgin olive oil, divided
2 large garlic cloves, chopped
1 tablespoon chopped Italian flat leaf parsley

1. Preheat the grill to high heat.
2. Place the onion powder, garlic powder, paprika, lemon pepper, and sea salt in a large bowl and stir to combine.
3. Dredge the fish in the spice mixture, turning until well coated.
4. Heat 2 tablespoons of olive oil in a small skillet. Add the garlic and parsley and cook for 1 to 2 minutes, stirring occasionally. Remove the skillet from the heat and set aside.
5. Brush the grill grates lightly with remaining 1 tablespoon olive oil.
6. Grill the fish for about 7 minutes. Flip the fish and drizzle with the garlic mixture and cook for an additional 7 minutes, or until the fish flakes when pressed lightly with a fork.
7. Serve hot.

Hazelnut Crusted Sea Bass Fillets

Prep time: 5 minutes | Cook time: 15 minutes | Serves 2

2 tablespoons almond butter
2 sea bass fillets
1/3 cup roasted

hazelnuts
A pinch of cayenne pepper

1. Preheat the oven to 425ºF (220ºC).
2. Line a baking dish with waxed paper.
3. Brush the almond butter over the fillets.
4. Pulse the hazelnuts and cayenne in a food processor.
5. Coat the sea bass with the hazelnut mixture, then transfer to the baking dish.
6. Bake in the preheated oven for about 15 minutes.
7. Cool for 5 minutes before serving.

Steamed Bass Fillets

Prep time: 10 minutes | Cook time: 8 minutes | Serves 4

1½ cups water
1 lemon, sliced
4 sea bass fillets
4 sprigs thyme
1 white onion, cut into thin rings

2 turnips, chopped
2 pinches salt
1 pinch ground black pepper
2 teaspoons olive oil

1. Add water and set a rack into the pot.
2. Line a parchment paper to the bottom of the steamer basket. Place lemon slices in a single layer on the rack.
3. Arrange fillets on the top of the lemons, cover with onion and thyme sprigs. Top with turnip slices.
4. Drizzle pepper, salt, and olive oil over the mixture. Put steamer basket onto the rack.
5. Seal lid and cook on Low pressure for 8 minutes. Release the pressure quickly.
6. Serve over the delicate onion rings and thinly turnips.

Lemon-Caper Sea Bass Fillets

Prep time: 10 minutes | Cook time: 7 minutes | Serves 4

4 (4 ounces / 113 g) sea bass fillets
Olive oil, for brushing
For the caper dressing:

3 tablespoons extra virgin olive oil
Grated zest of 1 lemon, plus
2 tablespoons juice
2 tablespoons small capers

2 teaspoons gluten-free Dijon mustard
2 tablespoons chopped flat-leaf parsley, plus a few extra leaves (optional)

1. To make the dressing, mix the oil with the lemon zest and juice, capers, mustard, some seasoning and 1 tablespoon water. Don't add the parsley yet (unless serving straight away) as the acid in the lemon will fade the colour if they are left together for too long.
2. Heat the oven to 220ºF (104ºC).
3. Line a baking tray with baking parchment and put the fish, skin-side up, on top. Brush the skin with oil and sprinkle with some flaky salt.
4. Bake for 7 minutes or until the flesh flakes when tested with a knife. Arrange the fish on warm serving plates, spoon over the dressing and scatter with extra parsley leaves, if you like.

Chilean Sea Bass Bake

Prep time: 15 minutes | Cook time: 15 minutes | Serves 4

For the Fish:
4 (6-ounce / 170-g) Chilean sea bass fillets
Kosher salt, to taste
Black pepper, to taste
Creole seasoning (or seasoned salt), to taste

For the Lemon Buerre Blanc:
¼ cup dry white wine
1 ½ tablespoons white wine vinegar
1 ½ tablespoons minced shallots
1 tablespoon lemon juice, to taste
1 teaspoon lemon zest
1 tablespoon heavy cream
6 tablespoons cold butter, cut into 1-inch pieces
Lemon wedges, garnish

1. Gather the ingredients
2. Preheat the oven to 425ºF (220ºC)
3. Oil a broiler pan and rack or baking pan with olive oil
4. Lightly sprinkle the sea bass fillets all over with kosher salt, pepper, and creole seasoning
5. Place the Chilean sea bass on the oiled broiler rack, skin-side down
6. Bake the fish fillets at 425ºF (220ºC) for about 15 to 20 minutes depending on the thickness of the fillets. The fish is ready when the temperature reaches 145ºF (63ºC) on an instant-read thermometer inserted into the center of a fillet.
7. While the fish is baking, prepare the lemon buerre blanc sauce
8. In a saucepan, combine the dry white wine, white wine vinegar, and minced shallots.
9. Bring the mixture to a simmer and cook until it has reduced to about 2 tablespoons.
10. Add the lemon juice, zest, and heavy cream.
11. Remove the pan from the heat and whisk in 1 piece of the butter.
12. Set it back over low heat and continue whisking until the butter has almost melted.
13. Continue with the remaining pieces of butter until all are incorporated.
14. Taste and add salt and pepper, as needed. Whisk until the well blended. If the sauce is too hot or too cold, it can separate, so keep it warm, at least 80ºF (27ºC) but no hotter than about 135ºF (57ºC), until serving time.
15. Arrange the fish on plates with lemon wedges and drizzle with the lemon buerre blanc.
16. Serve.

Roasted Sea Bass Fillets and Vegetable

Prep time: 10 minutes | Cook time: 32 minutes | Serves 2

300g red-skinned potatoes, thinly sliced into rounds	leaves removed and very finely chopped
1 red pepper, cut into strips	2 sea bass fillets
2 tablespoons extra virgin olive oil	25g pitted black olive, halved
1 rosemary sprig,	½ lemon, sliced thinly into rounds
	Handful basil leaves

1. Heat oven to 180ºF (82ºC). Arrange the potato and pepper slices on a large non-stick baking tray.
2. Drizzle over 1 tablespoon oil and scatter with the rosemary, a pinch of salt and a good grinding of pepper.
3. Toss everything together well and roast for 25 minutes, turning over halfway through, until the potatoes are golden and crisp at the edges.
4. Arrange the fish fillets on top and scatter over the olives.
5. Place a couple of lemon slices on top of the fish and drizzle with the remaining oil.
6. Roast for further 7 to 8 minutes until the fish is cooked through. Serve scattered with basil leaves.

Garlic-Herb Sea Bass

Prep time: 15 minutes | Cook time: 6½ minutes | Serves 4

3 tablespoons butter divided
1 tablespoon extra-virgin olive oil
1½ pounds (680 g) sea bass
¼ cup all-purpose flour
1 teaspoon kosher salt plus more if needed
½ teaspoon black pepper plus more if needed
2 garlic cloves, minced
¼ cup dry white wine such as savignon blanc

½ cup chicken stock/broth or water, in a pinch
Juice of one lemon about 2 tablespoons
1 tablespoon fresh oregano roughly chopped
1 tablespoon fresh thyme roughly chopped
1 tablespoon fresh parsley roughly chopped
lemon wedges for serving optional
Pat the fish dry with a paper towel.

1. In a shallow dish, mix together the flour (¼ cup), salt (1 teaspoon), and black pepper (½ teaspoon).
2. Dredge each piece of fish in the flour mixture, coating the entire surface, and shake off any excess.
3. In a large skillet, preferably stainless steel or nonstick, melt 1 tablespoon of the butter over medium high heat and add the olive oil (1 tablespoon).
4. Cook the fish in the skillet for 3 to 4 minutes on each side, until golden brown and fully cooked. Try not to move the fish too much, especially if you are using a pan that isn't nonstick, otherwise the fish may be more likely to stick to the bottom and not get browned as nicely.
5. Remove fish from the skillet to a plate.
6. Turn down the heat to low. Add the white wine (¼ cup) to the skillet to deglaze, stirring up any browned bits. Continue heating until almost all the wine has evaporated.
7. Add one more tablespoon of butter to the skillet. Once it's melted, add the minced garlic (2 cloves) and fresh herbs (1 tablespoon each of oregano, thyme, and parsley) to the skillet and sauté until fragrant, about 30 seconds. Add the chicken broth (½ cup) and bring to a simmer.

8. Turn off heat and stir in remaining 1 tablespoon butter and lemon juice (about 2 tablespoons). Taste and adjust seasoning if necessary.
9. Serve sauce on top of fish.

Honey & Orange Roasted Sea Bass

Prep time: 10 minutes | Cook time: 10 minutes | Serves 2

2 large skin-on sea bass fillets
zest and juice ½ orange
2 teaspoons clear honey
2 teaspoons wholegrain mustard

2 tablespoons olive oil
250g pouch ready-to-eat puy lentils
100g watercress
Small bunch parsley, chopped
Small bunch dill, chopped

1. Heat oven to 200ºF (93ºC).
2. Place each sea bass fillet, skin-side down, on individual squares of foil.
3. Mix together the orange zest, honey, mustard, 1 tablespoon olive oil and some seasoning, and drizzle it over the fillets.
4. Pull the sides of the foil up and twist the edges together to make individual parcels.
5. Place the parcels on a baking tray and bake in the oven for 10 minutes until the fish is just cooked and flakes easily when pressed with a knife.
6. Warm the lentils following pack instructions, then mix with the orange juice, remaining oil, the watercress, herbs and seasoning.
7. Divide the lentils between 2 plates and top each with a sea bass fillet.
8. Drizzle over any roasting juices that are caught in the foil and serve immediately.

Chapter 18 Haddock

Haddock Fillets with Cucumber Sauce

Prep time: 10 minutes | Cook time: 10 minutes | Serves 4

¼ cup plain Greek yogurt
½ scallion, white and green parts, finely chopped
½ English cucumber, grated, liquid squeezed out
2 teaspoons chopped fresh mint

1 teaspoon honey
Sea salt and freshly ground black pepper, to taste
4 (5-ounce / 142-g) haddock fillets, patted dry
Nonstick cooking spray

1. In a small bowl, stir together the yogurt, cucumber, scallion, mint, honey, and a pinch of salt. Set aside.
2. Season the fillets lightly with salt and pepper.
3. Place a large skillet over medium-high heat and spray lightly with cooking spray.
4. Cook the haddock, turning once, until it is just cooked through, about 5 minutes per side.
5. Remove the fish from the heat and transfer to plates.
6. Serve topped with the cucumber sauce.

Smoked Haddock and Saffron Kedgeree

Prep time: 15 minutes | Cook time: 24 minutes | Serves 6

300g basmati rice
50g butter
3 hard-boiled eggs, shelled and halved
1 cup double cream
500g naturally smoked haddock, skin removed
½ cup white wine
1 teaspoon cayenne

pepper
Pinch saffron strands
1 tablespoon mild curry powder
Freshly grated nutmeg
Small handful flat-leaf parsley, chopped
1 lemon, cut into wedges, to serve

1. Cook basmati rice, leave to cool. Heat oven to 160ºF (71ºC).
2. Grease a large ovenproof dish with some of the butter. Push the egg yolks through a sieve and roughly chop the whites.
3. Gently heat the cream in a frying pan until just below boiling point, then add the fish. Cover and poach for 4 minutes.
4. Place the wine in a pan with the saffron and warm to infuse.
5. In a large bowl, mix together the rice, cayenne, curry powder, nutmeg, seasoning, chopped egg whites and saffron-infused wine. Lift the fish out of the cream and flake into the bowl, removing any bones as you find them. Scrape in the cream and gently mix together once more.
6. Tip everything into the buttered dish and dot the top with the remaining butter.
7. Bake to heat through for 20 minutes, then serve scattered with the parsley and sieved egg yolk, with lemon wedges on the side.

Easy Haddock and Spinach Cheese Melt

Prep time: 5 minutes | Cook time: 15 minutes | Serves 2

200g baby spinach
85g low-fat soft cheese
2 (5-ounce / 142-g) pieces of skinless

haddock
1 large tomato, sliced
2 tablespoons grated Parmesan

1. Heat oven to 200ºF (93ºC). Pile the spinach into a large pan over a medium heat, turning it over and over until wilted. Remove from the heat and drain off the excess liquid.
2. Mix spinach with the soft cheese, then place in the bottom of a small baking dish and sit haddock pieces on top. Lay sliced tomatoes on top of the fish and sprinkle with the Parmesan.
3. Bake for 15 to 20 minutes (depending on thickness of the haddock), or until the fish flakes easily.

Savory Haddock Stew with Spice

Prep time: 15 minutes | Cook time: 33 minutes | Serves 6

¼ cup coconut oil
1 tablespoon minced garlic
1 onion, chopped
2 celery stalks, chopped
½ fennel bulb, thinly sliced
1 carrot, diced
1 sweet potato, diced
1 (15-ounce / 425-g) can low-sodium diced tomatoes
1 cup coconut milk
1 cup low-sodium chicken broth
¼ teaspoon red pepper flakes
12 ounces (340 g) haddock, cut into 1-inch chunks
2 tablespoons chopped fresh cilantro, for garnish

1. In a large saucepan, heat the coconut oil over medium-high heat.
2. Add the garlic, onion, and celery and sauté for about 4 minutes, stirring occasionally, or until they are tender.
3. Stir in the fennel bulb, carrot, and sweet potato and sauté for 4 minutes more.
4. Add the diced tomatoes, coconut milk, chicken broth, and red pepper flakes and stir to incorporate, then bring the mixture to a boil.
5. Once it starts to boil, reduce the heat to low, and bring to a simmer for about 15 minutes, or until the vegetables are fork-tender.
6. Add the haddock chunks and continue simmering for about 10 minutes, or until the fish is cooked through.
7. Sprinkle the cilantro on top for garnish before serving.

Keto Haddock Chowder

Prep time: 10 minutes | Cook time: 35 minutes | Serves 4

1 tablespoon extra-virgin olive oil
½ cup chopped onion
2 garlic cloves, minced
2 cups chopped turnips
2 cups vegetable broth
2 cups full-fat coconut milk
½ teaspoon salt
¼ teaspoon freshly ground black pepper
1 pound (454 g) firm haddock, cut into 4 pieces
1 tablespoon minced fresh thyme

1. In a large soup pot, heat the olive oil over medium-high heat. Add the onion and garlic and cook for 2 minutes, or until the onion has begun to soften.
2. Stir in the turnips and vegetable broth. Bring to a boil, then reduce the heat to medium-low and simmer for 30 minutes, or until the turnips are fork-tender.
3. Remove from the heat and use a potato masher to mash the turnips into the liquid.
4. Return the pot to the heat and add the coconut milk, salt, and pepper and bring to a boil.
5. Add the haddock to the pot, reduce the heat to medium, and simmer for 3 minutes, or until the fish flakes easily with a fork.
6. Sprinkle with the thyme before serving.

Smoked Haddock Fillet & Sweetcorn Stew

Prep time: 10 minutes | Cook time: 30 minutes | Serves 4

25g butter
1 onion, chopped
3 celery sticks, chopped
200g baby new potatoes, halved
2 cups chicken stock
2 cups semi-skimmed milk
300g frozen sweetcorn (or drained weight from a can)
400g undyed smoked haddock fillets, skinless and boneless
Small pack flat-leaf parsley, leaves only, chopped

1. Heat the butter in a large saucepan until melted.
2. Add the onion, celery and potatoes, and cook gently for 10 minutess until the onion is really soft.
3. Pour in the chicken stock followed by the milk and stir well. Bring to a simmer and cook for another 15 minutes, stirring occasionally. Season to taste.
4. Add the sweetcorn, then place the haddock fillets on top. Let the mixture simmer very gently for 5 minutess or until the haddock just starts to break up.
5. To serve, carefully stir in half of the parsley, ladle the chowder into individual bowls and scatter with the remaining parsley at the table.

Haddock Fillets & Jarlsberg Gratin

Prep time: 5 minutes | Cook time: 1¹/₁₂ hours | Serves 6

15g butter, plus extra for the dish	skin removed
½ tablespoon sunflower, groundnut or rapeseed oil	800g potatoes
	2 cups double cream
	1 cup soured cream
2 onions, finely sliced	160g Jarlsberg cheese, grated
600g haddock fillet,	

1. Heat the oven to 200ºF (93ºC) with a baking sheet inside. Heat the butter and oil in a heavy-bottomed pan over a medium-low heat, and cook the onions until golden and soft, about 15 to 20 minutes.
2. Cut the haddock into 2 x 4cm pieces. Cut the potatoes into wafer-thin slices using a mandoline or sharp knife, if the slices aren't thin enough, the potatoes won't become tender while the fish cooks.
3. Heat the double cream and soured cream in a saucepan large enough to hold all the potatoes. Bring to just under the boil, then add the potatoes and season well. Cook gently for about 10 minutes until the potatoes are just slightly softened.
4. Butter a 2-liter pie dish. Spoon in a third of the potatoes, then scatter over half the onions and a quarter of the cheese. Lay half the fish pieces on top, then season. Sprinkle over another quarter of the cheese, then add another third of the potatoes, then the remaining onions and another quarter of cheese. Add the remaining fish on top, season, then scatter over the remaining potatoes. Pour over any leftover cream mixture, then sprinkle over the remaining cheese.
5. Carefully slide the dish onto the hot baking sheet in the oven and bake for 40 to 45 minutes, or until golden and the potatoes are tender.

Battered Haddock Fillets & Pesto Wrap

Prep time: 15 minutes | Cook time: 4⅓ minutes | Serves 4

4 haddock fillets	Tortilla wraps, salad leaves and sliced cucumber, to serve
Plain flour, for coating	
vegetable oil, for frying	

For the Pesto:

50g basil , leaves picked	20 to 25 g chunk of Parmesan , roughly chopped
1 garlic clove	¼ lemon, juiced
Small handful of toasted pine nuts	½ cup olive oil

For the Lemon Mayo:

4 tablespoons mayonnaise
½ lemon , zested and juiced

For the Batter:

150g plain flour	10g baking powder
100g cornflour	

1. For the pesto, whizz all ingredients in a blender, slowly pouring in the oil while blending until it forms a smooth, nutty paste. Season well and add a splash of water if it's too thick. Set aside.
2. For the lemon mayo, mix all the ingredients together and season.
3. To make the batter, sift the flours together, then whisk, while slowly adding water. Continue until your batter is a thick but runny consistency. It should stick to your finger when you dip it in. Season.
4. Set a deep-fat fryer to 350ºF (180ºC), or in a large pan filled no more than a third full, heat the oil until a piece of bread browns in 20 seconds. Meanwhile, check the haddock fillets for bones, season them and coat them in plain flour. Then dip each fillet in to the batter until each has a good coating. Place the fillets in to the deep-fat fryer or pan (make sure you give it a gentle shake so it doesn't stick to the bottom). Cook until the batter becomes brown and crisp, around 4 minutes. Remove and place on kitchen roll to soak up any oil.
5. To assemble, spread each tortilla with some of the pesto, then a tablespoon of lemon mayo. Add a handful of salad leaves and the cucumber, then top with the fish and more pesto. Season, wrap up and serve.

Zesty Haddock with Vegetables

Prep time: 10 minutes | Cook time: 14 minutes | Serves 4

600g floury potato, unpeeled, cut into chunks
140 g frozen peas
2½ tablespoons extra-virgin olive oil
Juice and zest ½ of a lemon

1 tablespoon capers, roughly chopped
2 tablespoons snipped chives
4 (120 g) haddock
2 tablespoons plain flour
Broccoli, to serve

1. Cover the potatoes in cold water, bring to the boil, then turn to a simmer. Cook for 10 minutes until tender, adding peas for the final minute of cooking. Drain and roughly crush together, adding plenty of seasoning and 1 tablespoon oil. Keep warm.
2. Meanwhile, for the dressing, mix 1 tablespoon oil, the lemon juice and zest, capers and chives with some seasoning.
3. Dust the fish in the flour, tapping off any excess and season. Heat remaining oil in a non-stick frying pan. Fry the fish for 2 to 3 minutes on each side until cooked, then add the dressing and warm through. Serve with the crush and broccoli.

Baked Haddock with Truffled Macaroni

Prep time: 15 minutes | Cook time: 35 minutes | Serves 4

For the Macaroni:
250g macaroni
1 teaspoon olive oil
1 small onion , finely chopped
2 cups milk
300g smoked haddock

1 tablespoon truffle oil
50g soft butte , plus extra for the dish
25g plain flour
100g gruyère, coarsely grated

For the Breadcrumbs:
50g white breadcrumbs
Small pack parsley, leaves picked
Small thyme sprig, leaves picked
Small pack tarragon,

leaves picked
1 garlic clove, roughly chopped
Small piece of butter
Drizzle of truffle oil, plus extra to serve

1. Blend together all the ingredients for the breadcrumbs in a food processor until roughly chopped, season, then set aside.
2. Boil the macaroni 1 minute less than the time on the pack, drain, toss in the olive oil and set aside.
3. Tip the onion, milk and the smoked haddock into a pan and season. Simmer gently for 10 minutes, then remove the haddock. Flake the flesh and drizzle with the truffle oil and set aside.
4. Mix the butter and flour together to make a paste. Over a low heat, whisk the paste into the hot milk and bring to the boil, stirring all the time. Remove from the heat and add half the grated cheese and stir well.
5. Take the pan off the heat, tip the pasta into the sauce and mix well, then fold through the haddock and season with ground black pepper. The sauce may seem a little thin, but it'll thicken as it cooks. Butter a large ovenproof dish and tip in all the macaroni, then finish by scattering over the rest of the cheese and most of the breadcrumbs. This can be prepared a day ahead, covered and kept in the fridge.
6. To cook, heat oven to 200ºF (93ºC).
7. Bake for 20 minutes until bubbling and sprinkle with the rest of the breadcrumbs. Bake for 5 minutes more, then drizzle a little more truffle oil on top, and scatter some extra herbs, if you like.

Herb-Crusted Haddock Fillets

Prep time: 10 minutes | Cook time: 15 minutes | Serves 4

1 tablespoon olive oil, plus extra
4 (5-ounce / 113-g) skinless unsmoked or smoked haddock fillets
2 handfuls cherry tomatoes
3 tablespoons mayonnaise
1 teaspoon garlic paste or 1 garlic clove, crushed
100 g white breadcrumbs
Zest and juice of 1 lemon
2 handfuls flat-leaf parsley, leaves roughly chopped

1. Heat oven to 220ºF (104ºC). Lightly oil a large baking tray, then lay the haddock and tomatoes alongside each other. In a small bowl, mix the mayonnaise with the garlic paste or crushed garlic, then spread evenly over the fish.
2. In a separate bowl, toss together the breadcrumbs, lemon zest, juice and parsley, and season to taste. Top the fish with the breadcrumb mixture. Drizzle olive oil over the fish and tomatoes, and bake for 15 minutes or until the fish flakes slightly when pressed and the crust is golden and crunchy.

New England-Style Haddock

Prep time: 5 minutes | Cook time: 15 minutes | Serves 4

1- to 1½- pounds (454-to 680-g) haddock patted dry
1 cup plain breadcrumbs or seasoned
6 tablespoons salted
butter melted
Kosher salt and black pepper
Lemon wedges and fresh parsley for serving (optional)

1. Preheat oven to 350ºF (180ºC).
2. Put a spoonful of the melted butter in a baking sheet or dish and spread to coat the bottom.
3. Combine the bread crumbs (1 cup) with the rest of the 6 tablespoons of melted butter.
4. Salt and pepper both sides of the fish liberally (I used about 1 teaspoon kosher salt and ¼ teaspoon pepper), and lay in the buttered baking dish.
5. Spread all of the bread crumbs evenly over the fish
6. Bake for 15 minutes, or until fish is cooked thoroughly (and flakes easily).
7. Serve with a squeeze of lemon juice and a garnish of fresh parsley, if desired.

Chapter 19 Branzino

Roasted Branzino

Prep time: 5 minutes | Cook time: 13 minutes | Serves 2 to 4

2 whole branzino, cleaned, with head and tail intact
Extra-virgin olive oil
½ teaspoon salt

½ teaspoon freshly ground black pepper
1 lemon, sliced
6 garlic cloves, diced

1. Rinse fish, pat dry, and place on a lightly oiled baking pan or wood plank (increase baking time by 50% for wood).
2. Brush fish inside and out with olive oil, and sprinkle with salt and pepper. Stuff cavity of each fish with 2 or 3 lemon slices. spread garlic inside and over both sides of fish. Bake, uncovered, at 400°F (205°C) for 5 minutes.
3. Turn fish over; cook 5 more minutes. Turn oven to broil, and cook fish 3 to 5 minutes or until skin blisters and fish flakes easily with a fork.
4. Remove fish from oven, and transfer to serving plates. Drizzle with olive oil, serve.

Whole Branzino with Caper Butter

Prep time: 10 minutes | Cook time: 16 minutes | Serves 8

1 stick unsalted butter, softened
1 tablespoon finely chopped capers
1 tablespoon fresh lemon juice
1 tablespoon chopped parsley
Salt

4 (1-pound / 454-g) whole branzino, scaled and gutted
1 lemon, sliced into 8 rounds
4 large rosemary sprigs
3 tablespoons extra-virgin olive oil

1. Preheat the oven to 425°F (220°C). In a medium bowl, mix the butter with the capers, lemon juice and parsley and season with salt. Keep at room temperature.
2. Season the branzino cavities with salt and stuff 2 lemon rounds and 1 rosemary sprig in each. Season the fish with salt.
3. In a large, nonstick, ovenproof skillet, heat 2 tablespoons of the olive oil until shimmering.

4. Add 2 of the branzino and cook over high heat until the skin is browned and crisp, about 3 minutes per side. Transfer the fish to a large rimmed baking sheet. Repeat with the remaining 1 tablespoon of olive oil and 2 stuffed branzino. Roast the fish in the oven for about 10 minutes, until just cooked through.
5. Serve whole or filleted, passing the caper butter at the table.

Whole-Roasted Branzino

Prep time: 10 minutes | Cook time: 14 minutes | Serves 6

4 tablespoons melted butter
2 tablespoons soy sauce
juice and zest of ½ a lemon (plus 1 additional lemon, sliced into 9 rounds)
1 tablespoon parsley, chopped, plus more

for garnish
3 (16-ounce / 454-g) whole branzino, scaled, cleaned and gutted
salt
3 sprigs thyme
3 tablespoons extra virgin olive oil

1. Preheat the oven to425°F (220°C).
2. In a bowl, mix the butter with the soy sauce, juice and zest of ½ a lemon, and 1 tablespoon chopped parsley. Season the branzino cavities with salt and stuff 3 lemon rounds and a sprig of thyme into each. In a large, nonstick, ovenproof skillet, heat the olive oil until shimmering.
3. Add the branzino and cook over high heat until the skin is browned and crisp, about 2 minutes per side. You may need to do this in batches.
4. Transfer the fish to a large rimmed baking sheet. Drizzle with the butter mixture, season with more salt to taste and roast for 9 minutes. Finish under the broiler for 1 to 2 minutes. Keep an eye on it to prevent burning.
5. Garnish with more chopped parsley and serve!

Grilled Branzino with Rosemary Vinaigrette

Prep time: 10 minutes | Cook time: 9⅔ minutes | Serves 2

2 tablespoons onion, minced
1 teaspoon Dijon mustard
1 teaspoon kosher salt
3 tablespoons white wine vinegar
1 large garlic clove, chopped

1 heaping tablespoon fresh rosemary, minced
½ cup extra virgin olive oil, plus more for coating the fish
1 whole branzino
Salt, preferably sea salt

1. Put the minced onion, mustard, salt, vinegar, garlic and rosemary into a blender and pulse it for about 30 seconds. Use a spatula to scrape down the sides of the blender and purée it again for 10 to 20 seconds. Scrape the sides down again.
2. Turn the blender on low and take the removable cap off the lid. Hold your hand over the hole, as it might spit a little. Pour the olive oil in slowly and put the cap back on. Turn the blender off and scrape the sides down one more time. Turn the blender back on low, then high for 60 seconds.
3. Rinse the fish under cold water. Now make sure its gills and scales are all removed; your fishmonger is not always so diligent about this task, and no one wants a scale on their plate. Gills can impart a bitter taste to the fish, so they need to go, too.
4. Make cuts on the sides of the fish: Use a very sharp knife and make several slashes on the sides of the fish, maybe every inch or so. Make the cuts at an angle to the side of the fish, and slice down until you feel the spine. Do not sever the spine, however. These cuts will help the fish cook faster. Rub olive oil all over the fish and set it aside.
5. Prepare the grill for high, direct heat: Scrape down the grates well and close the lid. Salt the fish well. Now grab a paper towel, a set of tongs, and some cheap vegetable oil. Bring all of this out to the grill.
6. Fold the paper towel over several times, moisten it with the vegetable oil, and hold it with tongs to wipe down the grill grates.
7. Grill the fish: Lay the fish down on the grill and close the lid. Let this cook for 5 minutes without touching it.
8. Open the lid and, using tongs, gently see if you can lift the fish off the grates cleanly. Don't actually do this, but check for sticky spots. If you have some, get a metal spatula. Use the spatula to dislodge the fish from the sticky spots.
9. Using tongs in one hand, and the spatula in another, gently flip the fish over. If it sticks, no biggie. It happens sometimes.
10. Finish grilling the fish: Once the fish has been flipped, let it cook another 3 to 5 minutes with the lid on. Again, test for sticky spots with the tongs and spatula. Dislodge them gently and gently lift the fish onto a plate.
11. If the fish is too long or seems like it might break in half, use two metal spatulas instead of the tongs-and-spatula set-up.
12. Drizzle the vinaigrette over the fish and serve at once.

Easy Branzino Butter Recipe

Prep time: 5 minutes | Cook time: 7 minutes | Serves 4

4 (1 pound / 454 g) skin-on branzino fillets
2 tablespoons minced garlic
1 tablespoon fresh parsley leaves,

chopped
¼ teaspoon kosher salt
⅛ teaspoon ground black pepper
½ stick unsalted butter, melted

1. Sprinkle the fish on the fleshy side with the garlic, parsley, salt and pepper, and set aside.
2. Place a large skillet over medium-high heat, add the butter, and then place the fish skin-side down.
3. Cook for 4 minutes then carefully flip and cook for another 3 minutes.
4. Place the fish on a paper-towel-lined plate to remove any excess fat, then serve.

Mediterranean Branzino

Prep time: 10 minutes | Cook time: 25 minutes | Serves 4

2 tablespoons olive oil, divided
1 red onion, chopped
Salt and ground black pepper, to taste
2 whole branzino fish, cleaned
2 wedges fresh lemon
2 sprigs fresh rose-mary
½ cup white wine
¼ cup lemon juice
1 tablespoon fresh oregano leaves
¼ cup chopped Italian flat-leaf parsley
2 lemon wedges

1. Preheat oven to 325ºF (163ºC).
2. Drizzle 1 tablespoon olive oil into a large baking pan; add onion and season with salt and pepper.
3. Place the 2 cleaned fish into the baking pan and stuff each cavity with 1 lemon wedge, 1 rosemary sprig, and some of the red onion.
4. Pour white wine and lemon juice over each fish and sprinkle with oregano. Drizzle the remaining 1 tablespoon olive oil over the 2 fish.
5. Bake in the preheated oven until fish is opaque and flakes easily with a fork, about 25 minutes. Gently slide a spatula between the bones to separate fish, remove all the bones.
6. Serve fish on a platter and garnish with parsley and lemon wedges.

Bruschetta Branzino Fillets

Prep time: 10 minutes | Cook time: 8 minutes | Serves 4

For the Bruschetta:
1 cup chopped cherry or grape tomatoes
½ cup fresh basil chiffonade
2 tablespoons finely
For the Branzino:
1 tablespoon extra-virgin olive oil, divided
4 (6-ounce / 170-g) Branzino fillets, with
chopped red onion
1 garlic clove, finely chopped
⅛ teaspoon sea salt

skin
½ teaspoon sea salt
¼ teaspoon freshly ground black pepper

To Make the Bruschetta
1. In a large bowl, toss together the tomatoes, basil, red onion, garlic, and salt. Set aside.

To Make the Branzino
1. In a cast iron skillet, heat ½ tablespoon of the olive oil over medium-high heat.
2. Season the fish with salt and pepper on both sides.
3. Once the oil is hot, place two of the fillets, skin-side down, in the skillet. Sear for 5 minutes on the skin side before carefully flipping. Let cook for another 3 minutes, until the fish flakes with a fork. Repeat with the remaining oil and two other fillets.
4. Top the fish with bruschetta before serving.

Branzino Fillets with Citrus Gremolata

Prep time: 5 minutes | Cook time: 12 minutes | Serves 4

2 tablespoons olive oil, plus more for the pan
6 (3- to 4-ounce/ 85- to 113-g) branzino fillets, bones removed
Kosher salt and freshly ground black pepper
2 lemons
2 oranges
½ cup flat-leaf parsley, finely chopped
1 tablespoon good-quality extra-virgin olive oil
Pinch crushed red pepper flakes

1. Preheat the oven to 375ºF (190ºC). Generously grease a large rimmed baking sheet with olive oil.
2. Arrange the fillets on the baking sheet in one layer. Drizzle the 2 tablespoons of olive oil over the fish and season with salt and black pepper. Bake until the fish is flaky and just fully cooked through, about 12 minutes.
3. Meanwhile, finely grate the zest of 1 lemon and 1 orange into a small bowl and add the parsley, good olive oil, red pepper flakes, a pinch of salt, a few grinds of black pepper, juice of half the lemon and juice of half the orange. Stir gently to combine.
4. Slice the remaining lemon and orange. Serve the fish topped with the gremolata and citrus slices.

Branzino with Preserved Lemon Gremolata

Prep time: 10 minutes | Cook time: 9 minutes | Serves 4

1 (1- to 2-pound / 567- to 907-g) whole branzino, cleaned, gutted, descaled
1 tablespoon olive oil
1 teaspoon sea salt
½ teaspoon pepper
1 lemon
A small handful of fresh herbs- thyme, rosemary, sage or parsley

Preserved Lemon Gremolata:

1 bunch flat-leaf parsley, finely chopped
¼ cup chopped preserved lemons (rind and flesh)
2 garlic cloves, finely chopped
½ cup olive oil
cracked pepper
Chili flakes (optional)

1. When you buy a whole fish- make sure it is gutted and descaled.
2. Rinse it off inside and out and pat it extra dry.
3. Brush liberally with oil.
4. Season generously with salt and pepper, inside and out.
5. Slice some lemons and place inside the cavity of the fish. Tuck in some fresh herbs- thyme, rosemary, sage or parsley.
6. Using a sharp knife, cut 2 to 3 slits into each side of the fish at the thicker end. The tail end will cook faster than the head end, so this will help cook to evenly on the grill.
7. Heat the grill to medium-high heat, 400°F (205°C) and oil the grates. If possible, lower heat on one side.
8. Place the fish on hot, greased grill, with the tail end on the cooler side. Grill, covered, not moving it for about 5 minutes for a ½- to 2-pound fish, or until you see grill marks.
9. Use a thin metal spatula and tongs to carefully flip. Cover, grill until crisp with visible grill marks and eyes cloud, another 4 to 5 minutes.
10. While the fish is grilling make the flavorful Preserved Lemon Gremolata, placing all ingredients in a bowl and stir.
11. Place fish on a platter and right before serving spoon the flavorful Gremolata over top. Yes, please eat the delicious crispy skin!
12. Enjoy this with Everyday Quinoa and a leafy green salad.

Branzino with Shaved Fennel Salad

Prep time: 10 minutes | Cook time: 16 minutes | Serves 2 to 3

For the Fennel Salad:

1 medium (10-ounce/ 283-g) fennel bulb
¼ to ½ cup packed fresh flat-leaf parsley leaves, chopped
3 tablespoons extra-virgin olive oil
2 teaspoons white wine vinegar
Kosher salt and freshly ground black pepper

For the Branzino:

2 or 3 (1-pound / 454-g) whole branzino, cleaned
6 tablespoons olive oil
2 lemons, preferably Meyer, sliced, plus more for serving

Make the Fennel Salad

1. Trim the fennel, reserving the fronds. Halve the bulb lengthwise and cut away the core if it seems tough.
2. Using a mandoline or other handheld slicer, thinly shave the fennel into long ribbons. Finely chop the fronds.
3. In a medium bowl, combine the shaved fennel, fennel fronds, parsley, olive oil, and vinegar and toss to coat well. Season to taste with salt and pepper.

Make the Branzino

1. Position a rack in the upper third of the oven and preheat the oven to 400°F (200°C). Line a rimmed baking sheet with parchment paper.
2. Rinse and pat the fish dry. Place it on the prepared baking sheet. Drizzle 2 to 3 tablespoons of oil over each fish and rub it all over, being sure to get it into the cavity.
3. Generously season the entire fish, inside and out, with salt and pepper. Place the lemon slices in the cavity, overlapping them slightly.
4. Bake the fish until it's slightly opaque throughout and the lemons have wilted, 10 to 15 minutes. It should be almost but not quite completely cooked through.
5. Turn on the broiler to its highest setting and broil, flipping once, until the skin crisps and the fish is opaque when tested with the tip of a knife, 3 to 5 minutes per side.
6. Serve the roasted fish with the fennel salad and extra lemon slices, if desired.

Lemon Roasted Branzino Fillets

Prep time: 15 minutes | Cook time: 21⅙ minutes | Serves 2

4 tablespoons extra-virgin olive oil, divided
2 (8-ounce / 227-g) branzino fillets, preferably at least 1-inch thick
1 garlic clove, minced
1 bunch scallions (white part only), thinly sliced
10 to 12 small cherry tomatoes, halved
1 large carrot, cut into ¼-inch rounds
½ cup dry white wine
2 tablespoons paprika
2 teaspoons kosher salt
½ tablespoon ground chili pepper
2 rosemary sprigs or 1 tablespoon dried rosemary
1 small lemon, thinly sliced
½ cup sliced pitted kalamata olives

1. Heat a large ovenproof skillet over high heat until hot, about 2 minutes. Add 1 tablespoon of olive oil and heat for 10 to 15 seconds until it shimmers.
2. Add the branzino fillets, skin-side up, and sear for 2 minutes. Flip the fillets and cook for an additional 2 minutes. Set aside.
3. Swirl 2 tablespoons of olive oil around the skillet to coat evenly.
4. Add the garlic, scallions, tomatoes, and carrot, and sauté for 5 minutes, or until softened.
5. Add the wine, stirring until all ingredients are well combined. Carefully place the fish over the sauce.
6. Preheat the oven to 450ºF (235ºC).
7. Brush the fillets with the remaining 1 tablespoon of olive oil and season with paprika, salt, and chili pepper. Top each fillet with a rosemary sprig and lemon slices. Scatter the olives over fish and around the skillet.
8. Roast for about 10 minutes until the lemon slices are browned. Serve hot.

Spciy Branzino with Wine Sauce

Prep time: 15 minutes | Cook time: 15 minutes | Serves 2 to 3

Sauce:
¾ cup dry white wine
2 tablespoons white wine vinegar
2 tablespoons cornstarch
1 tablespoon honey

Fish:
1 large branzino, butterflied and patted dry
2 tablespoons onion powder
2 tablespoons paprika
½ tablespoon salt
6 tablespoons extra-virgin olive oil, divided
4 garlic cloves, thinly sliced
4 scallions, both green and white parts, thinly sliced
1 large tomato, cut into ¼-inch cubes
4 kalamata olives, pitted and chopped

1. Make the sauce: Mix together the white wine, vinegar, cornstarch, and honey in a bowl and keep stirring until the honey has dissolved. Set aside.
2. Make the fish: Place the fish on a clean work surface, skin-side down. Sprinkle the onion powder, paprika, and salt to season. Drizzle 2 tablespoons of olive oil all over the fish.
3. Heat 2 tablespoons of olive oil in a large skillet over high heat until it shimmers.
4. Add the fish, skin-side up, to the skillet and brown for about 2 minutes. Carefully flip the fish and cook for another 3 minutes. Remove from the heat to a plate and set aside.
5. Add the remaining 2 tablespoons olive oil to the skillet and swirl to coat. Stir in the garlic cloves, scallions, tomato, and kalamata olives and sauté for 5 minutes. Pour in the prepared sauce and stir to combine.
6. Return the fish (skin-side down) to the skillet, flipping to coat in the sauce. Reduce the heat to medium-low, and cook for an additional 5 minutes until cooked through.
7. Using a slotted spoon, transfer the fish to a plate and serve warm.

Chapter 20 Mahi-Mahi

Mahi-Mahi Fillets and Tomato Bowls

Prep time: 10 minutes | Cook time: 14 minutes | Serves 3

3 (4-ounce / 113-g) mahi-mahi fillets	lemon juice
1½ tablespoons olive oil	Salt and freshly ground black pepper, to taste
½ yellow onion, sliced	1 (14-ounce / 397-g) can sugar-free diced tomatoes
½ teaspoon dried oregano	
1 tablespoon fresh	

1. Add the olive oil to the Instant Pot. Select the Sauté function on it.
2. Add all the ingredient to the pot except the fillets. Cook them for 10 minutes.
3. Press the Cancel key, then add the mahi-mahi fillets to the sauce.
4. Cover the fillets with sauce by using a spoon.
5. Secure the lid and set the Manual function at High Pressure for 4 minutes.
6. After the beep, do a quick release then remove the lid.
7. Serve the fillets with their sauce, poured on top.

Baked Mahi-Mahi Fillets

Prep time: 10 minutes | Cook time: 0 minutes | Serves 4

4 (6 ounces / 170 g) mahi-mahi fillets	1 tablespoon olive oil
2 tablespoons butter	1 lemon

Kickin' Cajun Seasoning Mix:

½ teaspoons onion powder	1 teaspoon dried oregano leaves
1 teaspoon garlic powder	1 teaspoon fine grain sea salt
1 teaspoon smoked paprika	½ teaspoon freshly ground black pepper
1 teaspoon dried thyme leaves	½ teaspoon cayenne pepper, or to taste

1. Combine all Kickin' Cajun Seasoning Mix ingredients in a small bowl.

2. Pat fillets dry with paper towels. Season the fillets liberally with Kickin' Cajun Spice Mix on both sides, pressing the seasoning into the fish with your hands. Wash hands thoroughly.
3. Place a large saute pan over medium-high heat and add butter and oil. When the fat is nice and hot, add the seasoned fish. Cook, undisturbed, for several minutes, until golden brown on one side. Flip fish over and continue to cook until opaque and completely cooked through.
4. Squeeze lemon juice over the fish and serve.

Ginger Glazed Mahi-Mahi Fillets

Prep time: 10 minutes | Cook time: 8 minutes | Serves 4

3 tablespoons honey	or to taste
3 tablespoons soy sauce	2 teaspoons olive oil
3 tablespoons balsamic vinegar	4 (6-ounce / 170-g) mahi-mahi fillets
1 teaspoon grated fresh ginger root	salt and pepper, to taste
1 garlic clove, crushed	1 tablespoon vegetable oil

1. In a shallow glass dish, stir together the honey, soy sauce, balsamic vinegar, ginger, garlic and olive oil. Season fish fillets with salt and pepper, and place them into the dish. If the fillets have skin on them, place them skin side down. Cover, and refrigerate for 20 minutes to marinate.
2. Heat vegetable oil in a large skillet over medium-high heat. Remove fish from the dish, and reserve marinade. Fry fish for 4 to 6 minutes on each side, turning only once, until fish flakes easily with a fork. Remove fillets to a serving platter and keep warm.
3. Pour reserved marinade into the skillet, and heat over medium heat until the mixture reduces to a glaze consistently. Spoon glaze over fish, and serve immediately.

Mahi-Mahi Instant Pot Meal

Prep time: 10 minutes | Cook time: 5 minutes | Serves 4

1½ cup water
4 (4-ounce / 113-g) mahi-mahi fillets
Salt and freshly ground black pepper, to taste
4 garlic cloves, minced

4 tablespoons fresh lime juice
4 tablespoons erythritol
2 teaspoons red pepper flakes, crushed

1. Sprinkle some salt and pepper over mahi-mahi fillets for seasoning.
2. In a separate bowl add all the remaining ingredients and mix well.
3. Add the water to the Instant pot and place the trivet in it.
4. Arrange the seasoned fillets over the trivet in a single layer.
5. Pour the prepared sauce on top of each fillet.
6. Cover and secure the lid.
7. Set the Steam function on your cooker for 5 minutes.
8. Once it beeps, do a quick release then remove the lid.
9. Serve the steaming hot mahi-mahi and enjoy.

Mahi-Mahi Fillets and Asparagus

Prep time: 10 minutes | Cook time: 11 minutes | Serves 4

3 tablespoons butter, divided
2 tablespoons extra-virgin olive oil, divided
4 (4-ounce / 113-g) mahi-mahi fillets
Kosher salt
Freshly ground black pepper
1 pound (454 g) asparagus

3 garlic cloves, minced
¼ teaspoon crushed red pepper flakes
1 lemon, sliced
Zest and juice of 1 lemon
1 tablespoon freshly chopped parsley, plus more for garnish

1. In a large skillet over medium heat, melt 1 tablespoon each of butter and olive oil. Add mahi-mahi and season with salt and pepper. Cook until golden, 4 to 5 minutes per side. Transfer to a plate.

2. To skillet, add remaining 1 tablespoon oil. Add asparagus and cook until tender, 2 to 4 minutes. Season with salt and pepper and transfer to a plate.
3. To skillet, add remaining 2 tablespoons butter. Once melted, add garlic and red pepper flakes and cook until fragrant, 1 minute, then stir in lemon, zest, juice, and parsley. Remove from heat, then return mahi-mahi and asparagus to skillet and spoon over sauce.
4. Garnish with more parsley before serving.

Crispy Parmesan Mahi-Mahi

Prep time: 10 minutes | Cook time: 18 minutes | Serves 4

4 (20- to 24-ounce / 567- to 680.4-g) pieces of mahi-mahi
Flour mixture:
1/3 cup all purpose flour
½ teaspoon garlic powder
2 tablespoon grated Parmesan Cheese salt
Egg mixture:
2 eggs

Salt
Fresh cracked black pepper
Panko mixture:
½ cup Panko bread crumbs
½ cup grated Parmesan Cheese
1 tablespoon parsley
½ teaspoon garlic powder
Salt

1. Preheat the oven to 425ºF (220ºC) and line a rimmed baking sheet with parchment paper or aluminum foil.
2. Set three wide and shallow bowls in front of you.
3. Mix flour with salt, garlic powder, and grated Parmesan Cheese in first bowl. Whisk eggs with salt and pepper in another bowl.
4. Mix Panko bread crumbs, grated Parmesan Cheese, parsley, garlic powder, and salt in a third bowl.
5. Coat each piece of fish in flour first, then in egg, and last in the Panko mixture. Pat the coating onto the fish firmly and lay in on the prepared baking sheet.
6. Bake for 18 to 22 minutes, depending on the thickness of the fish.
7. Serve.

Roasted Mahi-Mahi Recipe

Prep time: 10 minutes | Cook time: 8 minutes | Serves 4

For the Lemon Garlic Mixture:

2 tablespoons salted butter, softened to room temperature
1 tablespoon freshly chopped chives or parsley
2 tablespoons garlic cloves, minced

⅛ teaspoon kosher salt
¼ teaspoon freshly ground black pepper
1 tablespoon juice from fresh lemon
1 tablespoon grated lemon peel

For the Fish:

2 tablespoons olive oil
4 (4 ounces / 113 g) mahi-mahi fillets, 1-inch thick

Kosher salt and freshly ground black pepper

1. Preheat oven to 400ºF (205ºC) with rack on middle position.
2. Lemon Garlic Mixture (can be made ahead), in a small pan, combine all Lemon Garlic Mixture ingredients and stir to fully combine. Set aside.
3. Pat-dry all excess moisture from the fish fillets with paper towels. This step is important, so be sure to pat off as much moisture as you can. Evenly sprinkle both sides of fillets with pinches of kosher salt and freshly ground black pepper. Set aside.
4. In a large oven-proof pan, heat the olive oil over high heat. Once oil is sizzling hot, add the fish fillets to pan and let cook until browned on one side, about 3 minutes, do not move fish around.
5. Carefully flip fish fillets over to the other side, turn stove burner off, and immediately transfer pan into already-hot oven.
6. Roast fish at 400ºF (205ºC) about 5 minutes or just until the top is golden and center is just cooked through. Take care not to overcook. A minute before fish is done cooking in oven, heat your small pan of prepared lemon-garlic mixture over medium high heat, constantly stirring, just until melted and bubbly.
7. Immediately turn heat off and pour mixture over the cooked fish. Be sure to pour on any juices from the fish pan as well. Serve with extra lemon slices for garnish.

Savory Mahi-Mahi and Pineapple Salsa

Prep time: 10 minutes | Cook time: 8 minutes | Serves 2

For the Pineapple Salsa:

1 cup of finely diced pineapple
1 tablespoon finely diced red onion
1 tablespoon of finely chopped cilantro

leaves
1 tablespoon of fresh lime juice
Sea salt, to taste
1 to 2 dashes of cayenne pepper

For the Mahi-Mahi:

2 (6-ounce / 170-g) skinless mahi-mahi fillets, patted dry
4 teaspoons of cooking oil
¼ teaspoon of sea salt
½ teaspoon of black

pepper
½ teaspoon of granulated garlic
½ teaspoon of Cajun seasoning
½ a lime, cut into wedges, for serving

1. Combine all the fruit salsa ingredients in a medium bowl, stir well, and set aside to macerate as you're fixing the fish.
2. Coat both sides of each mahi-mahi fillet with cooking oil, followed by the sea salt, black pepper, granulated garlic, and Cajun seasoning.
3. Place a 10 to 12-inch heavy-bottomed skillet over medium heat. When the skillet is warm, add the additional ½ tablespoons of cooking oil . When the surface of the oil is just starting to shimmer, add both fillets.
4. Cook the mahi-mahi fillets for about 5 minutes on the first side (watch the sides and you'll see them go from transparent to opaque halfway up the fish), then flip and cook another 3 to 5 minutes (depending on the thickness of the fillets) or until the fish is completely opaque, but not dry.
5. Promptly remove the fillets from the skillet (they will overcook if left in the pan, even with the heat off), top each one with ½ the pineapple salsa and serve immediately with lime wedges and your favorite side dishes.

Mahi-Mahi Fillets with Balsami Salad

Prep time: 10 minutes | Cook time: 4 minutes | Serves 4

4 mahi-mahi fillets
3 tablespoons olive oil
3 garlic cloves, finely minced
2 teaspoons dried ba-
For the Salad:
2 roma tomatoes, diced
2 tablespoons chopped fresh basil
½ tablespoon olive oil
1 garlic clove, minced

sil, or 2 tablespoons chopped fresh basil
½ teaspoon salt
¼ teaspoon fresh ground black pepper

Salt and fresh ground pepper, to taste
Fresh grated Parmesan
Balsamic glaze, for topping

Grill Method

1. Preheat an outdoor grill to medium-high heat; about 425ºF (220ºC) to 450ºF (235ºC).
2. Pat dry the fish fillets and set on a plate.
3. In a mixing bowl, whisk together the oil, garlic, basil, salt and pepper. Brush fish with the oil mixture.
4. Brush grill grates with oil so that the fish doesn't stick.
5. Grill the fish for 4 to 5 minutes per side, or until nice golden grill marks appear and the flesh is set. Don't overcook or the fish will be dry and rubbery.
6. In the meantime, prepare the salad by combining prepared tomatoes, basil, oil, garlic, salt and pepper in a mixing bowl; stir until well incorporated.
7. Remove fish from the grill and transfer to a plate. Add some salad over each fish fillet.
8. Grate fresh Parmesan cheese over the salad and drizzle with balsamic glaze. Serve and enjoy!

Mahi-Mahi with Avocado Salsa

Prep time: 15 minutes | Cook time: 8 minutes | Serves 4

1 tablespoon olive oil
4 mahi-mahi fish
Brown Butter Lime Sauce:
6 tablespoons Butter
3 tablespoons fresh lime juice
1 teaspoon honey
Avocado Salsa:
1 avocado chopped
1 roma tomato chopped
½ of a small red onion, chopped
½ cup corn

fillets
salt and pepper

1 garlic clove, minced
½ tespoon salt
½ teaspoon pepper

Juice from 2 limes
2 tablespoons cilantro, finely chopped
⅛ teaspoons dash of salt

To Make the Brown Butter Lime Sauce

1. In a large skillet over medium high heat, add the olive oil. Salt and paper the mahi-mahi and cook until golden, 4 to 5 minutes each side.
2. Heat the butter into a small saucepan. Swirl the butter occasionally until it has turned a light brown color and is fragrant. Remove from heat and whisk the garlic, honey, salt and pepper into the sauce.
3. Add the fish back to the skillet.

To Make the Avocado Salsa

1. Mix the avocado, Roma tomato, red onion, chopped cilantro, salt and juice from the limes in a small mixing bowl. Top the mahi-mahi with the avocado salsa.

Grilled Mahi-Mahi with Mojo Sauce

Prep time: 10 minutes | Cook time: 11 minutes | Serves 2

2 garlic cloves, chopped
2 tablespoons extra-virgin olive oil, plus extra for brushing
¼ cup freshly squeezed lime juice (about 2 limes)
½ teaspoon kosher salt
2 tablespoons chopped fresh cilantro leaves plus 2 sprigs for garnish
2 (5- to 6-ounce /142- to 170-g) mahi-mahi fillets
Extra-virgin olive oil
Kosher salt and freshly ground black pepper
Mixed greens, for serving

1. Put the garlic and olive in a small microwave-safe bowl, cover with plastic, and microwave on HIGH until the garlic is soft and aromatic, 1 to 2 minutes. (Alternatively, heat the oil and garlic in a small saucepan over medium heat until the garlic is softened.) Stir in the lime juice, cilantro leaves, and salt. Set aside until ready to serve.
2. Prepare an outdoor grill to medium high heat. Brush the fillets all over with olive oil and season generously with salt and pepper. Lay the fish on the grill, rounded-side down, and leave it until you can lift the fish without it sticking to the grill and there are distinct grill marks, about 5 minutes. (Test it by gently lifting a corner, if it sticks, cook it a bit longer and try again). Carefully turn the fish over and cook until firm to the touch, about another 5 minutes.
3. Place a bed of greens on 2 plates. Divide the fish between the plates and brush with some of the mojo. Garnish with cilantro sprigs and serve with the sauce.

Creole Mahi-Mahi Fillets

Prep time: 15 minutes | Cook time: 36 minutes | Serves 2

2 mahi-mahi fillets, skin removed
2 tablespoons butter, unsalted
1 small onion peeled & chopped
3 tomatoes, chopped
2 garlic cloves, peeled & chopped
2 tablespoons thyme, fresh
1 hot chilli pepper, chopped
½ green pepper, cut into strips
½ red pepper cut into strips
½ cup chicken stock
½ teaspoon cinnamon
½ teaspoon paprika
½ teaspoon salt
½ teaspoon black pepper
Season the fish with salt and pepper

1. Heat the butter in a large frying pan on a medium heat.
2. Fry the fish for 3 minutes per side, then remove and set aside.
3. Fry the onion, garlic, tomatoes and thyme for 5 minutes, stirring occasionally so that the vegetables do not dry out or stick.
4. Add the cinnamon, paprika, hot pepper and stock and cook for 5 minutes
5. Add the green and red pepper strips to the pan and cover it with a lid and cook for a further 5 minutes.
6. Add the fish and simmer for 15 minutes in the sauce.
7. Serve immediately

Chapter 21 Rockfish

Colorful Alaska Rockfish Tacos

Prep time: 20 minutes | Cook time: 5½ minutes | Serves 4

2 cups very thinly shredded cabbage
1 red onion halved and very thinly sliced
1 teaspoon minced seeded jalapeno pepper
2 tablespoons cider or rice wine vinegar
3 tablespoons vegetable or canola oil divided
Coarse salt and freshly ground pepper, to taste
12 (6-inch) corn or flour tortillas
½ pound (227 g) flaky Alaska rockfish, cut into 1-inch pieces
1 teaspoon ground cumin
1 teaspoon chili powder
1 clove garlic finely minced
3 teaspoons lime juice

To Serve (Pick and Choose):
Diced avocado
Fresh cilantro leaves
Lime wedges
Tomatillo or regular salsa
Sour cream

1. Toss the cabbage, onion and jalapeno with the vinegar and 2 teaspoons of the oil, and season generously with salt and pepper. Set aside.
2. Heat a large dry skillet over medium high heat. Heat the torillas one at a time, cooking for about 30 to 60 seconds on each side, until it is browned in spots and smells slightly toasty. Stack the tortillas on a plate as they are cooked, and repeat until all of the tortillsas have been toasted. Set aside.
3. Sprinkle the pieces of fish all over with the cumin, chili powder, and salt and pepper. Heat 2 tablespoons of the oil in the large skillet over medium high heat.
4. Add ⅓ of the fish and sauté until almost cooked through, turning it as needed, about 5 minutes in all. The pieces may fall apart a little as you cook them, that's perfectly fine. During the last minute of cooking each batch, add about ⅓ of the garlic and toss over the heat.
5. Place the fish on a serving plate as it is cooked and sprinkle each batch with 1 teaspoon of the lime juice. Keep going, adding a bit more oil as needed, and then adding the fish to the same plate as it is cooked, until all of the fish is sautéed and sprinkled with juice.
6. Serve the fish with the toasted tortillas, cabbage slaw, and the toppings you like. Let everyone assemble their own tacos.

Delicious Rockfish with Ginger Sauce

Prep time: 10 minutes | Cook time: 9 minutes | Serves 2

¼ cup neutral oil, plus more for sautéing
1 scallion, thinly sliced
1 inch ginger, peeled and cut into fine matchsticks
1 serrano or jalapeño chile, thinly sliced
1 tablespoon fish sauce
1 tablespoon toasted sesame seeds
1 to 2 portions rockfish, thawed
¼ cup cilantro leaves and tender stems
Lime wedges for serving

1. In a small skillet, heat ¼ cup oil over high. Add scallion and ginger and some or all of the jalapeño (depending on heat preference). Cook, stirring until sizzling and browned in spots, about 3 minutes.
2. Transfer to a small heat-proof bowl and stir in the fish sauce and sesame seeds.
3. Heat 1 tablespoon oil in a medium non-stick skillet over medium-high heat until shimmering.
4. Season rockfish lightly with salt and pepper and add to the pan.
5. Cook, turning once, until golden and the flesh gently flakes around the edges, about 6 minutes, depending on thickness.
6. Transfer fish to plates. Stir the sauce and spoon some over the fish. Sprinkle with cilantro and serve with lime wedges on the side.
7. Serve.

Blackened Rockfish with Avocado Sauce

Prep time: 15 minutes | Cook time: 6 minutes | Serves 4

Blackened Seasoning:

1 tablespoon paprika	thyme leaves
1 teaspoon cayenne pepper	1 teaspoon dried oregano leaves
½ teaspoon garlic powder	½ teaspoon salt
1 teaspoon dried	½ teaspoon ground black pepper

Rockfish:

1 tablespoon coconut oil melted, or avocado oil	4 (1 pound / 454 g) rockfish fillets

Avocado Fish Sauce:

1 avocado	½ lime juice of, or 1 teaspoon
½ cup non-fat Greek yogurt	1 large garlic clove
1 cup water	½ teaspoon salt
2 cups cilantro with stems	½ splashes of chipotle sauce optional

Make the Rockfish

1. In a small bowl mix all the ingredients for the blackened seasoning. Set aside.
2. Preheat the oven to broil. In a 9-inch by 13-inch baking dish, drizzle 1 tablespoon of oil.
3. Rinse the Rockfish in cold water and pat dry with a paper towel. Add it to the prepared baking dish.
4. Pour blackened seasoning on top of the fish and using hands rub it into the fish and around the sides and bottom.
5. Bake uncovered 6 to 10 minutes or until the center is cooked and flakes apart when pulled with a fork (bake 6 minutes for thin slices, thick slices might need about 10 minutes). If it starts to burn on top, cover in foil.

While The Fish Bakes, Make the Avocado Sauce

1. Blend all ingredients of the avocado fish taco sauce in a blender.
2. Drizzle the avocado fish taco sauce on top of the baked rockfish.
3. Serve with a side of vegetables and rice or into tacos.

Garlic Lime Rockfish Fillet

Prep time: 10 minutes | Cook time: 30 minutes | Serves 2

2 fillets of rockfish	2 tablespoons olive oil
Celery	1 green onion, sliced, both green and white parts
Salt	
Pepper	
Paprika	2 garlic cloves, minced
Juice of one lime	

1. Preheat oven to 370ºF (188ºC). Rinse and pat fish dry. Sprinkle well with salt, pepper and paprika. You should be able to see the seasonings on the fish.
2. Place in oven-proof dish. Drizzle with olive oil and lime juice. Sprinkle with green onion and garlic.
3. Bake for 30 minutes or until fish flakes at the touch of a fork.

Moroccan Spiced Rockfish Fillets

Prep time: 5 minutes | Cook time: 38 minutes | Serves 2

2 (6 ounces / 170 g) rockfish fillets	2 large garlic cloves, minced
⅓ cup extra virgin olive oil	1 teaspoon Moroccan spice
1 lemon, zested and juiced	¼ teaspoon kosher salt

1. Preheat oven to 400º F (205ºC).
2. In a bowl, add the olive oil, lemon juice and zest, garlic, Moroccan spice, and salt. Whisk together with a fork until cohesive.
3. Place the fillets into a large freezer bag or plastic container. Pour the marinade in over the fish, seal the bag or container, and gently toss around to coat.
4. Place in the fridge and marinate for 30 minutes.
5. Transfer the marinated rockfish to a baking dish. Pour the remaining marinade over the fish and bake, uncovered, for about 8 to 10 minutes, or until the fish is opaque, flaky, and has an internal temperature of 145ºF (63ºC). Rockfish fillets aren't overly thick, so they cook quickly. Better to check on it earlier and not overcook it.
6. Serve.

Pan-Seared Rockfish Fillets

Prep time: 10 minutes | Cook time: 5 minutes | Serves 2

2 (8 ounces / 227 g) rockfish fillets
1 tablespoon flour
Pinch salt, pepper
1 tablespoon olive oil
2 tablespoons butter, divided
1 lemon, juiced
1 tablespoon capers
Small handful fresh herbs (such as fresh rosemary, chives)

1. Pat rockfish fillets dry. Dust with flour, and shake off any excess. Sprinkle them on both sides with salt and pepper.
2. Prepare a heavy pan with the olive oil and 1 tablespoon butter. Heat on medium-high until butter is melted but not browned, then turn the heat down to medium.
3. Place the fillets in the pan and cook about 3 minutes. Don't touch the fillets until they're ready to flip. Use a thin metal spatula to test the fish. If you can slide the spatula under the fish without the fish sticking to the pan, it's ready to flip. If the fillets won't release, give them another 30 seconds. They'll release when they've finished cooking. After flipping, divide the remaining 1 tablespoon butter over both fillets.
4. Cook fish another 2 to 3 minutes until done. Fish will be golden on both the top and bottom and opaque all the way through when finished cooking. Transfer the fish to plates, leaving the excess butter in the pan. Cover fish to keep warm, or set fish in a 200ºF (93ºC) oven. Reduce heat to medium. Add the lemon juice and capers, and stir with a wooden spoon. Add half the herbs and stir again.
5. Serve fish hot with pan sauce and remaining herbs.

Savory Rockfish Fillets with Fresh Herbs

Prep time: 10 minutes | Cook time: 6 minutes | Serves 2

2 (5-ounce / 142-g) rockfish fillets
1 pinch salt, pepper and garlic powder
3 tablespoons butter
½ tablespoon olive oil
4 sprigs fresh dill
4 sprigs fresh rosemary
4 sprigs fresh thyme
For Garnish:
2 sprigs fresh dill
2 sprigs fresh rosemary
4 slices lemon, thinly sliced

1. Lightly season the fish on one side with salt, pepper, and a teensy bit of garlic powder.
2. Melt butter and olive oil in a large skillet on medium heat.
3. Add rosemary, thyme and dill to the butter as it melts to help infuse a little fresh herb flavor.
4. Add the fish to skillet, and place the herbs on top of each piece while they cook. It takes about 3 to 4 minutes to pan-sear the bottom of the fish to a golden brown color.
5. Transfer herbs to side of skillet, and carefully turn fish to the other side, and continue cooking. While the fish cooks, spoon some of the melted butter over the pieces of fish. After spooning butter over fish, place the herbs back on top, and continue cooking fish about 3 to 4 additional minutes until done, and fish flakes easily.
6. Transfer fish to individual serving plates. Garnish each fillet with two lemon slices and a fresh twig of rosemary and dill. Serve.

Crispy Panko Crusted Rockfish Fillets

Prep time: 10 minutes | Cook time: 7 minutes | Serves 2

2 (1-pound / 454-g) rockfish fillets
2 tablespoons olive or vegetable oil
⅓ cup flour
½ teaspoon salt
½ teaspoon pepper
1 egg
2 tablespoons milk
½ cup panko bread crumbs
3 tablespoons grated Parmesan Cheese
1 teaspoon Old Bay Seasoning

1. Place a large oven safe skillet into the oven and preheat to 425ºF (220ºC).
2. In a large bowl, combine together the flour, salt and pepper. Stir, then pour onto a large plate.
3. In the same bowl, combine together the panko, seasoning blend, and Parmesan Cheese. Stir, then pour onto a large plate.
4. Wipe out the bowl, then use it again to whisk together the egg and milk.
5. Check the fish fillets for any bones and remove as necessary. Slice fish in half if necessary.
6. Dredge first in the flour, shaking off any excess. Dip fish into the egg mixture, allowing any excess to drip off. Coat fish in the panko mixture, shaking off any excess. Place on a clean plate and allow to rest 1 to 2 minutes so the panko can adhere.
7. When the oven and frying pan are preheated, add the 2 tablespoons of oil to the hot pan. Allow to heat 1 minute. Carefully add fish fillets to the hot oil.
8. Cook in the oven for 3 to 4 minutes, then carefully flip over.
9. Cook an additional 3 to 4 minutes, then check with a meat thermometer for an internal temperature of at least 140ºF (60ºC).
10. While fish cook, set up a cooling rack over a couple layers of paper towels.
11. Remove fish from the pan and place on the cooling rack. Allow to drain 3 to 5 minutes prior to serving.

Broiled Rockfish with Pasta

Prep time: 10 minutes | Cook time: 8 minutes | Serves 4

½ cup olive oil plus 1 tablespoon, plus more for preparing the pan and fish
2 pounds (907 g) rockfish fillets, rinsed and patted dry
Kosher salt
6 garlic cloves, thinly sliced
6 baby bell peppers, any color, thinly sliced
3 tablespoons fresh rosemary leaves
1 cup cherry tomatoes, halved lengthwise
1 pound (454 g) dried capellini pasta

1. Preheat the broiler. Lightly coat a broiler pan with oil.
2. Place the fish on the prepared broiler pan. Brush it with oil and scatter salt on top.
3. Broil for about 5 minutes until opaque and cooked through. When done, the fish should flake easily with a fork.
4. While the fish cooks, in a large skillet over medium heat, heat ½ cup of oil. Add the garlic, letting it bathe in the oil for about 1 minute until deeply fragrant but barely taking on any color.
5. Tip in the bell peppers and rosemary. Cook, stirring occasionally, for 2 to 3 minutes.
6. Add the tomatoes. Cook for 1 minute. Using the back of a wooden spoon, lightly smash the tomatoes. Season with salt to taste. Remove from the heat and keep warm.
7. Cook the pasta according to the package directions. Drain and toss with the remaining 1 tablespoon of oil.
8. Distribute the pasta among 4 plates and top with the fish. Spoon the pepper-and-tomato sauce over each and serve.

Easy Buttery Rockfish Recipe

Prep time: 10 minutes | Cook time: 5 minutes | Serves 4

2 pounds (907 g) rockfish fillets
3 tablespoons vegetable oil
1 tablespoon fresh lemon juice
4 tablespoons butter

4 garlic cloves, minced
2 tablespoons finely chopped fresh basil
¼ teaspoon cayenne pepper

1. Marinate the fish in the oil and lemon juice for 30 minutes.
2. In the meantime, heat the butter in a small saucepan over low heat with the garlic, basil, and cayenne pepper.
3. Grill the fish over direct heat for about 5 minutes per side, depending on the thickness of the fish.
4. Serve with the butter, garlic, basil, and cayenne sauce.

Quick Panko Rockfish

Prep time: 5 minutes | Cook time: 12 minutes | Serves 3 to 4

1 pound (454 g) rockfish fillet
2 large eggs

1 cup Panko
1 tablespoon paprika
1 tablespoon salt

1. Spray your air fryer with non-stick cooking spray and preheat to 370ºF (188ºC).
2. Slice your rockfish fillet into 3 to 4 pieces and set aside.
3. Crack your eggs into a bowl and beat. Add your Panko to a separate bowl and mix in salt.
4. Coat your rockfish pieces in egg and then in the Panko mixture. Place into preheated air fryer and air fry for 12 minutes.

Grilled Rockfish Fillets

Prep time: 10 minutes | Cook time: 15 minutes | Serves 4

2 pounds (907 g) rockfish fillet
3 tablespoons vegetable oil
1 tablespoon lemon juice

4 tablespoons butter
4 garlic cloves
2 tablespoons basil, fresh and chopped
1 dash Cayenne pepper

1. Marinate the fish in the oil and lemon juice for at least 30 minutes before grilling. Grill for 10 to 15 minutes, turning only once. Time depends on the thickness of your fish.
2. Heat the butter and stew the garlic for 3 min stirring constantly to make sure it doesnt brown. Add the basil, cayenne pepper and remove from the heat. Either pour the garlic butter over the fish or serve it in a gravy boat on the side.

Appendix 1 Measurement Conversion Chart

VOLUME EQUIVALENTS(DRY)

US STANDARD	METRIC (APPROXIMATE)
1/8 teaspoon	0.5 mL
1/4 teaspoon	1 mL
1/2 teaspoon	2 mL
3/4 teaspoon	4 mL
1 teaspoon	5 mL
1 tablespoon	15 mL
1/4 cup	59 mL
1/2 cup	118 mL
3/4 cup	177 mL
1 cup	235 mL
2 cups	475 mL
3 cups	700 mL
4 cups	1 L

VOLUME EQUIVALENTS(LIQUID)

US STANDARD	US STANDARD (OUNCES)	METRIC (APPROXIMATE)
2 tablespoons	1 fl.oz.	30 mL
1/4 cup	2 fl.oz.	60 mL
1/2 cup	4 fl.oz.	120 mL
1 cup	8 fl.oz.	240 mL
1 1/2 cup	12 fl.oz.	355 mL
2 cups or 1 pint	16 fl.oz.	475 mL
4 cups or 1 quart	32 fl.oz.	1 L
1 gallon	128 fl.oz.	4 L

TEMPERATURES EQUIVALENTS

FAHRENHEIT(F)	CELSIUS(C) (APPROXIMATE)
225 °F	107 °C
250 °F	120 °C
275 °F	135 °C
300 °F	150 °C
325 °F	160 °C
350 °F	180 °C
375 °F	190 °C
400 °F	205 °C
425 °F	220 °C
450 °F	235 °C
475 °F	245 °C
500 °F	260 °C

WEIGHT EQUIVALENTS

US STANDARD	METRIC (APPROXIMATE)
1 ounce	28 g
2 ounces	57 g
5 ounces	142 g
10 ounces	284 g
15 ounces	425 g
16 ounces (1 pound)	455 g
1.5 pounds	680 g
2 pounds	907 g

Appendix 2 Recipe Index

CPSIA information can be obtained
at www.ICGtesting.com
Printed in the USA
LVHW061645160921
697978LV00003B/316